Iraq on the Brink of Civil War

Iraq on the Brink of Civil War

◆

The Plight of a Nation

Saleh Abbas Iraqi Human rights activist

iUniverse, Inc.
New York Lincoln Shanghai

Iraq on the Brink of Civil War
The Plight of a Nation

iUniverse books may be ordered through booksellers or by contacting:

iUniverse
2021 Pine Lake Road, Suite 100
Lincoln, NE 68512
www.iuniverse.com
1-800-Authors (1-800-288-4677)

ISBN-13: 978-0-595-41602-8 (pbk)
ISBN-13: 978-0-595-85950-4 (ebk)
ISBN-10: 0-595-41602-0 (pbk)
ISBN-10: 0-595-85950-X (ebk)

Printed in the United States of America

We aknowledge the contributions of Dhahr Jmail,
John Elmer, Joe Car and Jo Wilding.

Contents

Foreword

Iraqi people in the last 30 years have been oppressed, persecuted and many were forced into exile. They have suffered one of the tragedies in history, the nation had been through 3 wars in the last 25 years, and the nation had been under siege for 13 years under the strictest economic sanctions in history.

After the eight years war with Iran; which squandered the wealth of the country, the economy failed to recover. And out of arrogance and miscalculation Saddam invaded Kuwait that culminated in the Kuwait liberation war and the economic sanctions. Economic sanctions against Iraq were waged simultaneously by the United Nations and the United States, resulting in the most comprehensive siege against a country, targeting civilians while strengthening the regime of Saddam Hussein. Economic sanctions claimed the lives of hundreds of thousands of children, through water borne disease and through the denial of medical care and humanitarian infrastructure.

The two wars had taken a toll of hundreds of thousands of young lives; those were our brothers, fathers and relatives who could have been with us now. By the end of the second war and liberation of Kuwait the sanctions remained in place, which brought the nation to a total ruin. Forced the elite to seek better life abroad, killed many people by the lack of medical care and poverty. Yet had not affect Saddam a bit.

Mr Denis Halliday was Assistant Secretary General to the United Nations (UN) and Head of the UN Oil-for-food programme in Iraq; he resigned in November 1998 in protest at the effects of the sanctions.

At the time of his resignation Denis Halliday (UN coordinator of Oil for Food program) said: "I am resigning because the policy of economic sanctions is totally bankrupt. We are in the process of destroying an entire society. It is as simple and as terrifying as that...Five thousand children are dying every month...I don't want to administer a program that results in figures like these"

The sanctions were lifted only after a third war that through the nation into chaos and anarchy. It brought to reality the long feared civil and ethnic violence in a form that Iraq had never seen before. The freedom of the Iraqi people had been confiscated twice, once at the hands of one of the worst dictatorships in history and again by the ethnic violence that surfaced after a long time of oppression, poverty, and masked hatred.

1

About The Nation of Iraq

Republic of Iraq,

Al-Iraq was the name used by the Arabs to refer for the land since the 6th century. There are several suggestions for the origin of the name of Iraq; one dates back to the Sumerian city of Uruk. Another suggestion is that *Iraq* comes from the Aramaic language, meaning "the land along the banks of the rivers. is an Arabic country and part of Middle Eastern in southwestern Asia encompassing most of Mesopotamia as well as the northwestern end of the Zagros mountain range and the eastern part of the Syrian Desert. It shares a border with Kuwait and Saudi Arabia to the south, Jordan to the west, Syria to the northwest, Turkey to the north, and Iran to the east. It has a very narrow section of coastline at Umm Qasr on the Gulf.

History

Iraq is the land that is historically known as Mesopotamia (Beth Nahrain in Aramaic), which means 'land between the rivers', also largely comprising the eastern and bigger part of the Fertile Crescent (that involves syria and lebanon). This land was home to the world's first civilizations, including the Sumerian, Akkadian, Babylonian, Assyrian whose influence extended into neighboring regions as early as 5000 BC. These civilizations produced the first writing, science, mathematics, law and philosophy in the world, making the region the center of what is commonly called the "Cradle of Civilization". Ancient Mesopotamian civilization dominated other civilizations of its time.

Islam spread to what is now Iraq in the seventh century AD. The prophet Muhammad's cousin and son-in-law (Ali) moved his capital to Kufa when he became the fourth caliph. Baghdad was the capital of the Abbasid empire, was the leading city of the Arab and Muslim world for five centuries. In 1258, Baghdad was devastated by the Mongols who werecked all eliments of civilisation and slautered hundreds of thosands of civilians. Iraq was later occupied by the Ottoman Turks. Ottoman rule over Iraq lasted until World War I. During World War I, the Ottomans were driven from much of the area by the United Kingdom during the dissolution of the Ottoman Empire.

At the end of World War I, the League of Nations granted the area to the United Kingdom as a British mandate. It was formed out of three former Ottoman states Mosul, Baghdad and Basra, under the control of King Faisal. However, for three out of four centuries of Ottoman Turkish rule, all three states were administered from Baghdad.

Iraq was granted independence in 1932, though the British retained military bases and transit rights for their forces in the country. In response to a pro-Nazi coup by former Prime Minister Rashid Al-Gailani the British invaded Iraq in 1941 resulting in the Anglo-Iraqi War. A military occupation followed untill October 26, 1947.

The Hashemite monarchy was reinstalled by the British and lasted until 1958, when it was overthrown through a coup by the Iraqi army, known as the 14 July Revolution. The coup brought Brigadier General Abdul Karim Qassim's (Arabic and Shiites) government to power (which withdrew from the Baghdad Pact and established friendly relations with the Soviet Union) from 1958 till 1963. In 1963, he was overthrown by Colonel Abd-Alsalam Arif who died in 1966 in airpalne crash and his brother, Abd-Alrahman Arif, assumed the presidency.

In 1968, Rahman Arif was overthrown by the Ba'ath Party led by General Ahmed Hassan al-Bakr. Saddam Hussein was named vice-chairman of the Iraqi Revolutionary Command Council and vice president of Iraq. After years of consolidating rigidcontrol over the nation, Hussein formally acceded to the presidency in 1979 and, executed many of his opponents in the process. Saddam Hussein remained in power nearly 25 years. He brought highly tumultuous period for the country (probably the worst in itsa history), both domestically and internationally. Saddam implemented a harsh police state and personality cult with widespread torture and murder of dissident Iraqis.

From 1980 to 1988 Iraq was the aggressor in the devastating Iran-Iraq War. In the end both nations fought to a standstill and the status quo was restored on the expense of millions killed and furtunes destroyed. In 1990 Iraq invaded Kuwait resulting in the Gulf War, which saw a multi-national UN coalition led by the United States successfully liberating Kuwait.

In the aftermath of the Gulf War Iraq increasingly became an isolated among much of the international community. The United Nations implemented economic sanctions against the country, designed as leverage to press for Iraqi disarmament, The sanctions caused the deaths of thousands of Iraqi children during the period.

Iraq's relations with the United States continued to worsen and in March of 2003 Iraq was invaded and occupied by the United States and allies. Saddam Hussein was deposed, and later captured and tried for war crimes.

Ancient civilisation

An advanced civilization flourished in this region long before that of Egyptians, Greek, and Romans, it was here about 4000BC the Sumerian culture flourished. Calendars were used and the first written alphabet was invented in old Iraq. Its fertile land fresh waters contributed to the creation of deep-rooted civilization that had fostered humanity from its affluent fountain since thousand of years.

The civilized life that emerged at summer was shaped up by the two rivers. Thus, while the river valleys of southern Mesopotamia attracted people for the surplus food.

The people of the Tigris and the Euphrates basin developed sophisticated irrigation systems and created what were probably the first cereal agriculture as well as the earliest writing (the cuneiform).

Sumerians were able to pass on complex agricultural techniques to successive generations through the cuneiform writing. Writing evolved to keep track of property. Clay envelopes marked with the owner's rolled seal were. By 3,000 BC, the script evolved into a full syllabic alphabet.

The commerce of those times was recorded in great details. Double entry accounting practices were part of the records. It was the custom for all to pay for what they needed at a fair price. Royalty was not exception. The king may have had an edge on getting a "better deal", but it wasn't the law as it was in Egypt. In Egypt, all things, including the people and property, were owned by the pharaoh. Sumerians invented the wheel and the first plow in 3700 BC.

In Sumerian society women had a highly respected position in society. Banking originated in Babylonia out of temples and palaces, which provided safe places for valuables. Another important Sumerian legacy was the literature recording.

Poetry and literature were produced. The most famous Sumerian epic and the one that has survived in the most nearly complete form is the epic of Gilgamesh, who actually was king of the city-state of Uruk in approximately 2700 BC, is a moving story of the ruler's deep sorrow at the death of his friend Enkidu, and of his consequent search for immortality. Other central themes of the epic were about the devastating floods.

Sumerian had a local god or goddess, and a bureaucratic system was developed for their ritualistic and complex religion. High Priests represented the gods on earth. The priests ruled from their ziggurats, high rising temples of brick with outside staircases leading to the shrine on top. The Sumerians worshiped anu, the supreme god of heaven, Enlil, god of water, and Ea, god of magic and creator of man.

Sumerians battled another group of people, the Akkadians, who migrated up from the Arabian Peninsula. The Akkadians were a Semitic people, that is, they spoke a language drawn from a family of languages called Semitic languages and Babylonian (the term "Semite" is a modern designation taken from the Hebrew Scriptures; Shem was a son of Noah and the nations descended from Shem (Arabic Sam) are the Semites). Sumerians lost and Akkadian kingdom, which was based in Akkad. This great capital of the largest empire humans had ever seen up until that point that was later to become Babylon, which was the commercial and cultural centre of the Middle East for two thousand years. In 2340 BC, Akkadian military leader, Sargon, conquered Sumer and built an Akkadian empire stretching over most of the Sumerian city-states and extending as far away as contemporary Lebanon. In 2125 BC, the Sumerian city of Ur in southern Mesopotamia rose up in revolt, and the Akkadian empire fell. Mesopotamia is the suspected spot known as the "Garden of Eden." Ur of the Chaldees, and that's where Abraham came from, (north of the traditional site of the Garden of Eden, about twenty-five miles northeast of Eridu (south part of Iraq) was a great and famous Sumerian city, dating from this time. Predating the Babylonian by about 2,000 years was Noah, who lived in Fara, 100 miles southeast of Babylon. Babylonians developed a math system based on the numeral 60, which is the basis of time in the modern world.

The early Assyrians, some of the earliest people there, were known to be warriors, so the first wars were fought there, and the land has been full of wars ever since. The Assyrians were in the northern part of Mesopotamia and the Babylonians more in the middle and southern part. Iraq through the ages has seen so many conflicts, an almost all the disasters were man made unfortunately...

Current Demographics

Around 80% percent of Iraq's population are Arabs; the other major ethnic groups are the Kurds (around 15%), Assyrians, Turkomans and others around 5%. The minority groups mostly live in the north and northeast of the country. The Assyrians, Kurds, and Turkomans differ from Arabs in many ways, including culture, history, clothing, and language. Other distinct groups are Persians and Armenians. About 100,000–150,000 Mandaeans live in the southern Iraq.

Arabic and Kurdish are official languages; English is the most commonly spoken Western language. Assyrian is also used by the country's Assyrian population.

There are more members of the Shiite sect (65%), mostly Arab, than there are the Sunni Arabs (35%). Iraqi Christian comprise nearly 3% of the population, about 800,000 people. These are mostly ethnically Assyrian or Chaldean. Bahá'ís, Mandaeans, Shabaks, and Yezidis also exist. Iraq used to have a significant Jewish minority but emigration to Palestine has reduced this to a very small number.

General condition

While the country of Iraq holds great oil wealth, the vast majority of Iraqis have benefited little from this potential. When Saddam Hussein rose to power in 1979, the country plunged into endless wars and internal strife. First came the disastrous 1980-88 Iran-Iraq war (a million killed at an estimated cost of 100 billion dollars), followed by the Gulf War which was in response to Saddam's invasion of Kuwait in 1990, and most recently the United States-led war of 2003.

Following the 1991 Gulf War, the south of Iraq rebelled against the Iraqi regime. With the collapse of their rebellion in March of 1991, at least 100,000 Iraqi Shiites fled into neighbouring Iran, Saudi Arabia, and the U.S.-occupied zone along the Iraq-Kuwait border. Fearful of retribution against these refugees on the withdrawal of U.S. troops from the region, the U.S. brokered a deal with the Saudi government for the establishment of a Saudi-maintained refugee camp near Rafha, and another camp called Al Artawea. Many refugees report that conditions in the Al Artawea camp were poor, especially for Arabs (as opposed to Kurds who also were housed there). Eventually, Al Artawea was closed, and all the refugees were sent to Rafha. Rafha camp was divided between the former members of the Iraqi army, overwhelmingly comprised of single men, and the Iraqi families, most of whom were Shiites.

In the mid-1990s, it had became clear that Saddam Hussein's regime had not weakened, and repatriation for the tens of thousands of Iraqi refugees in neighbouring countries meant certain retribution, especially for the former members of the Iraqi army and dissidents in Saudi Arabia. With pressure from the Saudi government, the United States agreed to resettle the Rafha group en masse, beginning in 1994. The United States government's decision met with considerable opposition, especially from veteran's groups, who argued that the resettled former members of the Iraqi army had been potential adversaries to Allied troops during the war. Furthermore, the existing resettled Kurdish populations also were distrustful of these potential "agents of Saddam." Nonetheless, over 32,000 Iraqi refugees were resettled in the United States through 2002, adding to the population of non-refugee Iraqi immigrants, for a total of about 90,000 foreign-born Iraqis. The largest populations in the U.S. are in Detroit, Chicago, and San Diego.

Culture and Social Relations

Iraqi society on the whole can be viewed as having three classes: the political elite, the military and merchant class, and finally, peasants and labourers (Cultural Orientation, 2003). However, in rural parts of Iraq (estimated 60% of the population) allegiance to the extended family and tribe are stronger than allegiance to a central government.

Iraqi women on the whole enjoy more rights than other women from the Arabian Peninsula. Especially among Iraqi Sunnis, there are many educated and professional women. The husband controls the household finances, but women exert considerable influence over the children, including grown sons. Male relatives show concern over the treatment of their female kin after marriage.

Communication

Arabic is the universal language of Iraq. While there are over fifteen dialects of spoken Arabic throughout the world, defined by geographical and rural/urban differences. Iraqis in general have little difficulty in comprehending any Arabic speaker. However, literacy in Arabic is rather low in Iraq, at an estimated 58%; third drop from the seventies and eighties is largely attributed to the wars and the sanctions. Even though Iraq experienced significant British political influence earlier in this century, English language fluency is limited to professionals among Iraqis.

It is never acceptable for a man to shake the hand of a woman among the strict Islamic cultures. However Iraqi educated women are less restricted. Touching, and even full embracing, is quite common within (but not between) the sexes, especially when greeting. When greeting, deference is always given first to males.

Religion

Most Iraqis are Shiite Muslims or Sunni Muslims, but the political elite, the military and merchant classes, and those living around the capital area of Baghdad in general are Sunni.

Both Sunnis and Shiites adhere to halal laws regarding meat in their food. Any meat consumed by a Muslim must come from an animal slaughtered by another

Muslim in a prescribed way, or it is considered impure, haram. This ritual involves asking God for forgiveness for taking the life of the animal. Furthermore, pork and alcohol are especially haram and should never be consumed. Even in the West, most Iraqis do not buy meat or chicken in a grocery store but prefer to go to farms to buy the meat fresh, or from a few trusted halal markets.

References

Al-Mousawi, M., Hamed, T. & Al-Matouk, H. (1997). Views of Muslim scholars on organ donation and brain death. Transplantation Proceedings. 29(8), 3217.

Central Intelligence Agency (2003). World fact book 2002: Iraq. Retrieved April 10, 2003) from www.cia.gov/cia/publications/factbook Note that the 2002 Fact book has been updated in 2003.

Cultural Orientation (2003). Iraqis: Their history and culture. Retrieved April 10, 2003 from http://www.culturalorientation.net.

Geissler, E.M. (1998). Cultural Assessment, 2nd edition. Mosby: St. Louis, pp.129-131.

Glover, J. (1999). Humanity: A moral history of the twentieth century. New Haven: Yale University Press.

Griece, E. (2003). Iraqi immigrants in the United States. Migration Information Source. Retrieved April 10, 2003 from http://www.migrationinformation.org

Hawn, T.R. & Jung, E.C. (2003). Health screening in immigrants, refugees, and internationally adopted orphans. In E.C. Jong & R. McMullen (Eds.) the travel and tropical medicine manual (3rd ed.) (pp. 255-265). Philadelphia: Saunders.

Kemp, C.E. (2002). Infectious diseases. Retrieved April 12, 2003 from http://www3.baylor.edu/~Charles_Kemp/Infectious_Disease.htm

Population Reference Bureau. (2002). 2002 world population data sheet. Retrieved May 12, 2003 from http://www.prb.org/pdf/WorldPopulationDS02_Eng.pdf

World Health Organization (2002a). World health report. Retrieved June 5, 2003 from http://www.who.int/whr/2002/en

2

Invasion of Kuwait

People in Baghdad woke up on the 2nd of August 1990 to the radio news that the Iraqi army has invaded and annexed Kuwait permanently as the 19th governorate of Iraq. The claims that Kuwait is part of Iraq are not new and historically during the era of the Ottoman Empire was part of the state of Basra, which is the south most part of Iraq.

The morning of the 2nd of august was an ominous landmark in the history of the nation; the mood was sober in the streets of Baghdad; several generations were called back to the mandatory military service. Most of those people had just been released from the military after the end of the war with Iran. Men left their businesses and work to join the military.

The impact of that was awful on the average family income; in a nation that is already impoverished by the eight years of the war with Iran. Saddam lost the war and Iraq was pu back to the dark ages. Gen. Norman Schwarzkopf said, "We have bombed Iraq back into the *pre-industrial age.*" That was the great victory the world most powerful country, taking on an impoverished country with outdated weapons. But he was admitting what became a fact latter on: "We bombed a lot more than just the military targets"

Since then the Nation of IARQ has been in an ongoing turmoil, from a disaster to another; the rest of the world is silently watching.

THE UN

Since the U.N. adopted economic sanctions in 1945, as a means of maintaining world order, it has used them fourteen times. But only those sanctions imposed on Iraq were comprehensive, almost every aspect of imports and exports was tightly controlled, which was damaging to a country who just recovered from two wars. The sanctions killed 500,000 Iraqi children under the age of five; almost three times as many as the number of people killed during the U.S. nuclear attack on Japan.

Immediately after the invasion the United Nations had emergency meeting to demand immediate and unconditional withdrawal from Kuwait. This fell on deaf ears and Saddam was adamant that Kuwait is part of Iraq and urged the Iraqi people to defend it with their lives. On the 6th August 1990 another meeting of the security council of UN have imposed economic sanctions on Iraq, including a full trade embargo stopping all kinds of goods imports from and exports to Iraq with exception of medical supplies, food and other items of humanitarian needs, then a Security Council sanctions committee was established to determine the needs of Iraqi people and to follow the changes in the sanctions. The sanctions committee was chaired by the Ambassador of Ghana to the United Nations.

The main requirements were that Iraq has to get rid of all the weapons of mass destruction and its ability to produce them as an essential prerequisite for peace in the Middle East; however the American administration was trying to undermine Saddam to change his regime.

The nation was sagging under the embargo for 12 years to come; an embargo that was demanded by the United States and endorsed by the international committee. It left the Iraqi people not only impoverished but deprived of healthcare, education and basically food.

Saddam was the villain who was punished, but the IRAQI people who suffered the consequences. He enjoyed several years of prosperity; expanded his series of palaces and his cronies and particularly his two sons, have grown more fierce than ever, persecuting the society and growing their wealth.

The UN has extended and reinforced the sanctions under pressure of the United States, who was demanding that Saddam admits the UN inspectors to get rid of what they thought he had of weapons of mass destruction; that turned out not to exist!!

The poverty, lack of job opportunities and the uncertainties of the future of Iraq has pushed a large number of the Iraqi people to leave their country seeking a job opportunity abroad, hopefully to improve their living standards. That particular problem had compound the effects of the sanctions by further depleting the country of its professionals and educated people. Those who left are typically either doctors, engineers or university lecturers and professors.

The embargo had no affect on Saddam or his friends, they had billions of dollars in hard currency, easy access to modern high-quality health private health system and he remained indifferent to the suffering of the people. The regime stopped cooperating with Security Council weapons inspections in 1998. The United Nations withdrew its inspectors; Saddam did not allow them to return.

Soon after the economic sanctions, the international community, the united nations and the American people themselves have recognized the devastating effects of the embargo on the Nation; the fact that Saddam himself had enjoyed relative peace and stability has ascertained that sanctions will not directly affect Saddam and he did not yield to the demands of the UN and was not going to do so. Indeed he remained defiant for years to come.

Bill Clinton carried on the American policy of maintaining the sanctions. During his time the oil for food program was established, he ordered many air strikes against Iraqi targets.

The oil for food program was a disgrace Iraq's oil-producing equipment was badly damaged with lack of repair equipment, and never functioned to full capacity. The Clinton Administration had caused delays and flagrant blocking of contracts behind the scenes. The weapons inspection team that was established to get rid of the weapons of mass destruction was thought to be riddled with spies and covert agents. There was food in Iraq, however it was mostly smuggled and at black-market prices. People suffered were the poor, the elderly, the chronically ill and the children. The war and the sanctions had shown us the ugly face of the world.

U.S. officials have effectively turned the economic sanctions into a legitimized act of mass slaughter.

The Embargo continued (items banned)

(The Scourging of Iraq: Sanctions, Law and Natural Justice by Geoff Simons, St. Martins Press)

Ref

- Sanctions Against Iraq Are Genocide by George Bisharat, Seattle Post-Intelligencer (5/3/02)

- Iraq War: The Coming Disaster by Immanuel Wallerstein, LA Times (4/14/02)

- For a Lasting Peace In Iraq by

- Despite Ramadan, US war on Iraq continues by Ramzy Baroud, Arabia.com (11/25/01)

- Softening Public Opinion For All Out War On Iraq by Stephen Gowens, Swans (10/29/01)

- Iraqis know what New Yorkers are suffering by Stephanie Salter, San Francisco Chronicle (10/10/01)

- The price is worth it by

- BBC Wednesday, August 18, 1999

- Smart Bombs, Dumb Sanctions January 3, 1999 New York Times Article

WAR CRIMES

Ramsey Clark and Others had filed a lawsuit to prosecute the Bush administration after the Kuwait liberation war. Accused the administration of a number of war crimes committed against the people of Iraq. They applied the complaint to the Commission of Inquiry for the International War Crimes Tribunal

The Crimes (by Ramsey Clark and his group)

1. President Bush from August 2, 1990, intended and acted to prevent any interference with his plan to destroy Iraq economically

2. President Bush ordered the destruction of facilities essential to civilian life throughout Iraq.

3. The United States destroyed civilian life, schools, hospitals, mosques, churches, shelters, residential areas, historical sites and civilian offices.

4. The United States intentionally used excessive force, killed soldiers seeking to surrender, often unarmed and far from any combat zones

5. The US used prohibited weapons capable of mass destruction and inflicting indiscriminate death and unnecessary suffering against both military and civilian targets.

6. President Bush ordered U.S. forces to invade Panama, resulting in the deaths of 1,000 to 4,000 Panamanians and the destruction of thousands of private dwellings, public buildings, and commercial structures.

7. President Bush usurped the Constitutional power of Congress as a means of securing power to commit crimes against peace

8. The United States waged war on the environment.

9. President Bush encouraged and aided Shiite Muslims and Kurds to rebel against the government of Iraq causing l violence, emigration, exposure, hunger and sickness and thousands of deaths.

10. President Bush deprived the Iraqi people of essential medicines, water and food.

11. The US continued its assault on Iraq after cease fire

12. The United States has violated and human rights, civil liberties, in Kuwait, Saudi Arabia

13. The US, having destroyed Iraq's economic base, demands reparations which will permanently impoverish Iraq and threaten its people with famine and epidemic.

June, 1991

Within the American society there was a controversy about the conduct of the army in the war to liberate Kuwait form the Iraqi Army, about the humanitarian effects of the sanctions. An American congressman has shown a film of the American helicopters shooting at Iraqi troops that were running away and fleeing the battle field. Over 100,000 of those died, most of them while they were running away. This particular crime had its ramification latter.

It was only a year down the track from the United Nation's resolution to enforce the sanctions on Iraq and already hundreds of thousands of children died from illnesses and malnutrition issues. The death of those has been unreported and not documented by the western media. Even worse there were hundreds of thousands of those children who were at risk of dying for the same reason.

The international community watched and could do nothing for that. The US government took a solid stance against Saddam and was not going to yield to any international pressure to ease the sanctions. The UN inspectors have been and out, their work was interrupted by the Iraqi officials several times. Saddam was not going to change his position and continued to accuse the inspectors for spying to the US. His arrogance and ignorance of international politics had cost the nation dearly.

It is still not precisely known how many civilians have died as a direct result from the sanctions. The estimation was few hundreds of thousands. 60,000 Iraqi children under age 5 have already died according to human rights organizations.

At that point hundreds of thousands of young children were dying. Human rights groups have reported appalling sequels of the sanction on the Iraqi people. The United Nations, the International Red Cross, the Physicians for Human Rights, a Harvard study team, and Catholic Relief Services have all documented the fact that unless the economic sanctions imposed against Iraq are lifted immediately, tens of thousands, if not hundreds of thousands of Iraqi civilians will die in" the next few months".

The US Government by then knew those figures and was a ware of the consequences on the civilians in Iraq' yet they have done nothing to ameliorate the situation for the ordinary people, not even acknowledging that it happened.

A report by Harvard University medical team who surveyed Iraqi hospitals that year has concluded that the mortality rate of Iraqi children under 5 years old could double in the year1991 because of diseases compounded by malnutrition.

Ref

- Everything to do With Oil Prices by Charley Reese (Orlando Sentinel 11/09/97)

- Bay of Camals CIA Iraqi coup failure, by Eric Margolis (08/25/97)

- Iraq measures the health effects of sanctions by Dr Peter Kandela (The Lancet, 6/28/97 p. 1896)

- Iraqi Sanctions, Human Rights and Humanitarian Law by Roger Normand (Middle East Research and Information Project, 6/2/97).

- Patrick Tyler: Disease Spirals in Iraq as Embargo Takes Its Toll. New York Times; June 24, 1991

- The weapon of Economic Sanctions, Voices in the wilderness, July 2004

- Iraq paying the price, John Pilger.

- Sydney Morning Herald, 8th of April, 2000, p 31

Details of the suffering
RETURNING REFUGEES

The end of the gulf war was a shameful defeat for Saddam who turned on his own people. His army had kerbed the rebellion in the south of Iraq; them moved to subdue the Kurds in the north. That action by itself was a disaster that pushed hundred of thousands of people to flee the arrest and the persecution to the neighbouring countries, mainly Turkey and Iran.

Thousands of Kurdish refugees returned after few months of despair at the borders, to their homes from Iranian and Turkish border areas. They returned to a country whose economy was besieged by the sanctions, the inflation was spiralling because of the embargo. Many of those Kurds were reported to have brought their ill and malnourished children to hospitals; they are no longer able to afford the black-market prices for infant-milk formula, unable to feed them properly due to the rapidly increasing black market prices, which dominated the economy, a situation that went on from bad to worse for many years to come. Hospital resources were dwindling; with the ever increasing demand the level of medical care was one of the worst in the world; that is in a country who had the best medical establishment in the Middle East.

Reports by doctors and relief agencies during visits to Iraq hospitals across the country seem to bear out Iraqi Health Ministry figures showing a 25 percent increase in the admission of patients suffering from gastroenteritis in the two months following the Gulf War. Iraqi officials insisted that figures significantly underestimate the rise in gastrointestinal infections, since a large proportion do not reach hospitals. Iraq Health Ministry figures also confirmed what many Iraqi doctors reported in interviews—that more patients are dying from infectious diarrhoeal disease, largely because of their weakened general condition due to malnutrition. While death from such infections was rare in 1990, the death rate for patients suffering from those diseases in the two months after the first Gulf War was about 32 per 1,000 cases admitted to hospitals. Data from the Iraqi health ministry indicated that more than 17,000 people suffering from infectious diarrhoeal diseases were admitted to hospitals in April and May (the two months after the war). Other infective illnesses that was uncommon started to rise in incidence such as Cholera, Typhoid and malaria, mostly due to lack of clean drinking water. The death rate in reported typhoid cases had jumped that year from statistical insignificance to 60 to 80 deaths per 1,000, according to Iraq Health Ministry figures. Lack of immunization that particular year resulted in a surge of measles in children. This is in addition to the tens of thousands of children who have already died in Iraq in the few months following the war. Widespread and severe malnutrition was a rapidly increasing problem in Iraq.

New York physician, Joseph Thomas, visited 15 major hospitals (1991) across the country indicated that an earlier epidemic of cholera is now under control. But other infectious diseases, including typhoid, hepatitis, meningitis and gastroenteritis, have surged to what the world Health organization and relief agencies call epidemic levels. The course of those diseases in a population struggling to recover from a devastating war is complicated by the Iraqis' generally poor health and nutrition, since the country was already impoverished by the eight years war with Iran that ended in 1988.

In March 1991, more than two million Kurdish and other Iraqis refugees fled after their unsuccessful rebellions in the north and south. The international community responded with a delayed effort to save them from starvation, exposure and disease. The Bush Administration then sought to repatriate those refugees to their homes in Iraq. Eventually most of those returned to a country with damaged infrastructure and weakened economy with rapidly increasing inflation to face the consequences. Those who feared for their lives remained on the borders of other countries in camps run by the United Nations, notably the camp on the Saudi borders (Rafha) which was notorious for human right abuses by the Saudi authorities. Thousands of people lived there for several years waiting for a country that accept them as refugees.

The plight of the Kurds was ignored by the international community until the after the European press, particularly the French, who had the organization "Doctor Without Borders" that had volunteered and worked in the north of Iraq, have demanded some action. The whole plight of the Iraqi was not known to the world, there were hundreds of thousands, and probably millions who are suffering from starvation and were in a dire need for help.

The Kurds were lucky for their problem to be recognised by the UN, the international community worked on their behalf and the press showed their suffering to the world. Humanitarian action was taken. Saddam and his army were prohibited from controlling the north of Iraq, it was patrolled by the Allied forces, by both sky and ground patrols. The UN has taken responsibility of distributing the international aids. The north part of Iraq, in fact, had enjoyed prosperity for several years while the rest of the country was sagging under the embargo.

No action was taken to improve the wellbeing of the rest of the nation, perhaps until the Oil for Food program took place several years latter. The plight was far beyond any description. The inflation rate skyrocketed, jobs became almost impossibility, the medical care was a disgrace, there was no food and simply for most families selling their belongings was the only was to survive. The rest of the world sadly was watching a slow and painful process of disintegration of this unfortunate Nation.

Ref

- Amnesty international 1991

- UNHCR. 28.may 2003

- United Nations; Office for the Coordination of Humanitarian Affairs (OCHA) Integrated Regional Information Network (IRIN) 4 September 2003

- Whatever happened to Iraqi Kurds. Human Right watch, 11 March 1991

Baghdad, Iraq, June. 1991

American and other Western doctors have visited the country ana conducted wide inspections of health facilities and hospitals; they have reported that the strict the international sanctions on trade with Iraq has culminated in climbing levels of illnesses and increasing dearth rates among children.

Senior officials of international relief agencies began to criticize the policy of the international community for penalizing the innocent people as the sanction wasn't effective to make Saddam yield for pressure. The prolonged trade sanctions because had devastating effect on the general population and added a large burden on humanitarian organizations and relief agencies that was under strain from conflict in other parts of the world.

The U.N. embargo has devastated all of life of the people in Iraq. But the deprivation is more evident in what used to be a modern health care system, where sanctions denied patients the medicine and equipment they need, it denied their doctors the means they need to save their patients of the curable diseases burgeoning amid the wreckage of war. U.N. official's estimate more than 1 million Iraqis have died in more than decade long era of economic sanctions..

Towns and large cities without electricity

The national supply of pure water that is suitable for human consumption is in a precarious state. Most cities and towns across the country are pumping only about 10% of the drinking water they were a year ago; the national reserve of chlorine have dwindled to few weeks supply in most cities in the country. There was a breakdown in the medical care system with severe shortages of medicines, equipments, and staff, water purification, sewage-disposal plants, and electrical power. The entire infrastructure was incapacitated.

The entire country had no power supply in the first 2-3 months after the end of the war. Patched-up generating plants are struggling to meet the demand for power supply in a country with average daytime temperatures of 45° c. Power blackouts of 12 hours or more a day had been a commonplace in the summer of 1991.

In southern Iraq, where the forces of President Saddam Hussein crushed the rebellion of the south at the end of the first Gulf war, hundreds of thousands of people are still without running water or electricity. The south part of the country was badly neglected and paid heavily for their disloyalty. Stale ponds of sewage disposal and mountains of rubbish piled in the streets of those neighbourhoods in the south. Services were bad before that but just got worse. The boom of the black market and the surge in prices has made their plight even more desperate.

The American Administration decided to maintain the embargo despite the reports of relief agencies of the humanitarian impact of the sanctions.; the purpose they thought was enforce Saddam to get rid of his "Weapons of Mass Destruction", which after all did not exist. Perhaps as a hidden intention, but they thought he would be weakened and eventually forced to leave power. That carried on despite the investigations, which suggested that trade sanctions are hurting the Iraqi people far more than what was perceived in Washington.

Food rations have been established by the Iraqi government, they were subsidised and cheap, however it was not enough and the quality was very poor, the items included were rations of flour, oil, rice and sugar

By the end of 1991 those rations that had previously sustained many Iraqi families have been drastically reduced in quantity. The black market prices for food have increased more than tenfold. The high ranking Iraqi officials enjoyed comfort and lived affluently and were indifferent to the population suffering. Few people were wealthy, mainly merchants and professionals who were able to carry on by drawing on their savings

Oil was Iraq's main source of revenues, due to the embargo there was no oil export the United Nations lifted its embargo on humanitarian shipments of food to Iraq by the end of the Gulf War, the embargo continued on foreign financial transactions, added to that was the freezing of Iraqi assets abroad made it extremely hard to import but a small amount of medicine and food; the Iraqi government was accused that they were using this for their own agenda, while they were trying to build their own wealth and try to expand the armamentarium of weapons.

Ref

Civilian casualties of January—February 1991, BBC

Physicians for human rights; http://www.phrusa.org

Aftermath of the bombing

The war devastation only ended and the rebellion in the south and the north part of the country. Saddam was broke but wanted to hang on to the power as long as he could and did every thing that he possibly could to curb the rebellion. He survived the war and wanted to rejuvenate his control on Iraq after the loss of Kuwait; he was in a perilous situation at certain stages. Certainly he would not have been able to crush the south without the American help, who allowed him to use the space of the no fly zone. The American saw the Iranian influence on Iraq was coming should Saddam get overthrown and did not want another theocracy. Saddam had crushed the rebellion and thousands of people were killed and buried in mass graves. Tens of thousands fled the country to neighbouring Iran and Saudi Arabia. Bush administration kept the options opened for indeterminate sanctions and possible war if need be and the plight went on for another 13 years.

The heavy bombing attacks on Iraq's national electric power centres had badly damaged the country's power supply; water-purification and sewage disposal and treatment system. Failure of the sewage treatment system led raw untreated waste to and flow directly into the rivers. Given the fact that water purification ahs failed millions of Iraqis turned to those rivers for drinking water during the war and in the immediate period afterward. Poor sanitation was the direct reason for the epidemics of enteritis, cholera, typhoid, and other waterborne diarrhoeal illnesses.

The war has contributed directly to the crisis. It is a consequence of the war. The blanket destruction of Iraq's electrical facilities has made it almost impossible to treat sewage or purify water which means waterborne diseases flourish, and hospitals cannot function normally.

The heavy bombing of the civilian facilities was poorly planned by the American officials; it damaged the infrastructure badly; its impact on the sewage disposal, and water purification was devastating.

Dominique Dufour was the head of a large team sent to Iraq by the International Committee of the Red Cross (ICRC) after the war said, "*I am absolutely sure that no Pentagon planner calculated the impact bombing the electrical plants would have on pure drinking water supplies for weeks to come, and the snow-ball effect of this on public health".*

Iraqi officials also allowed Westerners to visit Baghdad's main hospital for infectious diseases after the war. Some doctors in the United States were suspicious that Iraq had hid some cholera cases at that hospital in April and May 1991. But the staff of the badly rundown hospital easily acknowledged the fact that they had treated many suspected cholera cases, as well as typhoid meningitis and hemorrhagic fever.

Dr. Michael Viola, a professor of medicine and microbiology at the University of New York at Stony Brook visited some of the hospitals; he said

'I think they were just embarrassed by the place,' said, who also visited Iraq to study the war's effects on public health. 'It's a disgrace. They ought to close it.'

New York based physicians who represented a group called Medicine for Peace, chaired by Dr Viola said that although no reliable statistics are available from reliable sources or organizations, a severe epidemic of several diseases is in progress and is being aggravated by malnutrition.

'You don't need statistics,' he said. 'It's everywhere.'

A reporter travelling through large number of paediatric, and infectious-diseases wards across the country saw more than 100 cases of marasmus, or progressive emaciation from advanced malnutrition. Children in this situation were malnourished with protruded abdomen. There were also large number of cases of kwashiorkor, which is an emaciating disease caused by lack of proteins in the diet; this disease is only seen in remote places in the African subcontinent.

Under Iraqi Government policy, advanced malnutrition alone does not entitle one to admission to a hospital; a patient must also have contracted a disease or developed other complications before admission is allowed.

A severe shortage of infant formula has put the price of that basic nourishment beyond the means of the average Iraqi family. The price of a can of infant formula milk had risen from about $1 to nearly $50. The average income for working class people was US $100 monthly.

Poor families get subsidized three cans of powder formula per month from Government rations at a very low and affordable price. Evidently the minimum nutritional requirement of one year old infant is 10 cans per month. It was estimated that children under age 5, were dying at the rate of 500 to 1,000 a day from infectious diseases and malnutrition. On the 30th of May 1991 the New York Times front page showed a baby with swollen abdomen from Kwashiorkor, a scene that only African impoverished children were suffering from. By reinforcing the sanction, the US and the UN were effectively perpetuating genocide.

'Ibn Baladi Hospital in Baghdad is the largest paediatrics hospital in the country, the wards all full with children who were admitted with infectious diarrhoeal diseases and variety of other conditions. The same group of New York physician reported that the hospital refused to admit any malnourished child unless the have contracted some disease; a step that was taken by the local official due to lack of resources and the strain the hospital suffered from increasing infectious diseases.

A reporter saw dozens of mothers diluting infant formula to half strength to stretch out their precious supplies. Even in hospitals, most patients are receiving only half the normal ration of food because of cutbacks by the Health Ministry in hospital food budgets. Food rations of doctors and nurses have also been reduced by 50%.

Bush (Senior) Administration officials questioned whether Saddam is spending any resources on the health sector. The officials suggested that Mr. Hussein was effectively allowing relief agencies to assume the public-health burden in Iraq, even though their resources are quite limited.

According Western relief officials and Iraqi ministry of health officials have by then indicated that the Iraqi Government had allocated some resources to import essential medicines and infant formula that are not being provided by the relief agencies.

Medical care cards

The Iraqi public used to utilise the public hospitals for any health issue, which placed a significant stress of a system strained by shortages of medications and funds. During summer 1991 all Iraqis were issued medical cards that forbid them to consult a hospital doctor directly. Each Iraqi was assigned to a local health centre where primary care was dispensed; only serious health problems could be referred to the hospitals.

In the public hospitals, doctors said they had been unable to supply adequate amounts of insulin to patients with diabetes. Medication for the treatment hypertension and heart diseases were unavailable in most cities. Kidney-transplant patients were left with no drugs to fight rejection of the organs after kidney transplantations. Kidney dialysis machine had no power to operate, there was shortage of other forms of dialysis. Many dialysis patients died as a squeal of lack of adequate treatment.

Relief agencies have provided significant shipments of medicines, mainly in the form of antibiotics that were needed to treat the epidemics of cholera, typhoid and other infectious diseases. Those agencies are used to supply medicines and treatment to places in the world that are hit with epidemics of infectious diseases or environmental disasters. They supply vaccinations and antibiotics and hydration solutions for children affected by gastroenteritis. They are unfamiliar with a condition like the problem they are facing in Iraq with 18 million people with a health system that was broke. Cancers and chronic illnesses were not part of the troubles that relief agencies would deal with. However the Iraqi population had a significant help in various aspects.

The cost of relief efforts in Iraq was estimated to be in excess of US $500 million by the year 1992. Admittedly that cost was all funded by western countries and come from governments and charitable organizations.

An interview was conducted by New York Times Reporter with a kidney specialist in Mosul said that "*28 of the 50 patients who were being treated in northern Iraq's only kidney dialysis program died during the gulf war or shortly after it ended because of a lack of transportation, electrical power or clean water for the delicate machinery*".

Cancer patients suffered from lack of specific cancer medications, unavailability of radiation therapy and chemotherapy. Most cancer patients were left to die, unless they can afford to have treatment abroad.

Within the country's medical establishment, the resentment against the west and in particular to Bush Administration for seeking to topple Mr. Hussein by inflicting pain on the Iraqi population. The Iraqi citizens themselves have lost hope of changing the Baathist government in a police state in which Saddam himself is protected by many tiers security forces. People lost faith in the American administration, the feeling among the populace is that the Americans have betrayed the Iraqi people and helped Saddam to quieten the rebellion in the south of Iraq by allowing the Iraqi National Guard and its helicopters to patrol the sky of the south, which was declared earlier by the UN as No Fly Zone.

Around the world the public opinion was the Iraqi citizens are being heavily penalized for the mistakes of their police state that made grave mistake by invading Kuwait the misery was a direct result of the United States-led imposition of UN sanctions against Iraq, which cut the country off the rest of the world. Calls throughout the world increased calling the American administration and the UN to lift those economic sanctions to save thousands upon thousands of innocent Iraqi civilians, especially children, by death from starvation and disease.

The massive destruction of Iraq's infrastructure by the allied forces bombing was too excessive and much more that enough to drive Saddam out of Kuwait. As Iraqi people we felt the world turned its back to us in a critical time where we wanted the most help we can get. The resentment grew against the United States as it was spearheading the campaign to topple Saddam by inflicting pain on the civilians of Iraq. Meanwhile President Bush in his turn asked the United Nations to continue to reinforce the sanctions which were killing the children of Iraq

Ref

- What Would the US do Without Saddam? by Eric Margolis (9/23/96)

- The War that Never Ended by Naseer Aruri (09/96)

- The UN: new dictators of Iraq by Hugh Livingstone and Kayode Olafimihan (Living Marxism issue 76, 2/95)

- Twisted Policy on Iraq by Sam Husseini (Washington Post 01/26/99)

- Democracy Disappears by Eric Alterman (Nation 01/11-18/99)

- It's Time to Put Away the Big Stick by Eric Margolis (01/11/99)

- US Missiles Target UN too by Phyllis Bennis, Baltimore Sun 01/10/99

- Arms Inspectors Helped US(Associated Press 01/06/99)

- US used UN to Spy on Iraq aides say by Colum Lynch (Boston Globe 01/06/99)

3

The depleted uranium

Fact

Dr. Doug Rokke, a U.S. Army health physicist assigned to help clean up depleted uranium after the War for liberation of Kuwait; Dr Rokke was recalled to active duty 20 years after serving in Vietnam, from his research job with the University of Illinois Physics Department, and sent to the Gulf to take charge of the DU cleanup operation. Today, in poor health, he has become an outspoken opponent of the use of DU munitions. We awe the information in this chapter to Dr Rokke.

He said he suffering from reactive airway disease, neurological problems, cataracts and kidney disease, and receives a 40 percent disability payment from the government. He believes that his health problems are caused by exposure to DU.

Rokke and his primary team of 100 people performed the cleanup task. According to Rokke at least 30 members of the team are dead, and most of the others—including him have serious health problems.

Uranium, a weakly radioactive element, occurs naturally in soil and water everywhere on Earth, but mainly in trace quantities. Humans ingest it daily in minute quantities. Depleted uranium, is a highly dense is the by product of the process during which fissionable uranium used to manufacture nuclear bombs and reactor fuel is separated from natural uranium. DU remains radioactive for about 4.5 billion years.

Depleted uranium is so cheap and effective—350 tonnes was used in weapons in the first Gulf War and possibly 500 tonnes in 2003 Iraq conflict—that Rokke says the US is reluctant to do proper studies of veterans or Iraqi civilians. "It's the arrogance. Once they acknowledge that there are actual health effects of depleted uranium munitions, then they can't use them any more; the house of cards falls apart."

In addition to direct radiation, potentially more serious hazard happens when a DU rocket hits the target, 70 % of it can burn up on impact, which makes a storm of ceramic uranium oxide particles. This is extremely fine particles that can be spread by the wind, then inhaled and absorbed into the human body, plants and animals will have the same exposure, so uranium becomes part of the food chain. Studies have shown that uranium can stay in the human body for years.

The US led allied bombing of Iraq started few weeks before the ground campaign, allied air fighters have bombed all military and most civil facilities all over the counter; it was to excessive to the extent it deprived the country's infrastructure from full recovery. Added to that was the use of depleted Uranium 238, which was used to boast the strength of the bombshells. Depleted uranium is radioactive and a health—hazard. The use of that uranium remained secret between the allied forces; no one knew it has been used. It was used throughout the entirety of Iraq,. Kuwait and with the munitions testing in Saudi Arabia, so it covered the entire region.

John Pilger (*antiwar and human rights activist*) had interviewed Doug Rokke, who was a health physicist responsible for cleaning up depleted uranium after the Gulf War. Hers is some of the points that were discussed. He had received a letter from the Surgeon General's office in the United States army that said "*think about DU and this uranium contamination*".

Doug Rokke job prior to the ground war was training and educating the medical professionals and soldiers on the effects of nuclear, biological, and chemical war. With the end of the ground campaign he was given the responsibility of cleaning up the depleted uranium or uranium 238 contamination. He said "*The contamination was extensive, the casualties were grotesque*". Apparently the bombs are so powerful, surviving them was almost impossible, those who did not die instantly were badly burned and deformed.

According to Dr Rokke the effect of depleted uranium depends on whether a person inhaled it, ate it, drank it, or if they got the uranium contamination into an open wound. The effect depends upon the dose that they had; it has caused respiratory problems, kidney problems. He had individuals of his team that were known to have exposed and they have died of different cancers or were dying of cancers. They had people with skin rashes, neurological problems. A lot of people have lost fine motor function, and neuropsychological problems and short term memory losses. Added to that depleted uranium is a heavy metal poison and also a radioactive poison, those effects added together results in serious health issues.

Dr Rokke carries on said "from my own experience, they didn't test or measure our team for years and they still haven't. It was a deliberate action to deny medical care".

The effects of uranium including respiratory problems, the kidney problems, cancers. It has affected the soldiers and that particular, team they were denied medical care. The American administration had denied any responsibility, the far-reaching and probably cumulative effects of Uranium on Iraqi people have not been scientifically studied.

The United Kingdom Atomic Energy Authority has certainly concluded that if only 8% of the depleted uranium used in the 1991Gulf war was inhaled it could cause 500,000 deaths.

Uranium effect on the civilian population:

John Pilger himself have visited Iraq and went to see the children hospital in Basra (southern Iraq) he was astonished to see the number of children affected by cancers that local doctors have not seen before, such as tumours of the nervous system and the muscles, which were extremely rare before the war.

Dr Rokke was appalled by the degree of the contamination that he found during the war. Even worse the research in 1994 and '95 has confirmed the contamination that was so sever 3-4 years after the war. He concluded that *"absolutely nobody should come within 25 metres, or climb on, or crawl in, or get anywhere near, depleted uranium destroyed or contaminated equipment, buildings or structures without full respiratory and skin protection"*.

The Iraqi people have been living there through and after the war with no protection and no knowledge of what was actually happening to them, yet few years after the war there was still severe degree of contamination with uranium

Numerous times, at various meetings and conferences, the Iraqi officials have asked for the medical treatment protocols after Uranium exposure. They've also asked for the environmental treatment protocols that were denied by the US Department of Defence and the British Ministry of Defence.

Dr Rooke says "With the extent of the contamination in Basra and all over Iraq where the DU was fired by the tanks and by the aircraft—over 300 tons—there's no doubt in my mind that, because that lasts forever unless it's been physically removed, that any woman or child, any soldier, any non-combatant, anybody that comes in the area that it gets into their body is going to have medical problems. The overall effects are the fact that we used a weapon that's indiscriminate for eternity and therefore unless the environmental clean up is totally completed and the medical care is provided, the effects are permanent and lasting forever and ever and ever that's wrong".

As far as I know there was no action to screen the Iraqi people for the effects of uranium neither an attempt to clean up the environment.

The Iraqi government made an appeal for help with the environmental catastrophe at a conference in Washington DC after the war. Because the conferences are open to the public, they had Iraqi representatives that came to the conference looking for help. They approached Dr Rokke and members of the United States Secretary of Defence, officials of the British Ministry of Defence, members of the VA, United States Veterans Affairs that provides care for the discharged or retired veterans—and asked for help, for medical protocols. According to Dr Rokke they were rebuffed.

By the end of the war in Iraq there were thousands and thousands of soldiers that were wounded and probably exposed that didn't get any medical help; and all the civilians, the women and the children. Medical official in Iraq have reported many times increased number of cases of variety of cancers and leukaemia among children; there was variety of weird congenital malformations in newly born babies. Those reports, although were not verified by independent sources, they do represent the truth; it is very evident that those are consequences of the war, and it consolidates the concerns of Dr Rokke about the public health effects of Uranium on the population in Iraq.

The US and British officials latter on and under pressure have acknowledged the problem and its consequences, they did that only partly and still denying responsibility for the Iraqi people.

The US Department of Defence was eventually ordered to prepare an education and training curriculum to deal with depleted uranium. That curriculum, which was completed by December of 1995 and fully approved by not only all of the military forces in the United States, by the British Ministry of Defence, the Canadians, the Australians and the Germans.

Although it was approved it didn't happen. This was to teach the soldiers and other civilians employed by the military about the hazards of the depleted Uranium. And how to properly work around depleted uranium contamination, and how to clean it up, it basically was only done in part.

There was constant procrastination from the officials in the American and British governments to do that and according to doctor Rokke it took a lot of effort to prompt its approval and it took three years (1993-1996) to happen.

Dr Rokke was certain it was a deliberate and planned action. Should everyone have known about the hazard of the uranium; they would seek medical treatment and the uranium levels would have been tested and found. However waiting was going to diminish uranium level in their system and eventually uranium will disappear. If they weight long enough to go through the required half lives of uranium to disappear, there will be no evidence of that even if they were sick from uranium exposure.

That's why medical care has been denied in England, in Canada, the United States and all over the world. If we don't check it we won't find out they're sick. But more importantly, what this is all about?

The bottom line they did not want to take responsibility of the civilians; the women and the children in that particular region that have been affected.

Because the country was under tight embargo, the Iraqi people were unable to import any kind of equipments, they could not measure how badly they were affected, and they could not even get a diagnostic machine.

It was a coward and criminal action to deny the innocent people the medical care they needed; unfortunately that was one of the actions taken against the civilians to force Saddam to step down, and he was not going to do so. The women and children and the rest of he civilians in Iraq could not possibly change a fierce regimen of Iraq. The women and children were sick and dying not only because of the depleted uranium exposure but because of the whole host of the toxic battlefield and the contributions of the sanctions. But they can't get medical supplies to provide simple medical care. That was a grave historical mistake, made by the West and endorsed by the United Nations.

The excuse of the west was that Saddam may turn the equipments of measures into equipment he would use to build nuclear weapons. "*It was very difficult to figure out how medical equipment can be turned into weapons*".

Scale of the Uranium disaster

In the Gulf War the allies have fired missiles and bombs that had well over 300 tons. It is important to understand that during the 1991 Gulf War that three types of weapons were used. *"A 30 millimetre round from an A-10 attack aircraft, the Warthog—over 900,000 rounds. Each individual round is approximately 300 grams of solid uranium 238. There were another 15,000 rounds—predominantly the 120 millimetre round—fired by the tank. And each individual round is over 4500 grams of solid uranium 238. These rounds are not coated, they're not tipped, and they're solid uranium 238"*.

Dr Rokke said

"Those areas where the destroyed or contaminated equipment is, unless that is physically removed and totally disposed of properly, the disaster is for eternity. You cannot have contaminated equipment in terrain where people can inhale, ingest or get uranium contamination into a wound".

For us as Iraqi people we are certain that no action was taken to remove those bombshells that contained heavy doses of uranium, neither the Iraqi officials nor the united nation has taken any measures to unsure that has happened. So the disaster is for eternity.

Depleted uranium causes neurological abnormalities, kidney stones and chronic kidney pain, rashes, vision degradation, lymphoma, various forms of skin and other organs cancer, neuropsychological disorders, and birth defects in off-spring.

That action by the allied forces led by the United States was deliberate with full knowledge of the long-lasting effects of the depleted uranium of the public health of the civilians and the environment. The Iraqi people did not deserve to be punished for ever because of the mistakes of Saddam.

Saddam Hussein did not use depleted uranium munitions, however he is ultimately responsible for that disaster. The United States and Great Britain decided to use depleted uranium munitions, they didn't have to use it, they could have destroyed the entire of Iraq with the conventional weapons they had; it is not that they didn't have a choice. The depleted uranium have a permanent effect to everybody, soldiers in the battlefield, civilians in the neighbourhoods that had been bombed and the whole environment.

So what we have is a deliberate use of a weapon that has a lasting and indiscriminate effect. That's wrong. The women and the children and non-combatants don't deserve to be affected for eternity.

Dr Rokke had put the sole responsibility of Washington and London and he thought they have two responsibilities; the first is either to complete the environmental clean up themselves for the areas that they deliberately contaminated, or provide the guidelines for environmental re-mediation. And the second was they have a moral obligation to provide either the medical care or treatment, or to provide the protocols and the equipment that will permit the medical care and treatment. "*That's an obligation under God*" he said.

The Iraqi people during the sanction era were kept in the dark about the magnitude of the uranium contamination, they were denied any help from the Americans and the British officials. Evidently health care was even denied to the alliance soldiers, who about the Iraqi people? They were left totally in the dark the uranium disaster remained only as rumours; during the sanction we had no internet, no foreign newspapers or journals, no satellite television. No one new how it is going to affect them, if it has not affected them already. The war veterans were denied medical care let alone the Iraqi people.

It seemed that the alliance imposed sanctions on Iraq to stop Saddam from producing weapons of mass destruction; however they themselves had weapons of mass destruction and have used them.

The Highway of Death in Basra

Iraqi doctors believe that depleted uranium is responsible for an increase in cancers and birth defects in the region. Many researchers outside Iraq, and several U.S. veterans' organizations, agree; they also suspect depleted uranium of playing a role in Gulf War Syndrome.

Basra is the south most cities in Iraq and part of Southern demilitarized zone. Twelve years after the war, a collection of tanks, armoured vehicles and other military equipments (from the withdrawing Iraqi army on the highway between Basra and the Kuwaiti borders) are rusting in the desert between Basra and the Kuwaiti borders, which was the war field in 1991. They also are a source of radiating nuclear energy.

In 1991, the United States and its allies blasted the Iraqi military vehicles with armour-piercing shells made of depleted uranium; that was a historical precedent, those uranium weapons were never used before. Those powerful weapons brought a quick victory for the allies. The battlefield remained a source of radioactive depleted uranium.

Extent of the of the problem

According to Geiger counter readings done for the Seattle Post-Intelligencer by Dr. Khajak Vartaanian In2002. DU shell holes in the vehicles along the Highway of Death are 1,000 times more radioactive than background radiation, the desert around the vehicles was 100 times more radioactive than background radiation..

The U.S. Army acknowledges the hazards of DU-contaminated equipment who will require wearing mask and skin protection if they come in 25m distance of contaminated equipments and indicated *"contamination will make food and water unsafe for consumption."*

Prior to the War, the Army released a report on DU predicting that large amounts of uranium dust could be inhaled by soldiers and civilians during and after the war.

According to Karen Parker (from International Educational Development Humanitarian Law Project, which is UN consultant group). In interview with Larry Johnsonian 1999, a United Nations sub-commission considered DU as a dangerous substance and recommended an initiative to prohibit its use in the future. The initiative was blocked by the United States.

She said *"there are four rules derived from all of humanitarian law regarding weapons:*

- Weapons may only be used in the legal field of battle, defined as legal military targets of the enemy in war. Weapons may not have an adverse effect off the legal field of battle.

- Weapons can only be used for the duration of an armed conflict. A weapon that is used or continues to act after the war is over violates this criterion.

- Weapons may not be unduly inhumane.

- Weapons may not have an unduly negative effect on the natural environ- ment".

"Depleted uranium fails all four of these rules,"

THE STUDIES

Of the 696,778 troops who served during the recognized conflict phase (1990-1991) of the Gulf War, at least 20,6861 have applied for medical benefits. As of May 2002, 159,238 veterans have been awarded service-connected disability by the Department of Veterans Affairs for health effects collectively known as the Gulf War Syndrome.

A published study from the Uranium Medical Research Centre in Canada and the United States appeared in the August 2002 issue of Military Medicine jour- nal. The authors used the very sensitive technique of thermal ionization mass spectrometry, which enabled them to distinguish between natural uranium and DU. They examined British, Canadian and US war veterans, who were suffering from Gulf War Syndrome, found that, nine years after the war, 14 of 27 veterans studied had DU in their urine. DU also was found in the lungs and bones of a soldier who was killed in the war.

BIRTH DEFECTS IN IRAQ

In an interview with Larry Johnson 2002, Dr. Jawad Al-Ali at the Teaching Hospital in Basra (Dr. Jawad Al-Ali, a British-trained oncologist), displayed, a photo albums of birth defects in Basra. The photos showed the sudden increase in birth defects after the war; the incidence in 1989 there were 11 per 100,000 births; in 2001 there were 116 per 100,000 births, according to Dr Al-Ali

Even before anybody new about DU, doctors in southern Iraq were making comparisons to the birth defects that followed the nuclear attack on Hiroshima and Nagasaki in the Second World War. Most of those abnormalities were nervous system malformations or what is medically called neural tube defects. Cancer increased dramatically in southern Iraq; mainly in the form of leukaemia, skeletal cancers and nervous system tumours.

"The cause of all of these cancers and deformities remains theoretical because we can't confirm the presence of uranium in tissue or urine with the equipment we have," said Al-Ali. *"And because of the sanctions, we can't get the equipment we need."*

Ref

WHO studies the depleted uranium in Iraq. BBC on day, 6 January, 2003

Truthout.org. Friday 29 April 2005

Larry Johnson. Seattle Post-Intelligencer, Tuesday, November 12, 2002

Scott Taylor the Weapon We Gave Iraq, common news dream centre. Monday, February 17

Lisa Ashkenazi CrokeTons of Depleted Uranium Polluting Iraq. Christian Science monitor. December 1, 2003

Dany Fahey, Current Issues—Depleted Uranium Weapons in the Gulf Wars (199

Glasgow Herald. Feb. 5, 20041, 2003

Kenneth H. Bacon. Toward A Human Disaster. Boston Globe. October 14, 2002

4

Iraq sagging under the Embargo

Then the situation got worse (Iraq sagging under the Embargo)
Late action by UN

The sanctions amended several times since 1990 and remain fiercely imposed. The United States has maintained its own sanctions against Iraq since Aug. 2, 1990, after Iraq's invasion of Kuwait, leading to the Gulf War On the14th of April 1995 the united nations have implemented the resolution of Oil for Food program to enables Iraq to export up to US$1 billion of oil every 90 days and use the hard currency revenues for humanitarian supplies to the country; it was basically for buying medicines and importing food.

May 1996, the UN and the Iraq officials had signed a Memorandum of Understanding that lead to the implementation of the Oil-for-Food program.

Late 1996, the humanitarian situation reached to its worst, the Iraq government accepted the terms of Security Council Resolution 986, which allowed it to sell a very small amount of oil to obtain the hard currency necessary to buy food and medicine—the so-called "Oil-for-food programme". Denis Halliday administered this program until his resignation in November 1998.

Halliday states: *"The theory was that sanctions diminish the leadership and sustain the people. In fact it's the reverse. The leadership has been strengthened by economic sanctions and the middle-class, the professional classes, the very people who might change governance in Iraq, has been wiped out, and those that remain are struggling to stay alive and keep their families alive."*

The embargo committee subsequently adopted on the 8th of August 1996 the procedures for the implementation of Resolution 986. On the 9th of December 1996, the Secretary General of the UN reported to the Security Council that all the steps necessary to ensure the effective implementation of Resolution 986 had been completed. As a result the resolution of Oil for Food went into effect on the 10th of December 1996.

The whole story took a lot of towing and throwing around the desks of the UN while the Iraqi people were basically dying. The first food shipment arrived in Iraq on the 20th of March 1997.

Under the rules of the oil for food program, Iraqis were allowed less than $200 US per person to survive for an entire year.

Larry Johnson, from the Post-Intelligencer and its foreign desk editor, and Post-Intelligencer photographer Dan DeLong had visited Baghdad and spend two weeks in Baghdad, during April 1999. They were accompanied a group of delegation of medical workers, which sponsored by the *Washington Physicians for Social Responsibility*, who attempted to gauge the effect of sanctions on the civilians in Iraq and especially children. They were exempt from State Department regulations banning travel to Iraq by Americans.

The have called for attention to the effects of the sanctions. The group brought medicine, equipment and medical textbooks without obtaining the required U.N. approval. They defied the sanctions and did not obtain the required U.S. government permit to visit to Iraq.

Around that time the US Government had threatened another group of Americans with tens of thousands of dollars in fines and prison sentences for taking "medicines and toys" to Iraq. The crime was violation of the sanctions.

In addition, a UN official based in Iraq said, "Even the Oil for Food programme is hardly working since most of Iraq's pumping capacity has either been deliberately targeted by bombing raids or rendered useless by the absence of spare parts, which are prohibited by the sanctions programme on the off chance that they might benefit Iraq's military programme".

Sanction and health

Among the deprivations Iraq had experienced, none was closely correlated with infant deaths as the damage to the water purification system. Prior to 1990, 95 percent of urban households in Iraq had access to clean drinking water, Soon after the Gulf War, there were widespread outbreaks of cholera and typhoid—diseases that had been largely eradicated in Iraq; as well as massive increases in child and infant dysentery, and increasing child and infant mortality rates. By 1996 all sewage-treatment plants had broken down. As the countries economy collapsed, salaries to employees were very low, Iraqi currency rendered nearly worthless by inflation. Between 1990 and 1996 more than half of the employees involved in water and sanitation left their jobs. By 2001, after five years of the Oil for Food Programme's operating at full capacity, the situation had got worse.

Iraq had the best medical system in the Middle East in the 1970s and 80s; hospitals were among the best equipped hospitals in the world. They had CT scanners, ultrasound machines, incubators to nurture premature babies; they were equipped to world standard hospitals.

During the sanctions much of the equipment has worn out, spare parts were unavailable. The hospital had no electric power, blackouts happen every single day for may hours, emergency generator have been constantly used since the gulf war; however those generators were only capable of powering only the operating theatre and the emergency departments. In the scorching heat of summer, patients lied on their beds with no conditioning, not even a fan was there to help fighting the desert type of summer heat, and windows were left open for a little possibility of a breeze.

Without consistent electricity to run air conditioning or transfer systems in other parts of the hospital, antiseptics were not available, to clean the floors (you would not believe it) the hospital workers sweep the floor of the hospital with gasoline to clean it. Doctors earned the equivalent of US$4 a month. They shared worn photocopies of decades-old textbooks. They had little access to current research or journals and no access to the Internet.

Nurses earn less than doctors. Many have abandoned the profession, leaving family members to look after their sick people, administering medicines and watching for changes. The hospital had shortages of even simple instruments like scalpels and clamps for surgery, antibiotics for infections and drugs for chemo-therapy. There is not enough specialized formula to treat underweight babies. Syringes and surgical gloves were washed and reused. Patients had to by antibiot-ics, surgical sutures and intravenous lines from the black market that prevailed at that time.

Child Mortality surveys conducted by UNICEF in 1999 showed that mortal-ity of children under the age of five was escalating at a rapid rate and reached to more than twice the rate it was ten years ago. The current rate of 131 deaths per 1000 live births is comparable to that of Haiti or Pakistan. The health care sys-tem is in a decrepit state and there has been a tremendous deterioration in pure water supply. Since 1991, hospitals have gone without maintenance. The func-tional capacity of the health care system has deteriorated further by shortages of water and power supply, lack of transportation and the collapse of the telecom-munications system. Communicable diseases such as water borne illnesses and malaria, previously under control, came back in epidemic portions in 1993. Diar-rhoea and acute respiratory infections account for 70 per cent of all child deaths.

Although the oil-for-food programme has ameliorated the situation by reduction of malnourishment, there was no change in the quality of consumed food. Malnutrition rates remain high, especially for children. An assessment by the Food and Agricultural Organisation (FAO) and the World Food Programme (WFP) in 2000 found that 10 per cent of children under the age of five had acute malnutrition compared with a rate of 3% in 1991. One in five children remains so malnourished that they were in need for hospital level care and nourishment.

That humanitarian crisis went on and got worse by the continuous decline in essential social infrastructure. It needed the implementation of a cash component for south and central part of Iraq, to upgrade the infrastructure and improve managerial and technical skills of local professionals. It is not known how much of those UN suggestions were implemented.

R. Watkins, head of the International Federation of Red Cross and Red Crescent Societies in Iraq, calls the situation *"a natural disaster not caused by the forces of nature, but by the forces of man."*

Hans von Sponeck, the United Nations Humanitarian Coordinator for Iraq, said in an interview.

"The sanctions are turning the social structure upside down—the middle-class is every day more impoverished."

Before 1990 and the imposition of sanctions, Iraq had one of the highest standards of living in the Middle East. In the mid nineties UNICEF reported that at least 200 children are dying every day. They are dying from malnutrition, a lack of purified drinking water and a lack of medical equipment and medications to cure common treatable diseases.

The evidence was scientifically proved beyond doubt; we need to look in the top medical journals studies:

A study reported in the *American Journal of Public Health* (April 2000) found that the sanctions that started in 1990 increased "substantially" the probability of death among Iraqi children. The study concluded; the pre-war sanctions period—from August to December 1990—resulted in a 4-fold increase in the mortality hazard rate among Iraqi children.

The *New England Journal of Medicine* in 1992 reported that Harvard researchers had found that 46,700 Iraqi children under the age of five had died from the effects of war and sanctions in the first seven months of 1991

The UNICEF report has concluded the subsidized food rations were enough for daily caloric supply, however they lack vitamins and minerals; there were no proteins included in those rations, so children were not getting the proteins they need for growth. Malnutrition was endemic amongst children. Diseases like kwashiorkor or marasmus are common in paediatric wards. Before 1990 the most important problem faced by Iraqi paediatricians was childhood obesity.

Many sewage treatment plants were targets of the air strikes during the war. Others have since disintegrated without equipment and spare parts because of the sanctions. Chlorine and other water purification chemicals were now banned under the embargo due to the possibility of "Dual use".

The health system disintegrated under embargo. Hospitals had significant shortages of staff with doctors' and nurses' salaries insufficient to support them and their families. There was a mass exodus of doctors, the left the country for better work op Morphine, the most effective painkiller has been banned by the Security Council. At the same time the number of cases of cancer among both adults and children had increased sharply especially in southern parts of the country.

Medical equipment like incubators, X-ray machines, radiotherapy equipment and heart and lung by-pass machines were banned according to the UN resolutions...The Security Council blocked vaccines, analgesics and chemotherapy drugs, the American administration have managed to convince the world that those materials could be converted into chemical or biological weapons. Problems with transportation and refrigeration and power supply meant that even drugs that were available such as antibiotics could only be obtained on irregular basis.

Children with leukaemia, even if they manage to get chemotherapy they still died from common infections that could complicate chemotherapy treatment. The unavailability of regular supply of antibiotics made it very difficult for them to survive the infectious complications.

After the Gulf war Iraq was not denied the equipments to clean up the polluted environment. More than 1 million rounds of weapons coated in depleted uranium were used by the US led alliance during the 1991 war. As much as 300 tonnes of DU now still lies (many years after the war) scattered throughout Iraq. Depleted uranium dust gets into the food via water or the soil. Inhalation can cause serious lung disease such as lung cancer. Added to it breakdown of the immune system, leukaemia and bone cancer. Cases of cancers in Iraq have risen tenfold since 1990. If cancers continue on the present upward curve and worse still is the estimation that 45% of the population could develop cancer within ten yea

At Ibn Al-Baladi Paediatric Hospital in Baghdad, the ward was dirty with the smell of stale urine and a large number of malnourished children, with flies every where. They were lying in the corridors, the beds the emergency unit on dirty mattresses, they were just miserable. The only weapon they had to kill the flies was to swat them; insecticides were prohibited under the embargo. Medications were in short supply.

Doctors have indicated that most of the illnesses were typhoid fever, pneumonia, leukaemia, tuberculosis, cholera. Even polio and measles were a common place due to lack of vaccination.

Elsewhere in Baghdad all the hospitals were in a dire situation, wards were dilapidated, the hospitals were dark; blackout happen everyday for several hours, sometimes the power was shut off on daily basis to save resources. The usual antiseptic odour of medical facilities has been replaced with the stench of urine, faeces and decay. Children regularly died from lack of adequate medical facilities.

The hospitals, ran out of almost everything they need, the were doctors exhausted and grieving, the hospitals became a place to die for the thousands of children suffering from diseases and Infections resulted from malnutrition and contaminated water.

The U.N. Security Council decided to keep the sanctions in place until it is convinced that *"Iraq's long-range missiles and chemical, nuclear and biological weapons have been dismantled or destroyed"*

Saddam had earlier agreed to destroy all his possession of those weapons by the treaty that was signed between the military generals at the end of the Gulf War. However Saddam's arrogance and ignorance had led him to believe he can evade the conditions of the truce, he would let the inspectors do their work on one occasion and refuses at another. The sanctions continued and involved a ban on commercial flights to and from Iraq to an oil embargo; however that was eased slightly in 1997 by the oil for food agreement when the United Nations allowed Iraq to export a limited amount of oil to buy food and medicine.

After daily work most people (doctors and engineers) had a second job, mainly driving taxis to boast their income to meet their needs for survival; the inflation was uncontrollable, the average salary for doctors was US$3-5 dollars.

Saddam Hussein himself was not affected a bit by the sanctions, despite the hopes of the American administration. He remains in full control, occasionally executing nay enemy, the Security Council efforts to find and destroy his weapons were in limbo. The embargo had devastating consequences on Iraq's 20 million people.

Ref

- Everything to do With Oil Prices by Charley Reese (Orlando Sentinel 11/09/97)

- Bay of Camals CIA Iraqi coup failure, by Eric Margolis (08/25/97)

- Iraq measures the health effects of sanctions by Dr Peter Kandela (The Lancet, 6/28/97 p. 1896)

- Iraqi Sanctions, Human Rights and Humanitarian Law by Roger Normand (Middle East Research and Information Project, 6/2/97).

- Patrick Tyler: Disease Spirals in Iraq as Embargo Takes Its Toll. New York Times; June 24, 1991

- The weapon of Economic Sanctions, Voices in the wilderness, July 2004

- Iraq paying the price, John Pilger.

- ABC Radio Current Affairs The World Today, 7 April 2000)

5

Clinton administration

The Year 1999

U.S. Secretary of State Madeleine Albright (under Clinton) was a staunch supporter of the sanctions. When she was asked by the press whether the American administration is responsible for the death of children because of a lack of food and medicine, Albright said: *"No, Saddam Hussein bears full responsibility for that. It is actually the United States that was the author of the oil-for-food program which permits Saddam to sell oil for food. If we had not done that, and if the sanctions weren't in place, then he would be selling oil for tanks. So it is the United States and our allies that have made sure that the people of Iraq have food."*

The same year 1999 Peter Burleigh (the American ambassador to the United Nations), in a speech to the Security Council, acknowledged that the sanctions had inflicted grievous suffering on the civilians in Iraq, but emphasized that Saddam was mostly to blame.

Regardless of who thinks what; the innocent were caught in a fierce conflict for along time, a conflict they had nothing to do with, and they certainly paid with their lives heavily.

Reports from UN, world religious leaders and officials of humanitarian organizations point out how the economic sanctions have left most people struggling for survival. The unemployment rate in Baghdad itself was over 50% and in the second largest city Basra was 75% as estimated by the United Nations 1999.

"Anupama Singh, the United Nations Children's Fund representative in Baghdad was interviewed by Larry Johnson he said *"Ten years ago, malnutrition was almost non-existent,"*

He carried on; from 1991 to 1998, children under 5 were dying from malnutrition-related diseases in numbers ranging from a conservative 2,690 per month to a more realistic 5,357 per month. "Malnutrition in Iraq is not just epidemic, it is endemic,"

During 1999 the international community became increasingly concerned about the alarming figures of the effects of the sanction on Iraq; humanitarians and politicians at the United Nations and in many world capitals. Russia, France and China, together with several Arab countries, have called for new approaches to deal with Saddam, the weapons and to lift the sanctions that were badly hurting the people.

Seattle Postintelligencer a nation sagging under the weight of sanctions caught in a spiral of poverty and death. *Tuesday, May 11, 1999*

Admittedly the embargo alone was not the responsible reason for the misery of the people of Iraq. The country's economy was weakened by the eight years war with Iran and then again by the invasion of Kuwait and the Gulf War. But the sanctions were the straw that broke the camel's back, it had speeded the deterioration of the economy, which went down a slippery sloop of disintegration.

Watkins (a Canadian) the Red Cross and Red Crescent leader in Iraq, described Iraq before the sanctions as an "oil-rich country with a sophisticated infrastructure. Well-designed highways linked its cities to the surrounding countries, hospitals were state-of-the-art, education was free through the college level and malnutrition was almost non-existent".

During the Iraq-Iran Iraq was importing most medicines and food from other countries, young men were all in the military service and the service industry had relied on foreign non skilled workers; this possibly had bad consequences to the local economy.

Poverty became the norm in the society, that only 10 years ago had one of the best economies in the world, the irony of that is the country still has the second most abundant oil reserve in the world. People started looking for any thing to sell, any work they could possibly do and masses had fled seeking a job opportunity of refuge abroad. By the year 1999 it was estimated that 5 million Iraqi people were scattered everywhere under the sun, from Canada to Argentina and from Japan to New Zealand; those were all from a country of around 20million people.

Larry Johnson have described a man who digs in the rubbish looking for old tires to patch them and perhaps make some money out of them and probably earned one US dollars for several hours of work. Around the same man hundreds of other Iraqis, mostly school-age boys, scramble through the refuse for something of value, just to survive.

The Iraqi government was described as been caught in Catch-22. It needed revenues to rebuild the infrastructure and import enough food and medicine for the people. Although they were allowed to sell oil, the sanctions on equipment limit the government's ability to pump oil to get that money.

The denial of Iraqi patients any access to medical care that was party of the sanction was a crime against humanity, committed in the twentieth century right in front of our eyes, and the American Administration could not care less.

The Ominous stigma

The American administration have managed to convince the rest of the world that Iraq under the Saddam regimen was a real threat to the international peace; indeed there was solid evidence of Saddam possessing some chemical and biologic weapons that he had used against the Iranians in the eight years war and latter against the Kurds. The US was demanding full cooperation with the UN inspectors; Saddam was still defiant and has not complied with their demands; leaving his own people to suffer while he was busy building palaces and occasionally making rhetoric speeches condemning the west.

The UN Security Council imposed comprehensive economic embargo against Iraq on August 6, 1990, just after Saddam had invaded and annexed Kuwait. When the coalition war had ousted Iraq from Kuwait (March 1991), the Council did not lift the sanctions, keeping them in full power as leverage to twist Saddam's arm and force him to get rid of the alleged weapons of mass destruction. Another aim of the sanction was to push Saddam around and force him to give up power in Iraq. In that sense the end of the war was effectively a temporary ceasefire and the alliance was going to strike back anytime if Saddam was not going to abide by their rules.

The sanctions remained in place thereafter, despite the heavy impact on innocent Iraqi people and the evident lack of pressure on Saddam Hussein.

A UN "Oil-for-Food Programme," started in 1997, offered some relief to Iraqis, but the humanitarian crisis continued. The US and UK governments always made it clear that they would veto any lifting or radical reforming of the embargo as long as Saddam remained in power.

Officials in the United States, and their allies who supported the enforcement of the embargo against Iraq, blamed the suffering on Iraqi President Saddam Hussein. The alleged weapons of mass destruction was used as an excuse to maintain the sanctions. It was used as a leverage to put pressure on Saddam to allow U.N. inspections to ensure Iraq is not developing nuclear, chemical or biological weapons

In January 1999, the Security Council decided to establish three panels on disarmament, humanitarian issues and prisoners of war and Kuwaiti property to discuss options that would lead to the full implementation of all relevant Security Council resolutions concerning Iraq. Ambassador Amorim (Brazil) chaired all three panels. He submitted the panels' reports in the spring of 1999 (S/1999/356), and the Council considered the recommendations contained therein.

Pressure was increasing in the (UN) Security Council for lifting the sanctions. U S and the UK were adamant that the sanctions remain in place. Of the permanent members of the Security Council, only the US and the UK voted for the resolution; France, China and Russia abstained.

On 17 December 1999, the UN Security Council passed a new resolution on the sanctions against Iraq. That resolution had appointed new monitoring body of inspectors of Saddam weapons, UN Monitoring, Verification and Inspection Committee (UNMOVIC), and for the suspension of the sanctions for limited periods (120 days) if the head of UNMOVIC reports favourably to the Security Council on Iraq's compliance with the process of inspections. Hans Blix of Sweden was appointed as head of UNMOVIC; he was a former head of the International Atomic Energy Agency.

Hans Blix during his time as the head of the UNMOVIC was very optimistic and thought that Iraq was slowly complying with the inspections. However the US officials blocked his efforts as a part of their agenda to prepare for the coming attack on Iraq. After more than twelve years of embargo had passed, the US and the UK waged another war on Iraq again in March 2003, toppling Saddam Hussein's regime. Soon after, the sanctions were lifted; Iraq resumed its relations with the west step that gave the American occupation the authority of full control over Iraq's oil industry.

Endurance of the Iraqis

Pentagon officials stated that Iraq's electrical grid had been totally destroyed by bombing in order to undermine the civilian economy. "People say, 'You didn't recognize that it was going to have an effect on water or sewage,'" said one planning officer at the Pentagon. "Well, what were we trying to do with sanctions—help out the Iraqi people? No. What we were doing with the attacks on infrastructure was to accelerate the effect of the sanctions."

The Food and Agriculture Organisation (FAO) had reported in 1995: "The situation throughout the country is increasingly disastrous with economic decline spreading across almost all sectors of Iraqi society".

The embargo was harvesting children. Before the Gulf War, when food was plentiful and clean drinking water was readily available, the greatest paediatric health problem in Iraq was obesity. Now, with widespread food shortages and contaminated drinking water, undernourished children were affected by cholera and typhoid. UNICEF blamed the sanctions for the deaths of more than 500,000 Iraqi children under 5.

"The most serious situation in Iraq," he said, "is the plight of the young people—we are grooming a generation that is deprived of the ability to prepare for the future."

"The fact is, educational items are embargoed" under the sanctions, von Sponeck said.

Both Watkins and U.N humanitarian coordinator von Sponeck pointed to the Iraqis' lack of experience for the delays in distributing food and medical supplies. Those delays made officials in the West to say that the Iraqi government's officials were attempting to make the humanitarian situation worse in Iraq in an effort to gain international support for lifting the sanctions.

Von Sponeck said "It is very clear that there is a willingness on the part of the Iraqis to get the supplies to the people," "Every day I am amazed at how they manage with so little."

He said "absolutely no evidence" that shipments under the UN administered Oil-for-Food program, which allows Iraq to sell up to US$5.2 billion dollars of oil every six months to buy equal amount in value of food and medicine, is being diverted to the government or to the black market.

Von Sponeck also said that Iraq, because of a lack of oil-industry-related parts, has never been able to pump enough oil to meet the $5.2 billion mark allowed under the oil-for-food program. The maximum amount that Iraq had exported evidently was US$3 billion, of which 35% went to the UN to run the program. The remainder of the money is deposited in an UN-controlled account to pay for food and medicine shipments.

"Even the most conservative, independent estimates hold economic sanctions responsible for a public health catastrophe of epic proportions. Malnutrition, disease, poverty and premature death now ravage a once relatively prosperous society whose public health system was the envy of the Middle East. I went to Iraq in September 1997 to oversee the U.N.'s "oil for food" program. I quickly realized that this humanitarian program was a Band-Aid for a U.N. sanctions regime that was quite literally killing people. Feeling the moral credibility of the U.N. was being undermined, and not wishing to be complicit in what I felt was a criminal violation of human rights, I resigned after 13 months."

Denis Halliday: humanitarian aid coordinator for Iraq

He resigned in protest to the impact of the sanction, afterward Halliday had spent much of his time talking about the impacts of the sanctions on the ordinary people of Iraq. He went to Australia in April 2000 as part of the campaign to have the sanctions lifted.

Ref

- Washington Post article June 23, 1991

- Seattle Post-Intelligencer, 12th of February 1999

- Agence France-Press. FAO urges UN committee to unblock agricultural-related contacts for Iraq; Jan 7 2002

- UNMOVIV, globalsecurity.org

- CBS—60 Minutes: Madeleine Albright on Iraq Sanctions, 1996, 12th May: "Killing half a million children was worth it". Albright was then the US ambassador to the UN.

- Kenneth R. Bazinet Daily News Washington; Bubba: Iraq war's 'a quagmire'. October 6. 2005

- Justin Brown, Clinton rethinks Iraq sanctions; Humanitarian concern stirs criticism, but many defend sanctions as a prod for weapons monitoring…The Christian Science Monitor; 3/1/2000;

- Barry Grey Clinton administration blocks easing of sanctions against Iraq. 28 September 1999

6

Lost Generations

At the end of the 1970s, Iraq was promising as a powerful and respected state in the international community; it began to emerge as a regional power and booming on oil revenues from one of the world's largest oil reserves. Two decades later the situation has drastically changed due to two devastating wars and the effects of international sanctions.

The United Nations Security Council imposed economic sanctions on Iraq on 2 August 1990. Under the economic sanctions, all imports to and exports from the Iraq were prohibited unless the Security Council agrees. Those sanctions were the toughest, most comprehensive sanctions known in history.

Mounting evidence had proved that the sanctions were having an immense humanitarian impact on Iraqi people. Since 1990 there has been a severe and persistent deterioration in the standards of living of the overwhelming majority of Iraqis. The country has seen a clear shift from affluence to crushing poverty. The economy was badly declining In addition to the immediate horror of thousands of children dying from malnutrion-related causes, von Sponeck said, there is a more long-term tragedy among students.

UNICEF's Executive Director, Carol Bellamy, stated that *"if the substantial reduction in child mortality throughout Iraq during the 1980s had continued in the 1990s, half a million fewer children under the age of five would have died during the eight year period from 1991 to 1998"*.

In December 1996, the United Nations and the Iraqi government agreed to an 'oil-for-food' programme. Iraq used its own resources to import essentials as a temporary measure to ease the burden of the sanctions. The programme was organised in six month 'phases'.

In 1997, the United Nations Human Rights Committee noted that *"the effect of sanctions and blockades has been to cause suffering and death in Iraq, especially to children"*.

The oil-for-food programme had not had a positive impact on the Iraqi economy although it was never meant to act as an adequate substitute for the independent efficacy of the economy. About 200 companies established direct working relations with Iraq, the national economy did not recover as hyperinflation, unemployment and the depreciation of the national currency continued to rise relentlessly.

In Northern Iraq, the economy continued to be completely dependent on informal trade with goods brought in from Turkey and Iran.

Humanitarian agencies have reported that while the humanitarian crisis in south and central Iraq continues, there has been a decline in infant and child mortality rates in the autonomous Northern Iraq. There were several factors that had contributed to that. The north has benefited from the heavy presence of aid agencies helping the Kurdish population. The north has also received 22 per cent more per capita from the oil-for-food programme and about 10% of this assistance in cash while the rest of the country can only use these funds to import commodities. In Northern Iraq, a cash component has been used to implement projects more effectively while in the south and centre; local authorities have received water pumps but have not had the money to pay contractors to install them. The sanctions were not implemented rigorously in the north because of a more vast and porous borders with Turkey and Iran than in the south and centre.

The specifics of the original oil-for-food programme have been changed in subsequent Security Council resolutions. In December 1999, Security Council Resolution (SCR) 1284 removed a cap on oil sales by Iraq, created 'green lists' of supplies which could be imported without prior approval by the UN sanctions committee and allowed a cash component to pay for local costs of implementing the programme.

The oil-for-food programme effectively stopped the humanitarian crisis from worsening, as it has helped to provide improved food rations for ordinary Iraqis. The programme however has not been able to solve the severe humanitarian problems, which needed more solid investment in other sections of the economy. Although food rations delivered by the government are in principle covering the caloric intake of the population, people have become so poor that in some cases, they are selling their rations to buy other necessities of daily life.

UNICEF has continued to support the physical rehabilitation and reconstruction of primary schools in four governorates in Iraq. In 2000 a further 55 schools were rehabilitated in various parts of the country. This has brought the total number of rehabilitated schools over the past two years to some 325, benefiting over

35,000 students and 1600 teachers. This project has benefited from substantial funding from the European Community Humanitarian Organisation (ECHO) during 2000.

UNICEF also tried persistently to improve the quality of teaching in primary schools. More than 400 school supervisors have been trained as trainers and 554 teachers were trained in teaching English, maths, health, ecology, special education and in teaching large classes.

UNICEF also helped to strengthen the skills of professionals working with street children through specialist training and study visits to other countries. UNICEF also supported a community-based programme for detecting and helping children with disabilities. Officials involved in this project were sent on a study round to Jordan where they visited successful community projects for children with disabilities. UNICEF and Enfants du Monde have set up libraries in more than 60 schools and children's homes, benefiting around 3750 disabled children, orphans and street children. Each library has been provided with 270 books and more than 100 titles of books recorded on tape.

The cumulative effects of the two wars and the sanctions have taken their toll on the Iraqi population in particular the centre and the south of the country. This region hosts 85 per cent of the country's population. The delivery of social services for women and children has greatly deteriorated. The emotional and psychological stress on children and women living with war and deprivation has been so severe. The WHO pointed out that the number of mental health patients visiting health facilities rose by 157 per cent from 1990 to 1998. The social cohesion of Iraqi society has become fragile, there was rising juvenile delinquency, begging, criminality and cultural and scientific impoverishment. A whole generation of Iraqis is growing up disconnected from the rest of the world.

The substantial progress made (during 1978-1985) in reducing adult and female illiteracy has stopped and regressed to mid-1980 levels. More and more pupils and teachers were leaving the school system, could not afford to stay in the system. More than half of all schools did not qualify for teaching and because they needed substantial reforms. The Ministry of Education statistics showed that 23 per cent of children between the ages of 6 and 15 are now working in the street to provide for their families and that Iraq can no longer implement its laws on compulsory education. Most schools had two shifts of classes and the curriculum was the same as in the seventies.

The country was badly hit by a wave of drought in 1998-99 has greatly reduced the capacity to generate electricity. Entire fields of crops died and the soil was so dry and salty in some places, it was no longer suitable for agricultural purposes. The drought had decreased crop production and more food needed to be imported under the oil-for-food programme during the summer months power cuts last up to 18 hours a day in most towns, severely affecting water and sewage treatment plants, health centres and other vital social services. Reduced water supplies had contributed to frequent infectious illnesses complicating child mal-nutrition...

Education

Michael Wolff is a San Diego activist and writer who works for the International Action Centre. He writes for television and radio. In January of 2001 he travelled to Iraq with Ramsey Clark's delegation to witness the effects of war and sanctions on the Iraqi people.

He Said

"During the war, Iraq's infrastructure was completely destroyed. The devastation was total."

Many students from different par of the world studied and continued to come to Iraq for university education, despite the impacts of the sanctions. Students came from all over the Middle East countries for quality teaching that is still affordable. Student from Yemen had particular interest in Iraq; they came to study medicine, computer science, engineering etc.

Yemenis had strong link to IRAQ with passion and love for the people of the country. They had real compassion to the Iraqi people and they expressed their solidarity with them against the sanctions.

In fact most of the Arabs and Muslims around the world have expressed their support to the civilians in Iraq. The education system was badly affected by the sanctions. There were no scientific journals, new books or references, not even news papers. Clearly the students were the innocent victims that had to suffer the consequences of the war.

The economic strife that Iraq went through is very evident to those who saw Baghdad in the era of economic sanctions. His buildings were in a various state of conditions, mostly dilapidated and may were deserted, chipped paint, rust, weeds, abandoned stores, garages and gas stations. It was like travelling through a place where time had stood still. The deterioration probably started in the late eighties; but the clock of development had stopped on August 6, 1990; the day the economic sanctions were imposed.

The Iraqi people have adapted, somehow to their desperate condition. Despite the years of Iran war, despite the tremendous impact of the strictest economic embargo in modern history, life in went on. The Iraqi people are truly survivors.

Mr Wolf went to the Moustanserya University, which is one of the oldest universities in the world with a history of at least 800 years; he spoke passionately about the students and the teaching staff who welcomed them warmly and generously. During that period of time of the embargo, most Iraq universities had the American flag painted on the floor of the main gates so people step on it as a protest to the harsh treatment they got from America.

In 1980, there was an Iranian assassination attempt on Tariq Aziz who was giving a lecture at the university that was one of the events that precipitated the Iran-Iraq conflict. The tertiary education was completely subsidized by the Iraqi government which allowed students from poor economic background to have an equal opportunity with their more fortunate peers to have an education chance. Variety of modern sciences was taught includes languages from French to Spanish and sciences from physics to computer science, medicine and engineering.

Getting into university was highly competitive and requires high grades at the secondary school level to attend the University. During the strict economic sanctions imposed by the United Nations all educational materials were banned by the sanctions committee.

Despite the long twelve years of sanctions, universities in Iraq were well taken care of. I went to Baghdad in October 2000; I went to visit the Medical school in Baghdad university; I was surprised to see the positive attitude of the students, their moral was high, they knew the challenges the will have to face in the future and still remained in good spirits with hope and optimism toward the future. It was very refreshing to see the hope in their eyes; they were well-dressed with their particular university uniform (white shirts, grey pair of trousers and navy jacket), and full of vitality and friendly smiles. Their optimistic views were a remarkable thing to see.

Before the war, the University of Baghdad had drawn students from throughout the Middle East and had the reputation of being the best medical school in the region. During the years of sanctions, it had the impact, textbooks were old, no current journals and university professors were leaving for a better opportunity abroad.

Mr Wolf in his visit had confirmed that and said "There are not enough words to describe how pleasant it was to be interacting with these fine individuals".

In his comment on education said "All of the students seemed genuinely thankful that the Iraqi government was paying for their education. It's really quite a testimony to the Iraqi educational system—that despite a military blockade, despite the war, the almost daily bombings, the famine, the lack of medicine and the enduring poverty, young students from all around the world still strive to come to Moustanserya University to get an education and better their lives".

The main concern of the student that I have seen (most of them were friends of my brother), was about the education materials they had, references were outdated, some of them were obsolete, textbooks were photocopied locally and yet were sold for high price.

I found that the UNSCOM inspectors had entered the central library, confiscated the chemistry books and burned them that were quiet concerning.

The sanction has turned the socioeconomic makeup of the society upside down, many people made fortunes by fraud, theft and using loophole of the law. Bribery and corruption was a commonplace in a society that was proud of their purity. Despite all the troubles university students were happy at the level of education they were getting, but that it had been negatively affected by the sanctions.

They are faced with difficulties that most people who live in the west cannot even imagine. They were in a country that has been ravaged by war and the embargo. They had to deal with emotional and financial hardship, their family difficulties, unemployment, a bleak outlook, poor medical care, obsolete education materials.

The country then was facing constant threat of American bombings and possibly renewed American invasion. And yet the young students of continued to go to school and they continued to learn. The studies to have better quality of life; they wanted to have a degree and possibly get a job and be a productive members in their society.

Mr Wolf said in his visit "We owe these students and enormous amount of gratitude. They are a reflection of ourselves and of the ability of all of us to persevere in the face of staggering adversity. They are students battling against genocide sanctions. Their story is an epic and heroic struggle. I hope they succeed".

Most of the students appeared healthy and well-dressed in school uniforms, but there were notable exceptions of poor-looking students without uniforms.

The new problem that had faced the nation was that young people were dropping out of school in alarming numbers; they were forced to do that because they had to work and support their families to survive.

Primary school level had truly suffered the most, schools were packed with large number of students, and classes were small, unhygienic, lacked electric power most of the times. Desks were in a shortage, some students sat on the floor, the country had no money for repair, or resources to renovate or build schools in a country that had grown from 18 to 26 million people during the years of the sanction. Two and three students shared desks designed only for one student.

Paper and pencil were their only instruments of learning. Most schools were in a dire situation and barely suitable, they lacked resources, buildings were old, and walls are dirt, graffiti of many generations written on the walls.

At the University of Baghdad's medical school, that had and still has special memories for me, students were the elite of the entire country. Often they came from an affluent background, it was evident on their dress, and the school looked vibrant with its youth who have just started a new year. The future looked bleak to the young people who were going to be doctors within few years. Doctors were paid poorly, the hospitals had minimal resources, their more senior colleagues were fleeing the country; the quality of a specialty education was poor. They knew I just came from New Zealand, I knew everyone was going to ask me about the wok opportunity and specialty training abroad and sure enough they did.

Sponeck had noticed that large number of people were leaving their lives behind and described the phenomenon of immigration of professional people from the country as "*immigration without noise*".

Ref:

- Scott Ritter and Von Sponeck on Iraq: accuracy.orgJuly 29, 2002

- Mark Tran Hans von Sponeck Former UN humanitarian coordinator for Iraq, The Guardian Thursday March 18, 2004

- UN sanctions rebel resigns BBC, Monday, 14 February, 2000,

- Un.org

- Laurie Mylroie. Special Report: Iraq in the Absence of Weapons Inspectors. Middle East Intelligence Bulletin. July 1st 2000

7

The Situation in Northern Iraq

The UN statement that described the north was:

From the mid 1970s to the mid 1980s, social services like health, basic education and water and sanitation were readily available, at least in all the urban centres of Northern Iraq. They were well managed and maintained, often by expatriate technical personnel. A reasonable portion of the country's oil wealth was invested in providing social services to all its citizens. There were also investments in agriculture and food production and not only was Northern Iraq self sufficient in food grains but also supplied the rest of the country.

The eight years Iraq/Iran War changed Northern Iraq for the worse. Northern Iraq's border with Iran became a battle front in the war. The Iraq/Iran War, the Gulf War in 1990, local political conflict between the Kurdish leaders and the economic sanctions cut off the investment in essential social services. The conflict between the two leading Kurdish political parties led to further disruptions during 1994-97. Extensive use of mines along the Iraq-Iran border as well as within the three governorates led to further problems.

According to the UN the health status of the population declined from 1991 onwards. The mortality rate for children under five give rose from 80 deaths per 1000 live births in the period 1984 to 1994 to 90 deaths per 1000 live births for 1989 to 1994. This has since improved to 72 deaths per 1000 live births, after the work of the UNICEF.

After the 1991 war Saddam lost his authority on the north to the United Nations and the Americans, the north enjoyed some relative prosperity compared to the rest of then country; the economy remained stable, the inflation was less and the food rations were distributed by UN personnel. However the health system has deteriorated In addition to the damage caused to hospitals during these conflicts, essential medical supplies were not available and trained health professionals left the country. Similarly the fighting disrupted the education system and schools were also destroyed and lacked educational materials. Working children and orphan children emerged as a new phenomenon in the mid 1980s, not only in the north but it was also in the rest of the country; it continued to increase as many families lost their prime breadwinner in the wars or due to financial hardships. Many villages were displaced and had to resettle in new places with lack of infrastructure.

Since 1997 and the beginning of the oil-for-food programme, the situation has gradually and significantly improved.

The UN Security Council allowed the import of food and essential supplies for all social services. Free food rations have ensured that basic food needs are met for all the population; malnutrition declined. Intensive efforts by UN agencies, NGOs and the other international donors have made the population healthier through immunisation and disease control campaigns. Clean drinking water supply was provided to towns and big cities. Schools, primary health care centres and drinking water supply systems were rehabilitated. More than 90 per cent of children attend primary school.

Even though infrastructure and supplies have been restored, services to remote rural areas were neglected and the urban-rural divide in Northern Iraq has widened; however this phenomenon is well known fact in the entire of the country

Free food rations, combined with the drought in 1998-1999 led to sharp decline in food prices, but at the expense of local food production. The oil-for-food programme six month resource allocation cycles militate against any long term planning. This has created greater dependency on the programme at the expense of sustainability and self reliance.

Education

It is estimated in 1999 that 90 per cent of children are enrolled in the first grade of primary school. It was less evident in remote areas. UNICEF rehabilitated 384 primary schools, mostly in urban areas. Another project was set up to increase access to primary education in rural areas. With UNICEF support, the local Ministry of Education and community members build 298 schools in villages. This admitted 7450 students. UNICEF provided more than 7000 desks to newly rebuilt schools. Around 690,000 children have received school stationary kits that contained pencils and copy books to use for educational purposes.

By the year 2000 1000 teachers were trained in maths, Kurdish, English, sciences and modern teaching methods by the UNICEF. UNICEF has also been strengthening the capacity of Ministry of Education staff to collect data on the current state of affairs in primary education and to plan for future programmes.

In 1999, 1.3 million text books were printed, an output fivefold greater than the annual average. UNICEF supported this process by providing computer equipment and software for Kurdish fonts. Software training was also conducted for printing staff. UNICEF helped education authorities transport two million textbooks from Baghdad to the north.

Amid such conditions, more than one in eight children in southern and central Iraq die before reaching his or her fifth birthday.

Water and Sanitation

The UN water and sanitation programme endeavoured on secure an access to safe water and sanitation and reducing differences in access between rural and urban areas. They provided appropriate technology, training, provision of equipment and supplies and water quality monitoring.

UNICEF has helped install water pumps, provided generators and transformers to pumping stations to the main cities of the north. This helped increase water availability from 110 litres per person in 1996 to 150 litres in 2000. The installation of more than 449 chlorinators and the provision of other water treatment chemicals have helped improve water quality. Some 1000 pump operators and engineers have been trained in pump operation and maintenance. UNICEF has also provided 171 sanitation vehicles to help dispose solid and liquid waste and has constructed 28 kilometres of sewage channels up to December 2000.

In rural areas, UNICEF has built or rehabilitated more than 1200 rural water schemes, benefiting 378,000 people. This has raised access to water for rural people from 63 per cent in 1996 to 82 per cent in 1999. The number of villages that had safe water has increased from 1,788 in 1996 to 2,599 in 2000. UNICEF supported training for 4,718 village operators in charge of managing village water pumps.

UNICEF runs a pilot project on school sanitation and hygiene education to improve hygiene practises amongst children, families and communities. Schools are used as a vehicle to promote hygiene messages. School toilets and water supply systems have been rehabilitated, mobile health teams visit the schools and conduct health check-ups and teachers give lessons in six different hygiene topics.

To help local authorities cope with the diminishing water supplies, UNICEF sent 100 water tankers to 475 villages and 25 towns. New wells were drilled.

Health

The UN program had distributed immunisation against six infectious child diseases, polio eradication; strengthened the primary health care.

In 2000, routine immunisation activities took place despite shortages of some vaccines. UNICEF supported National Polio Immunisation Days and provided 1.5 million polio doses. Mobile vaccination teams inoculated children in high-risk communities, and remote villagers. In 2000, 100 per cent of children less than one year of age were immunised against tuberculosis, 74 per cent against diphtheria, 76 per cent against polio 3 and 92 per cent against measles.

UNICEF held courses for 652 traditional birth attendants in rural villages. In addition, 164 health workers in antenatal clinics were trained in maternity care. Despite the lack of female staff in remote health centres.

To help control diarrhoeal diseases, one of the leading causes of child deaths, UNICEF gave support to 15 cholera watch teams. Health staff in clinics was trained in oral rehydration therapy.

To increase access to primary health care, UNICEF helped rehabilitate health centres. More than 60 health centres were rehabilitated during 2000. Eleven mobile health teams also visited primary schools throughout the north, carrying out check-ups and teaching children and teachers about proper hygiene.

Nutrition

The nutrition programme helped to improve the nutritional status of children under five and pregnant and lactating women. Large-scale screening for malnutrition and targeted nutrition programmes helped to reduce deficiency of iodine and vitamin A.

\Between 1994 and 2000, eight surveys were carried out. These studies not only measure the prevalence of malnutrition but also help build the skills of local experts involved in the surveys and advocate for greater efforts in reducing malnutrition. Between 1994 and 1999, acute malnutrition has dropped from 4.2 per cent to 1.8 per cent. Similarly chronic malnutrition has decreased from 37.3 per cent to 18.3 per cent.

UNICEF trained more than 4000 primary health workers in the use of growth monitoring equipment, breastfeeding promotion and prevention of vitamin and mineral deficiencies. Mobile monitoring teams are in the field to oversee the nutrition and preventative health care programme in primary health care centres...Mobile health teams travelled around schools and villages, teaching communities how to prevent malnutrition. After the entire situation in the northern Iraq was heaven compared to the rest of the country that was impoverished and people were reduced to mere existence.

8

War of attrition

In order to survive the impoverished people of the nation of Iraq started to sell their belongings; whatever they had, their television, their furniture, if they had a car, they were steadily and quickly reduced to crushing poverty.

The nation of Iraq was dying a slow death. The society was demoralised, crime rates has raised; the law disintegrated; people lost faith in the future; they lost interest in education. The rate of illiteracy had skyrocketed.

It was a brutal but silent war, regardless of who was the perpetrator, let it be Saddam or the Americans; the victim was an entire nation that steadily lost its integrity, its moral, its resources and its own people.

The sanctions were a collective punishment for a nation in its entirety. A punishment that was afflicted by the American policies and endorsed by the international community.

Sadly we lived to see another unjust war, a real war with more uranium bombs, destruction, misery and collective death inflicted on the people of Iraq.

Here are some eye witness accounts of the effects of the Sanctions:

"We call on the president of America, the vice president and the congressmen to come to Iraq and see the little children and Tony Blair, the U.K. government and Kofi Annan to come and to go to the cancer ward and give us an answer, what was their crime?"

Nobel Peace Prize scholar, Adolfo Perez-Esquivel, visited Iraq in March 1999.

"Where do the rights of children fit in here? Why should any, but especially children under the age of five, suffer so much and die in such numbers?"

"You kill people without blood or organs flying around, without angering American public opinion. People are dying silently in their beds. If 5,000 children are dying each month, this means 60,000 a year. Over eight years, we have half a million children. This is equivalent to two or three Hiroshima's."

U.S. officials were determined to keep the sanctions; it was seen as necessary deterrent to ensure that Iraq was obtaining military equipment. They accused the regime of hoarding medicine to worsen the plight of the people in order to gain support for lifting the sanctions without dismantling its weapons programs.

National Security Council spokesman P.J. Crowley said in an interview with New York times, Jan 1999 "There is enough food and enough medicine to care for and meet the needs of the Iraqi people,". "It is a manipulation by Saddam, using the suffering of the Iraqi people that he could solve if he wanted to…. We care more about the Iraqi people than he does."

Yet the UN officials who were monitoring the food and medicine distribution have not seen any evidence that the regime is withholding humanitarian supplies. They said the deterioration of storage and transportation systems sometimes slow distribution; however those were he results of the sanction itself.

Her mother, 21-year-old Said Naim, explains that the family lives in the al-Moufakia Flats, a notoriously poor housing development that has no drinking water. The water the family draws from a neighbourhood nearby is contaminated with sewage. Marium now suffers from gastroenteritis. Mohammed says the hospital is giving the baby medicine to clear up her diarrhoea and protein to improve her weight, but he expects the problem to recur when she returns home and resumes drinking the water.

The reporter of New York Times continues saying:

"The large stainless-steel box in the morgue at Basra Maternity and Paediatrics Hospital is called a refrigerator, but without power, it keeps no cooler than room temperature, which has risen to more than 100 degrees. The stench of decay fills the dusty, tiled room.

Dr. Abed al-Kareem Hussein opens the doors and pulls out the trays. Cardboard boxes made to ship packets of cereal and rolls of aluminium foil now hold the bodies of babies.

This is where the hospital keeps the corpses of children whose parents are unable to pay the $3 required for burial. The hospital will keep each for a few weeks before burying them in a pauper's field.

Hussein has counted 13 tiny corpses when an orderly arrives with another box. This one is marked "Tiffany Milk Biscuits." Inside is the body of a newborn that died after delivery, the fourth death in the hospital today".

Ref

- Ashraf Bayoumi, head of the World Food Programme Observation Unit (Al-Ahram Weekly, 24 December 1998).

- From: Smart Bombs, Dumb Sanctions January 3, 1999 New York Times Article

- Margarita Skinner, UNICEF Health Coordinator in Baghdad, 'Between Despair and Hope. Windows on my Middle East Journey 1967-1992'. The Radcliffe Press. London and New York 1998.

- National Security Council spokesman P.J. Crowley, interview with New York times, Jan 1999

Middle East Views

The Arab and Muslims throughout the world have condemned the United States officials for maintaining the sanctions it was thought of as being a low-intensity war of attrition against the Iraqis in the guise of sanctioned police action authorised by the United Nations.

There is no doubt that the Iraqi regime itself was condemned for providing the US with the opportunity of waging the war by invading and occupying Kuwait. Saddam and his military and political supporters in Iraq did not bear the brunt of the tremendous impact of the sanction imposed by the US on the people.

The Iraqi government by then made grave mistake and miscalculated the consequences of their act, it invaded a neighbour nation who was a sovereign member of the United Nations, regardless of what we thought were Kuwait belongs on the political map previously. Saddam had squandered the fortune of the nation in the war with Iran, the economy failed to recover after that war and yet he made another fool decision by invading Kuwait, using the slumping petrol prices as an excuse; blaming the Kuwaitis and the Gulf States for the decline of oil revenues. Those two wars had ruined the nation and forced considerable numbers of professionals to leave the country.

Saddam' regime had mocked the international community trying to evade the inspections warranted by the Security Council, this gave the world a reason to believe that he had weapons of mass destruction. The west used that as a pretext to maintain the sanctions, which had far exceed in proportionality and savagery of the rule of Saddam.

We were outraged that Mrs Albright when asked by television reporter whether US policies were worth the genocidal number of deaths of Iraqi civilians, which was in hundreds of thousands, she replied confidently, "*I think it is worth it.*" This was seen by the Arab nationalist as an act of genocide and mass murder of civilians.

The war during the sanction carried on by bombing targets in May parts of the country, it went on in silent but steady aggressions.

More damage had been done and more civilians were killed, more missile and anti-aircraft sites have been targeted, more civilians were killed. The American administration continued to reassure the world that it was not targeting the civilians in Iraq.

Dennis Halliday, the UN director of the Oil for Food programme in Iraq, resigned from his post and in his letter said "*the casualties of Iraq are mostly children, old people, women and the sick. The army, Baath Party officials, Saddam's entourage are spared the worst ravages of the war as well as the sanctions*"

The lifeline of Iraq has truly continued through Jordan; a steady trade with Jordan, Syria, and Turkey was there despite the sanctions, but only a relatively small number of people could benefit from that; the vast majority of the population has neither the means nor the mobility to get anything out of this smuggling.

Edward Saed (political analyst, university professor) Said "*The nation continued declining to the worse, Iraq's infrastructure was being slowly destroyed. Sewage, electrical power, communications, food distribution, water, medicine, education; access to all these is impaired to such a degree that most people now suffer the ravages of isolation, disease, darkness, and desperation without hope or respite*".

As the years went by, the stated US goal has changed; they clearly wanted to change the regime in Iraq and replace Saddam. This fuelled the anger of the Arab populace as it was seen as another war and more carnage. There were no candidates to replace Saddam; he made sure to kill anyone who opposed him. The opposition was in disarray, mostly in exile and can't stand each other.

As another war loomed after September 11 2001; the Arab distrust to the American officials had escalated. The bush administration started to talk about "the axis of evil". A disaster was inevitably coming. Widespread anger has taken the Middle East; the overwhelming majority was outraged by the American policy and questioned whether the American officials had the right to meddle in the region policies and changed the governments that it does not like. Some Iraqi, unfortunately, was hopeful that it will mean the end of Saddam; however most of us have miscalculated the price that we were going to pay.

The American officials were looked upon as the upcoming Mongols who ravaged Baghdad (Holago 1258). We knew a ruthless war was coming.

Edward Saed "*the Americans had history of reducing whole peoples, countries and even continents to ruin by nothing short of holocaust deserves to be better known by non-Americans, who believe despite all the evidence that the US is a country dedicated to enlightened Wilsonian ideals of liberty and democracy*".

Glance at the history shows the ruin brought on by US intervention in Latin America, the Caribbean, Asia (Philippines and Vietnam), Africa, and the Middle East. There is an attitude of murderous righteousness in most cases, the same whether it is the New England Puritans killing Indians or Henry Kissinger ordering the bombing of Laos and Cambodia. Iraq to Us (as Arab people) is 6,000 years of civilisation, modern Iraq was secular and most advanced of Arab countries before the endless wars. Iraqis throughout history were poets, artists, doctors, architects and above all generous and warm fine people; they are a source of pride to any Arabic person.

The mere thought of occupying Baghdad was dreadful, another war that is going to ruin Baghdad again, hundreds of tons of depleted uranium bombs, another blow to the infrastructure!! Was just inconceivable.

That thought was sadistic aggression; it was a continuation of a sadistic dehumanisation of an entire nation.

Ref

- Edward Said "Barbarians at the gates" Al-Ahram Weekly

- 11–17 March 1999

- Catherine Starr. IRAQ: UN SANCTIONS, U.S.-BRITISH AIR STRIKES DRAW FIRE FROM ARAB, digest. August 24, 1999

- Shari Silberstein Sanctions in Iraq: A Weapon of Mass Destruction December 19, 1998

9

The Diaspora of Iraqi people

OCTOBER 31, 2002

For over 30 years Iraqi people have been forced into exile: approximately (by 2001) three million people, out of twenty-three million people, have left Iraq. Despite its extent and seriousness, the issue of Iraqi refugees was largely ignored or forgotten. The conditions of their exile, their survival were in an appalling situation. Their psychological conditions were ignored; the reason for their exile was not dealt with. There were more people that left Iraq than what the United Nations and other international organisations did not include in their statistics, those were professionals, who managed to find jobs and immigrated to different parts of the world such as Yemen, Libya, New Zealand, and Australia. Many people managed to find a work opportunity in Europe and America, mostly those were the elite that the Iraqi society had lost and probably forever.

Several thousands of Iraqi people have died, either drowned in the Aegean Sea (trying to escape to Europe) or between Indonesia and Australia, killed while crossing borders or summarily executed. Some of Iraq's neighbouring countries have jailed and deported Iraqis, thus exposed them to great risks, while other countries have placed landmines in neighbouring regions, which caused some loss of lives. The economic plight imposed on the Iraqis left most of them to living in appalling conditions. The number of Iraqi refugees in Western countries continued to increase, while these countries were trying to stop the arrival of migrants on their soil. Some neighbouring countries were worried about massive influx of refugees in case of a war; they have reinforced the controls at their borders, in order to prevent people from crossing them.

That had imposed a grave danger to the life of the refugees, and prompted international human right organisations such as International Alliance for Justice, the International Federation of Human Rights League, Foundation France Libertés, and the French Human Rights League to call upon the neighbouring countries to comply with the international conventions on the right of asylum and to provide the necessary means of survival to the refugees in case of massive influx.

The governments of Jordan, Kuwait, Syria, and Saudi Arabia are not members of the Refugee Convention, they have no local rules or laws that deal with or protect refugees. All four governments of those Arab brothers had regulations ranging from just neglect to outright hostility towards the Iraqi refugees present in their countries. Kuwait was particularly hostile to Iraqi refugees because they are often suspected of previous collaboration with the Saddam government during the Gulf War of Kuwait invasion. However, Kuwaiti government had an agreement that was endorsed by the Kuwaiti National Assembly agreement with UNHCR in 1996 and accepted the UNHCR mandate to host and protect refugees.

Jordan hosted about 300,000 Iraqis, the number was probably higher, because most Iraqi people were not registered with the UNHCR because they either doubt the benefits of registering with UNHCR, or waiting for opportunities elsewhere or just worried they could get persecuted if they had to go back ti Iraq.

In accordance with an agreement signed between UNHCR and Jordan in April 1998, refugees were granted temporary asylum for Iraqi refugees in Jordan for a maximum period of six months, by the end of six months if they did not manage to find a refuge they were regarded as illegal immigrant and had to pay daily fines and run the risk of being forced to go back to Iraq. The refugees waiting for resettlement were accepted by the Jordanian government pending their departure; they had no permission to work and were subjected to periodic checks and scrutiny.

Kuwait hosted 15,000 Iraqi refugees in 2001. There were 5,200 Iraqi refugees are in the Rafha camp in Saudi Arabia. Syria, meanwhile, has over 1,700 recognized refugees registered with UNHCR, awaiting resettlement. Refugees in Syria were allowed to remain for a period of nine months, but they were not allowed to stay any longer. The U.S. Committee for Refugees estimates that there are 40,000 Iraqis in Syria who were not registered and were not formally recognized as refugees or asylum seekers.

The Saudi camp of Rafha was notorious for maltreatment of refugees. Although Saudi Arabia provides health care, air conditioning, and primary and secondary schooling in the Rafha camp, it remained largely a prison a prison located in the desert in a military zone. The Iraqi refugees lived totally isolated, the authorities only occasionally allowed them to access some markets in local towns. Dozens of Iraqi refugees held at this camp in Saudi Arabia were maltreated and went on a hunger strike in July 2001 to draw the world and the media for their misery. They had a program to resettle those refugees in different other countries; however that program was broken off in 1997, no country in the world was willing to accept them.

As of October 2002 the Saudi government has agreed to allow 2,000 Iraqis to settle permanently in Saudi Arabia, on a strict condition that the remaining 3,200 should be resettled permanently in other countries.

In Jordan and Syria, the access UNHCR offices was not straight forward, many refugees who would have had an acceptable reason to be a refugee under the Refugee Convention Regulations did not register UNHCR. Corruption made some of those non-registered refugees vulnerable to harassment and punishment by the Jordanian and Syrian police; they were exposed to abuse and some of them were repatriated by force.

Although the Syrian government denies forcibly repatriating refugees, there were reports that a significant number of Iraqis were forcibly returned to northern Iraq in 1999 and that several hundred were expelled in December 2001.There is evidence that the Jordanian police has done similar expulsion; such actions were very intimidating and prevented other refugees from coming forward to register with UNHCR.

Refugees (Iraqi people displaced far away)

At the end of 2001, the largest populations of Iraqi refugees outside the Middle East region were hosted by Sweden (25,900), the Netherlands (26,100), and the United States (19,100). Denmark (12,600), the United Kingdom (12,000), Norway (8,200), Australia (10,000) and Canada (6,000) also hosted significant numbers of Iraqi refugees.

As a result of armed conflicts and sanctions in Iraq, governments all over the world had hosted Iraqi refugees and offered them with respite and protection. Often those people had left the country and stayed fro variable duration at countries in the Gulf region (mostly Jordan, Iran and Syria).

United Nations urged the international community to keep their borders open to refugees, and immediately apply immigration measures. Other countries have applied strict policies including visa restrictions, carrier sanctions, detention and interception policies that effectively denied access to those seeking safe haven. Due to the flood of immigration, Australia and European Union member countries have in the late 1990s increasingly adopted "third country" policy, which implies that asylum seekers should find refuge in the first country they entered upon fleeing their country of origin; those who travel on are swiftly sent back to that country.

In November 2002, the E.U. states mandated the European Commission to negotiate asylum agreements with Turkey, E.U. member states wanted Turkey to be the third country to which Iraqi asylum seekers can be deported...

Turkey had a bad record of harsh treatment to asylum seekers from Iraq, based on that reputation of treating asylum seekers, Turkey could not be counted on to provide protection In the event of threatening war in Iraq.

It was a difficult task for the UN to accommodate Iraqi refugees no third country rules could be applied to Iraqi refugees, who will inevitably have to transit other countries to reach Australia, North America and Europe. And worse many countries including Australia and European countries were planning to repatriate Iraqi refugees.

Under present Australian policy, refugees, including those from Iraq, can only arrive in Australia by air; those who came by boat were frequently forced to return to Indonesia. This practically meant that only those holding valid travel documents are able to apply for humanitarian asylum In Australia. Any new arrivals by sea would either be detained in Christmas Island, then they had their claims examined without reference to Australian law, or they would be detained in one of the Australian-funded "offshore" sites in the Pacific (Nauru or Papua New Guinea).

Before that refugees arriving by boat have been intercepted and sent back to Indonesia. By January 2001, there were hundreds of Iraqis in Indonesia who had been turned back. Indonesia is not a signatory to the Refugee Convention and there are no local rules to host or protect refugees.

Many Iraqis who had already got to Australia have been granted only a temporary visas for variable times, they were going to be repatriated at a latter date, a status which requires them undergo to periodic evaluation of their need for continued refugee protection. Some refugees were given a form of protection that will only be reviewed when the situation in Iraq will be stabilized. If the hearings occur after the end of the war, individual refugees would have to prove that their return to Iraq was going to expose them to persecution. That made their future hanging and uncertain.

Even before the second war the Australian government had put considerable pressure Iraqi asylum seekers (those whose request of asylum were turned down) to return home, despite the terrible consequences likely to happen to them when they return to Iraq. Most of these rejected asylum seekers remained in detention camps, either in Australia or in the remote Pacific island where they had no mean to communicate with the rest of the world and no access to lawyers. Some of them spent many years in detention under harsh conditions. The Australian government offered them assistance with "voluntary return" to countries in the Middle East of which they are not nationals, such as Syria or Yemen.

European states had expressed willingness return rejected asylum seekers to Iraq. Germany, Denmark, Luxembourg and Switzerland, there was an "internal relocation alternative" for certain Iraqis in the Kurdish-controlled zone of northern Iraq, which was protected by the UN from the Iraqi authorities. The European Union had planned to return the refuges to the northern part of the country that was seen as an internal relocation alternative for those who fear persecution at the hands of the regime in Baghdad. E.U. countries have rejected a number of asylum seekers claims on that basis and returned them to the north.

In August 2002 Denmark planned to send home Iraqis whose asylum requests have been turned down, despite the imminent threat of a U.S. attack on Iraq, stating that *"the potential risks of war do not in themselves justify asylum."* According to the Danish immigration minister Bertel Haarder. Danish immigration office indicated that some Iraqi refugees can return to the country without facing any risk. Denmark announced in May 2002 that it would not deport twenty-six Iraqis on hunger strike in the Copenhagen cathedral, who was protesting the slow treatment or rejection of their asylum status. Integration Minister Bertel Haarder stated that Denmark would *"try to send back as many refugees as possible but will not force them to leave."* And their plight continued so did the uncertainty.

The burden of the refugees was obvious that On November, 2001 prompted Greece to sign an agreement with Turkey, which allows the Greek government to intercept individuals who departed from Turkey, and return them to Turkish territory. One such event happened on November 21, 2001, forty-two refugees were intercepted as they were heading from Turkey for the Greek island of Kos. Following the readmission agreement, Greece acquired several patrol boats for the purpose of intercepting refugees trying to reach its territory.

In April 2002, the Swedish Migration Minister Jan Karlsson indicated that Sweden would start repatriate asylum seekers from Iraq. Several thousand Iraqi asylum seekers who have been refused refugee status in Sweden were waiting to be deported to Iraq. According to Karlsson, April 2002, the situation in northern Iraq had stabilized, making it possible to people to that region, even if they were not Kurd. At the same time, Sweden granted Kurds from the Kurdish-controlled zone in northern Iraq permanent permission to remain in the country!

In 2001, the United Kingdom determined that the Kurdish-controlled zone of northern Iraq was increasingly stable and was exploring the options of repatriating refugees, a result of which was a drop in its recognition rate for Iraqi refugees. In July 2002, the British government announced that it planned to deport Iraqi Kurdish refugees who failed to acquire a refugee status.

Over 3,000 new Iraqi refugees arrived in the United States in 2001. Of these, about 815 were individuals who arrived at US airports or borders. The remainder arrived through the resettlement program of the UN, from countries in the immediate region and neighbours of Iraq. United States had allocated 70,000 places for resettled refugees from throughout the world in 2003. Refugees from Iraq have been especially affected by an increase in background checks on resettled refugees that has slowed down resettlement processing and left many refugees in dangerous situations. On January 10, 2003, the U.S. State Department introduced—and withdrew without comment less than twenty-four hours later—a policy that would have denied admission to Iraqis already identified as refugees in need of resettlement

Ref

- Shannon Meehan and Ada Williams, Refugees are Iraqi forgotten people LA Times

- 07/14/2003

- http://www.hrw.org/backgrounder/mena/iraq

- SARAH KERSHAW A NATION AT WAR: IRAQI EXILES; In Saudi Desert, '91 Iraqi Refugees Long to Return; April,11, 2003

- UNHCR

- Jonathan Victor Marshall; the Lies We Are Told About Iraq. Los Angeles Times. January 5, 2003

- www.un.org/apps/news/story. asp

- ELIZABETH OLSON World Briefing | United Nations: Concern over Danes' Proposal on Foreigners. New York Times. January 23, 2002

10

The Plight of Iraqi refugees

The Plight of Iraqis in Saudi Arabia's Rafha refugee camp
The UNHCR In May 1993 released the following statement about the refugees camp in Rafha

A pattern of torture and ill-treatment, particularly of former members of the Iraqi armed forces, emerges from the evidence gathered by Amnesty International, including testimonies provided by scores of former inmates of Areaways and Rafha camps. Refugees detained in both camps have described various forms of systematic torture and ill-treatment. Their accounts are consistent with information gathered from independent sources and by other non-governmental organizations such as the Lawyers Committee for Human Rights (LCHR). The victims have described systematic beatings all over the body, being forced to stand for prolonged periods of time, the administration of electric shocks and being dowsed with cold water while naked. In addition some have also endured tale (hanging by the wrists from the ceiling or a high window), falaqa (beatings on the soles of the feet) and deprivation of sleep for prolonged periods. Such methods of torture are known to have been used against political opponents in the Kingdom. In most cases, the refugees are tortured or ill-treated for a wide variety of perceived offences, including criticizing the camps' authorities, protesting living conditions, being "disobedient" or in order to extract "confessions".

Torture in Artawiyya

On at least two different occasions groups of refugees in Artawiyya camp were physically and psychologically abused after they peacefully protested their living conditions. In August 1991 and again in July 1992 groups of refugees went on hunger strikes demanding improvements in their living conditions and their resettlement in a third country. As a form of protest some of the refugees stitched their lips shut while others buried themselves with only their head above the ground. Many of those involved in these protests were later subjected to torture or ill-treatment"

After the Gulf war and the rebellion in the south that followed the war large numbers of people from the south of the country ran away for fear of their lives to neighbouring countries, thousands of them went westward to Saudi Arabia; they encountered appalling treatment by the Saudi authorities. The refugees are the last group of 33,000 Iraqis who fled to Saudi Arabia after the second Gulf war. The Rafha camp was built on a military base 12 kilometres from the Saudi-Iraqi border.

It is estimated that around 90,000 Iraqis were originally granted temporary asylum in the US-occupied zone of southern Iraq and Saudi Arabia after the war. The majority of them were prisoners of war, military deserters and others who fled the country, some with their families, after having taken part in the anti-Saddam uprising in southern Iraq after the war. Most of the refugees did not seek asylum or refuge in Saudi Arabia. The western Allies airlifted them to Rafha from a transit-camp in Aswan, in the occupied zone along the Iraqi-Kuwaiti border, shortly before they evacuated the area. Some 66,000 of them returned to Iraq in a subsequent exchange of POWs. But 33,000 refugees refused to return and were housed in two camps, Artawiyyah and Rafha. Conditions in the Artawiyyah camp, which housed captured Iraqi soldiers who refused to return to Iraq, were very poor. It was eventually closed in 1992 and its residents were transferred to Rafha.

The Saudis have kept them confined like prisoners to the camp, for more than ten years. For all this time, the refugees had lived in temporary mud-brick barracks. They were canvas-roofed units with simple schools; they had some medical care and other facilities. As such, the refugees had lived as prisoners in the militarily guarded camp. The camp is run by the Saudi military with supervision from the UNHCR, which had intensified its presence and services in the Kingdom since 1992 to provide the needs for the refugees. Saudi military regularly patrol the camp enforcing a nightly curfew.

UNHCR report 1993

"At least seven people were reportedly shot and killed and many more injured in March or April 1991 in al-Salman, one of the holding areas where refugees from Iraq were gathered before being transferred to Rafha camp. At the time, the refugees were under the military jurisdiction of the French army and the administrative jurisdiction of the Saudi Arabian army. One morning in late March or early April 1991 as some of the refugees were queuing for water from a water truck, an argument ensued between Saudi Arabian army personnel and the refugees. The refugees were demanding an increase in their water allowance. Saudi Arabian soldiers reportedly fired into the crowd, killing one man and injuring many others. Following this incident the ref-

ugees began a peaceful protest and delegated some of them to negotiate with the Saudi Arabian military authorities. The crowd grew and the protestors reportedly began chanting their demands. Saudi Arabian soldiers are then said to have indiscriminately opened fire at the crowd killing at least six people. Among those killed was Muhammad Ne'mah Salman, a student in his mid-20s from the city of Diwaniyya"

Flogging in Rafha (Amnesty international report)

"The judicial punishment of flogging is widely used in the camp. It is imposed for a wide range of offences including sexual acts between unmarried heterosexual couples and the consumption of alcohol. Refugees in Rafha camp who are charged with offences punishable by flogging are tried by a Shari'a court judge, who visits the camp on a regular basis. Individuals are brought before the judge in the absence of any defence counsel and, more often than not, are convicted solely on the basis of a "confession "signed under duress".

The vast majority of the refugees had a reason to fear persecution if the went back to Iraq and had been granted political asylum. The two camps were established in accordance with deal between the Americans and the Saudi government. However, from the very beginning the Saudi government had made it clear that the camps were built on the condition that no refugees will be offered local integration in the kingdom, and that they would not leave the fenced-in 20-sq kilometre area. The refugees can only leave their camp on a temporary basis with special permits provided in urgent situations such as for medical treatment in hospitals outside the camp. The Saudi Authorities had assigned them the term guest.

In 2001 more than 5,000 Iraqis remain stranded and forgotten in the Rafha refugee camp in north-eastern Saudi Arabia.

Many Iraqis around the world protested, the Canadian Iraqi community protest was the most noticeable, they took to the streets of Ottawa with their friends and supporters, held a demonstration on July 28th in front of the offices of the United Nations High Commission for Refugees (UNHCR). They were protesting against the horrible conditions of Iraqi refugees in Rafha camp in the barren desert of north-eastern Saudi Arabia. The protesters called on the international organization *"to act immediately to resume the resettlement program" for 5,200 Iraqi refugees who are still in the Rafha camp.* They also called on the UNHCR "to approach interested countries to help resettling all the refugees." Similar demonstrations were also held in Stockholm (Sweden), Copenhagen (Denmark) and New York (US).

A month earlier refugees at Rafha started a hunger-strike that lasted for a month demanding resettlement in suitable country. Many of those refugees were treated for dehydration, exhaustion and heat strokes. More than 250 people were treated at the Rafha centre.

More than 25,000 refugees have been resettled to other countries, mostly in America, Australia and Scandinavian countries. But s 5,200 remains there in limbo, still waiting in the barren desert for a lasting solution to their plight, amid dwindling hope and increasing frustration. They are unable to return to Iraq for fear of persecution.

Resettlement from Rafha had stopped in 1997. According to the UNCHR, about 40 percent of the camp's population in 2000 was under the age of eighteen and one fourth was under the age of ten, who had seen no land they could call home. According to UNHCR sources the Saudi authorities provided a high level of material assistance to the refugees. Yet the desert was inhospitable, nothing could ameliorate the suffering.

Many of them had not heard from their families back in the country since they left the Iraq in 1991...Women refugees faced excessive restrictions. The Saudi authorities prevent women from moving freely within the camp unless they are wearing a niqab (a veil that covers the head, face and neck of women in the Saudi culture) and should be accompanied by a male relative. Single men lived in a different section from the families.

There were many reports of systematic abuse of the refugees by the Saudi guards.

Eventually the harassment and the frustration they faced pushed them for a confrontation in 1993 with the camp guard. Thirteen people were killed and many others injured. Those particular refugees in Rafha had none of the l rights and protections granted to other refugees under international laws.

The geographic location of the camp did not comply with the UNHR and international regulations that require refugees to be protected in a place further away from their country of origin to ascertain their safety. Saudi was not a party to the 1951 Convention for refugees.

Amnesty International had a press release in July 2001:

"The treatment the Saudis to Iraqi refugees contrasts sharply with their open-arms policy toward Kuwaiti refugees during the Gulf crisis. During the seven-month-long Iraqi occupation of Kuwait, tens of thousands of Kuwaitis sought refuge in Saudi Arabia, where they were housed in public housing units and given the right to move freely around the kingdom".

The refugee's life at the camp of Rafha, the poor prospects of resettlement to a third country, and the uncertainty of their future put the refugees under enormous psychological stress. The frustration and the despair had led some of them to attempt suicide, obviously many of them saw the only way out of the misery and hopelessness was death. Many had suffered depression or post traumatic stress disorder.

An estimated 3,200 refugees have returned to Iraq out of despair. The majority however feared for their lives from the brutal regime in Baghdad...Some of those who returned have reportedly suffered severe punishment. Many of those who returned were said to have been arrested and jailed. The whereabouts of many others remained largely unknown, probably persecuted by Iraqi Mukhabarat. Many of them are believed to have been executed.

Rafha Camp was elegantly described as *"a place where there are no dreams any more, a monument to human suffering, endurance and wounded pride".*

References

UNHCR Briefing Notes October 15, 2002. "Iraqi refugees go on hunger strike in Saudi camp," Agence France-Presse, July 2, 2001.

"Lubbers Impressed by Saudi Efforts to Rehabilitate Iraqi Refugees," Saudi Press Agency, October 17, 2002.

U S Committee for Refugees World Refugee Survey 2002 UNHCR only counted 300 Iraqis in Kuwait in 2001. *See* UNHCR Statistical Yearbook 2001, October 2002, p. 92.

UNHCR, Statistical Yearbook 2001, October 2002, p. 92.

The Iraq foundation, July 2001

Amnesty International July 2001

See U.S. Committee for Refugees, *World Refugee Survey 2002*

U S Committee for Refugees World Refugee Survey 2002.

Red Crescent International, August 16-31, 1993).

Géraldine Chatelard, "Iraqi Forced Migrants in Jordan: Conditions, Religious Networks, and the Smuggling Process" September 2002

UNHCR, Statistical Yearbook 2001, October 2002, p. 92.

Correspondence from UNHCR, December 3, 2002 (Human Rights Watch).

Jordan does have a few provisions in its Constitution that recognize the existence of "political refugees."

U.S. Committee for Refugees, World Refugee Survey 2002, p. 178.

U.S. Committee for Refugees, World Refugee Survey 2002, p. 182.

UNHCR's "Saudi Arabia: Country Profile" (September 1999

11

Iraq, casualty of the Sanctions

Iraqi people fell as a mass casualty of the Sanctions

There was no doubt that the UNSCOM weapons inspections teams eliminated the majority of Iraq's weapons and its capability to produce them, UN Resolution 687 also mentions that Iraq's disarmament should represent a step towards "the goal of establishing in the Middle East a zone free from weapons of mass destruction and all missiles for their delivery." That was an essential prerequisite for peace in the Middle East. However Israel's arsenal of nuclear weapons remained unchallenged.

George W Bush took power in 2001, the search for evidence of the weapons of mass destruction, their existence and their potential continued as a mean for pressuring Saddam to give up power in Iraq, which became more evident as a goal in the American foreign policy.. Because the sanctions had indefinite term, ending them would require another resolution by the Security Council. The US and UK would be in a position to veto any such resolution even though the sanctions on Iraq have been opposed France, Russia, and China. The sanctions, in effect were not going to be lifted unless the United States wanted to do so.

Joy Gordon (an academic who studies the ethics of international relations from Harper Magazine) said in November 2002 "*If any international act in the last decade is sure to generate enduring bitterness toward the United States, it is the epidemic suffering needlessly visited on Iraqis via U.S within that body*".

The sanctions were indeed a deadly weapon, and the victims were the innocent Iraqis.

Joy Gordon (an academic who studies the ethics of international relations from Harper Magazine) said in November 2002

"*I have acquired many of the key confidential U.N. documents concerning the administration of Iraq sanctions. I obtained these documents on the condition that my sources remain anonymous. What they show is that the United States has fought aggressively throughout the last decade to purposefully minimize the humanitarian*

*goods that enter the country. And it has done so in the face of enormous human suffer-
ing, including massive increases in child mortality and widespread epidemics. It has
sometimes given a reason for its refusal to approve humanitarian goods, sometimes
given no reason at all, and sometimes changed its reason three or four times, in each
instance causing a delay of months. Since August 1991 the United States has blocked
most purchases of materials necessary for Iraq to generate electricity, as well as equipment for radio, telephone, and other communications. Often restrictions have hinged
on the withholding of a single essential element, rendering many approved items useless. For example, Iraq was allowed to purchase a sewage-treatment plant but was
blocked from buying the generator necessary to run it; this in a country that has been
pouring 300,000 tons of raw sewage daily into its rivers".*

The oil for food program and the subsequent changes in the sanctions allowed
Iraq to have some development projects. However the United States and Britain
subjected hundreds of contracts to intense scrutiny, other members of the Security Council was not involved; and after that scrutiny the US, only occasionally
involved Britain, and consistently blocked hundreds of humanitarian contracts.
United States always demanded detailed information about the goods and how
they would be used, and continuously expanded its monitoring system, tracking
each item from contracting through delivery and installation, ensuring that the
imports are used for legitimate civilian purposes. Despite all these measures. In
September 2001 nearly one third of water and sanitation and one quarter of electricity and educational-supply contracts were on hold by the US demand.
Between the springs of 2000 and 2002, holds on humanitarian supplies tripled.

A couple of months later, a Syrian company asked the committee to approve a
contract to mill flour for Iraq. Whereas Iraq ordinarily purchased food directly, in
this case it was growing wheat but did not have adequate facilities to produce
flour. The Russian delegate argued that, in light of the report the committee had
received from the UNICEF official, and the fact that flour was an essential element of the Iraqi diet, the committee had no choice but to approve the request
on humanitarian grounds. The delegate from China agreed, as did those from
France and Argentina. But the U.S. representative, Eugene Young, argued that
"there should be no hurry" to move on this request: the flour requirement under
Security Council Resolution 986 had been met, he said;

The British delegate stalled as well, saying that he would need to see "how the
request would fit into the Iraqi food programme," and that there were still questions about transport and insurance. In the end, despite the extreme malnutrition
of which the committee was aware, the U.S. delegate insisted it would be "prema-

ture" to grant the request for flour production, and the U.K. representative joined him, blocking the project from going forward.

The American hold on supplies was outrageous; a French contract for the supply of ventilators for intensive-care units stayed on hold for more than five months, despite his government's prompt and detailed response to a request for additional technical information and the obvious humanitarian character of the goods.

Thus millions in humanitarian contracts had been delayed not because of security concerns but simply because of U.S. disinterest in spending the money necessary to review them. In other cases, after all U.S. objections to a delayed contract were addressed (a process that could take years), the United States simply changed its reason for the hold, and the review process began all over. After a half-million-dollar contract for medical equipment was blocked in February 2000, and the company spent two years responding to U.S. requests for information, the United States changed its reason for the hold, and the contract remained blocked.

U.S. policy on water-supply contracts was very aggressive. For every such contract unblocked, three new ones were put on hold. A 2001 UNICEF report to the Security Council found that access to clean drinking water for the Iraqi population had not improved much under the Oil for Food Programme, and specifically cited the half a billion dollars of water—and sanitation-supply contracts were blocked. UNICEF reported that up to 40 percent of the purified water run through pipes is contaminated or lost through leakage. [Yet the United States blocked or delayed contracts for water pipes. Chlorine, the United States blocked the safety equipment necessary to handle the substance, not only for Iraqis but for U.N. employees charged with chlorine monitoring there.

In early 2001, the United States had placed holds on $280 million in medical supplies, including vaccines to treat infant hepatitis, tetanus, and diphtheria, as well as incubators and cardiac equipment. The rationale was that the vaccines contained live cultures, albeit highly weakened ones. The Iraqi government, it was argued, could conceivably extract these, and eventually grow a virulent fatal strain, then develop a missile or other delivery system that could effectively disseminate it.

Security Council: Russia, Britain, China, and France—vetoed the proposal. In the face of this new political agenda, U.S. security concerns suddenly disappeared. In early June of last year, when the "smart sanctions" proposal was under negotiation, the United States announced that it would lift holds on $800 million of contracts, of which $200 million involved business with key Security

Council members. A few weeks later, the United States lifted holds on $80 million of Chinese contracts with Iraq, including some for radio equipment and other goods that had been blocked because of dual-use concerns.

In the end, China and France agreed to support the U.S. proposal. But Russia did not, and immediately after Russia vetoed it, the United States placed holds on nearly every contract that Iraq had with Russian companies.

Under the new system, UNMOVIC and the International Atomic Energy Agency make the initial determination about whether an item appears on the GRL, which includes only those materials questionable enough to be passed on to the Security Council. The list is precise and public, but huge. Tallied together from existing U.N. and other international lists and precedents, the GRL has been virtually customized to accommodate the imaginative breadth of U.S. policymakers' security concerns. Yet when U.N. weapons experts began reviewing the $5 billion worth of existing holds, they found that very few of them were for goods that ended up on the GRL or warranted the security concern than the United States had originally claimed.

To counter this, the United States and Britain devised a system that had the effect of undermining Iraq's basic capacity to sell oil: "retroactive pricing." Taking advantage of the fact that the 661 Committee sets the price Iraq receives from each oil buyer, the United States and Britain began to systematically withhold their votes on each price until the relevant buying period had passed. The idea was that then the alleged surcharge could be subtracted from the price after the sale had occurred, and that price would then be imposed on the buyer. The effect of this practice has been to torpedo the entire Oil for Food Programme.

Ref

Joy Gordon Harpers magazine, November 2002, Cool War: Economic sanctions as a weapon of mass destruction

http://www.unicef.org/emerg/iraq/index.html

Smart Bombs, Dumb Sanctions January 3, 1999 New York Times

http://www.un.org/Depts/unmovic/Bx27.htm

Barry Grey. US and Britain combine to maintain crippling sanctions on Iraq; World socialist Website; 5 January 2000

12

September 11

The undeclared war after September 11

The wrangling over the issues of weapons of mass destruction went from 1991-2003; it was 13 years of uncertainty that damaged the economy, businesses and education. The uncertainty had brought life in the country to a complete halt. After September 11 the situation got even worse and it was evident that another war was almost certain. The American and British 2nd Gulf war on Iraq started silently immediately after September 11, 2001. Royal Air Force and US fighters had changed tactics and escalated their "patrols" over Iraq preparing for an assault on both military and civilian targets in the country. Bombing of Iraqi targets increased by 300 per cent. According to Ministry of Defence reply to MPs, Between March and November 2002, the Royal Air Force dropped more than 124 tonnes of bombs. Tony Blair government continued to claim in the British Parliament that no final decision has been taken

From August to December 2002, there were 62 attacks by American F-16 and Royal Air Force Tornadoes. Those attacks were claimed to be on Iraqi air defence; however civilian deaths definitely happened. Those attacks were breach of the truce and were illegal under the United Nations Charter and the conventions of war and international law. The bombing is a "secret war". Although such attacks happened before September 11, they were escalated after that date.

The US and British officials claimed they have a UN mandate to patrol "no-fly zones" which was the south of Iraq after the first Gulf war. That gave them total control of the air space in Iraq. The Anglo-American axis claimed that they were always targeting military facilities, however, John Pilger said in 2002" *I have seen the result of these attacks. When I drove from the northern city of Mosul three years ago, I saw the remains of an agricultural water tanker and truck, riddled with bullet holes, shrapnel from a missile, a shoe and the wool and skeletons of about 150 sheep. A family of six, a shepherd, his father and his wife and four children, were blown to pieces here. It was treeless, open country: a moonscape. The shepherd, his family and his sheep would have been clearly visible from the air".*

Whether the American or British aircraft had done that was not clear. British Ministry of Defence official in London said, "*We reserve the right to take robust action when threatened.*" This attack was investigated and confirmed by the senior United Nations official in Iraq at the time, Hans Von Sponeck, who drove there especially from Baghdad. He confirmed that nothing nearby resembled a military installation. Von Sponeck recorded his finding in a confidential internal document entitled, "Air Strikes in Iraq", prepared by the UN Security Section. Many reports described similar attacks that happened on innocents people.

Advertisement

In 1999, Tony Blair said the no fly zones allowed the US and Britain to patrol the skies of the north to protect the Kurds and the ethnic Marsh Arabs in the south. In fact, the allied air force has provided cover for Turkish army to invade the northern part of Iraq. Turkey was a strong ally to the US; the B52 Bombers were stationed in Turkey in the first war. That is all despite the fact that Turkey has a bad record of human rights, hundreds of thousands of Kurds have been displaced and tens of thousands killed in the last few decades.

For joining the US "coalition" against Iraq, the Turkish regime is to be rewarded with a bribe worth $6billion, in order to allow the American Army to invade Iraq via Turkey.

It was clear by 2002 that the United States is preparing for another attack and invasion in Iraq. The Pentagon's "Doctrine for Joint Urban Operations" says that unless Baghdad falls quickly it has to be the target of "overwhelming firepower".

Their were prior plans to use Cluster bombs, deep penetration "bunker" buster bombs and depleted uranium again. By 2002 the human cost of the American-driven embargo of Iraq was tremendous; it does mount clearly to the effects of weapons of mass destruction, yet the American using the WMDs as an excuse to invade Iraq.

"The country's regression over the past decade is by far the most severe of the 193 countries surveyed.

Ref

John Pilger, foreign policy correspondent 18 December 2002

Barry Grey. US and Britain combine to maintain crippling sanctions on Iraq; World socialist Website; 5 January 2000

Anthony Arnove Iraq under Siege the Deadly Impact of Sanctions and War

WMDs (the roots)

On June 7, 1981, in an attempt to prevent Iraqi acquisition of a nuclear weapons capability, Israeli aircraft bombed Iraq's nuclear reactor, by then the reactor was in the stages of being built by a French company.

It is very much doubted whether Iraq was able or not after that attack to acquire any nuclear technology. Certainly nothing has been proved so far that it was advanced in that type of technology. In the latter years of the sanctions and after Bush took power in the US, the American officials were determined to deny Saddam Acquiring any nuclear capabilities; and that was used to convince the world about the imminent dangers posed by Saddam regime. Eventually in 2003 US waged a war to overthrow Saddam based on his capability of and acquisition of weapons of mass destruction, which was never proved.

This Chapter is devoted to quotes form politicians about the issue of WMDs

"One way or the other, we are determined to deny Iraq the capacity to develop weapons of mass destruction and the missiles to deliver them. That is our bottom line (Bill Clinton say 17. feb.1998)

"Iraq is a long way from [here], but what happens there matters a great deal here. For the risks that the leaders of a rogue state will use nuclear, chemical or biological weapons against us or our allies is the greatest security threat we face" (Madeline Albright 18.feb 1998)

Hussein has chosen to spend his money on building weapons of mass destruction and palaces for his cronies."(Albright, 10.nov.1999)

"If I found in any way, shape or form that he was developing weapons of mass destruction, I'd take 'em out. I'm surprised he's still there." Asked if that meant he would overthrow Saddam, Bush said he was only talking about "the weapons of mass destruction."

(Presidential candidate George W Bush, New Hampshire 2 Dec 1999)

"The Secretary of State is going to go listen to our allies as to how best to effect a policy, the primary goal of which will be to say to Saddam Hussein: we won't tolerate you developing weapons of mass destruction, and we expect you to leave your neighbours alone

President George W Bush. 22 Feb 2001

"He's been a menace forever, and we will do—he needs to open his country up for inspection, so we can see whether or not he's developing weapons of mass destruction

President George W Bush 7 Aug 2001

Then September 11, 2001 happened

Shortly after September 11, 2001, the Bush administration (and Tony Blair, and several members of Congress) suddenly began telling everybody that Saddam Hussein definitely possessed weapons of mass destruction, and that those things constituted a clear and present danger against the United States. That particular conclusion was made after attempts to link Saddam to September 11 attack on the world trade centre in New York.

"There is no doubt that Saddam Hussein has reinvigorated his weapons programs. Reports indicate that biological, chemical and nuclear programs continue apace and may be back to pre-Gulf War status. In addition, Saddam continues to redefine delivery systems and is doubtless using the cover of a licit missile program to develop longer-range missiles that will threaten the United States and our allies."

(Letter to President Bush, Signed by Joe Lieberman, John McCain and others, Dec. 5, 2001)

"Simply stated, there is no doubt that Saddam Hussein now has weapons of mass destruction. There is no doubt that he is amassing them to use against our friends, against our allies, and against us

Vice President Dick Cheney 26 Aug 2002

"The last UN weapons inspectors left Iraq in October of 1998. We are confident that Saddam Hussein retains some stockpiles of chemical and biological weapons. Intelligence reports indicate that he is seeking nuclear weapons"

(Sen. Robert Byrd (D, WV), Oct. 3, 2002).

"I will be voting to give the President of the United States the authority to use force—if necessary to disarm Saddam Hussein because I believe that a deadly arsenal of weapons of mass destruction in his hands is a real and grave threat to our security."

Sen. John F. Kerry, Oct. 9, 2002.

"In the four years since the inspectors left, intelligence reports show that Saddam Hussein has worked to rebuild his chemical and biological weapons stock, his missile delivery capability, and his nuclear program. Saddam Hussein will continue to increase his capacity to wage biological and chemical warfare, and will keep trying to develop nuclear weapons."

Sen. Hillary Clinton, NY, Oct 10, 2002.

: "Some people say, 'Oh, we must leave Saddam alone, otherwise, if we did something against him, he might attack us.' Well, if we don't do something he might attack us, and he might attack us with a more serious weapon. The man is a threat…He's a threat because he is dealing with al Qaeda…And we're going to deal with him." President George W Bush (press conference), 7 Nov 2002

: "He already has other weapons of mass destruction. But a nuclear weapon, two or three our four years from now—I don't care where it is, when it is—to have that happen in a volatile region like the Middle East is most certainly a future that cannot tolerate." Condoleezza Rice, 13 Nov 2002

: "I am absolutely convinced, based on the information that's been given to me, that the weapon of mass destruction which can kill more people than an atomic bomb—that is, biological weapons—is in the hands of. Senate majority leader Bill Frist, 10 Jan 2003

"It should be noted that biological weapons—which Iraq and North Korea both possess—can be as deadly, and arguably more immediate a danger—because they are simpler and cheaper and deliver, and are even more readily transferred to terrorist networks than are nuclear weapons."

Defence Secretary Donald Rumsfeld declares 20 Jan 2003

"Without question, we need to disarm Saddam Hussein. He is a brutal, murderous dictator, leading an oppressive regime. He presents a particularly grievous threat because he is so consistently prone to miscalculation. And now he is miscalculating America's response to his continued deceit and his consistent grasp for weapons of mass destruction. So the threat of Saddam Hussein with weapons of mass destruction is real"

Sen. John F. Kerry (D, MA), Jan. 23. 2003.

Then a landmark in history

Secretary of State Colin Powell went to the United Nations for a presentation about the WMD. He passed around recent surveillance photos taken of Iraqi WMD sites. According to Powell, the black-and-white pictures depicted a chemical weapons complex in Al-Musayyib, as well as 15 chemical weapons bunkers in Taji just north of Baghdad. Although the briefing was vague, Powell's exhibits were too specific and numerous to be ignored. Taken in total, they seemed to portray an ongoing biological and chemical weapons production under way in Iraq.

"Our conservative estimate is that Iraq today has a stockpile of between 100 and 500 tons of chemical weapons agents. That is enough agents to fill 16,000 battlefield rockets."

During his U.N. presentation, Secretary of State Colin Powell 5 Feb 2003

"Saddam Hussein has longstanding, direct and continuing ties to terrorist networks. Senior members of Iraqi intelligence and al Qaeda have met at least eight times since the early 1990s. Iraq has sent bomb-making and document forgery experts to work with al Qaeda. Iraq has also provided al Qaeda with chemical and biological weapons training. And an al Qaeda operative was sent to Iraq several times in the late 1990s for help in acquiring poisons and gases. We also know that Iraq is harbouring a terrorist network headed by a senior al Qaeda terrorist planner. This network runs a poison and explosive training camp in northeast Iraq, and many of its leaders are known to be in Baghdad." During a radio address, President George W Bush declares 8 Feb 2003

: "The people of the United States and our friends and allies will not live at the mercy of an outlaw regime that threatens the peace with weapons of mass murder

During an address to the nation, President George W Bush, 19 Mar 2003

War Started march 20, 2003

We know where they are. They are in the area around Tikrit and Baghdad.

(D. Rumsfeld March 30, 2003)

Saddam's removal is necessary to eradicate the threat from his weapons of mass destruction (Jack Straw, British Foreign Secretary 2 April, 2003)

Obviously the administration intends to publicize all the weapons of mass destruction U.S. forces find and there will be plenty.

(Neocon scholar Robert Kagan April 9, 2003)

In a message to the Iraqi people, President George W Bush declares: "The goals of our coalition are clear and limited. We will end a brutal regime, whose aggression and weapons of mass destruction make it a unique threat to the world."

10 Apr 2003

In a message to the Iraqi people, British Prime Minister Tony Blair declares: "We did not want this war. But in refusing to give up his weapons of mass destruction, Saddam gave us no choice but to act."

10 Apr 2003

I think you have always heard, and you continue to hear from officials, a measure of high confidence that, indeed, the weapons of mass destruction will be found.

(Ari Fleischer April 10, 2003)

"We are learning more as we interrogate or have discussions with Iraqi scientists and people within the Iraqi structure, that perhaps he destroyed some, perhaps he dispersed some. And so we will find them".

(George Bush April 24, 2003)

"Before people crow about the absence of weapons of mass destruction, I suggest they wait a bit".

(Tony Blair 28 April, 2003)

There are people who in large measure have information that we need so that we can track down the weapons of mass destruction in that country.

(Donald Rumsfeld April 25, 2003)

"We'll find them. It'll be a matter of time to do so".

(George Bush May 3, 2003)

"I am confident that we will find evidence that makes it clear he had weapons of mass destruction".

(Colin Powell May 4, 2003)

"I never believed that we'd just tumble over weapons of mass destruction in that country".

(Donald Rumsfeld May 4, 2003)

I'm not surprised if we begin to uncover the weapons program of Saddam Hussein—because he had a weapons program.

George W. Bush May 6, 2003

The tone started to Change a little and the doubt started

On May 1st, President Bush declared the end of the war from the flight deck of the USS *Abraham Lincoln*. The doubt of existence of WMD started, indeed the matters were very perplexing. Early during the invasion of Iraq, American troops were cautious so they don't get hit by those weapons. In the aftermath of the war, none of the alleged weapons were found to contain the slight traces of the alleged materials of mass destruction. The sites shown by Collin Powel had no trace of any biologic or chemical weapons.

After more search the officials tried to at put on a brave face, but nothing had shown up, they began to try and find excuses.

Defence Secretary Donald Rumsfeld tells *Fox News Sunday*: "we never believed that we'd just tumble over weapons of mass destruction in that country…We're going to find what we find as a result of talking to people, I believe, not simply by going to some site and hoping to discover it

4 May 2003

Secretary of State Colin Powell declares: "I'm absolutely sure that there are weapons of mass destruction there and the evidence will be forthcoming. We're just getting it just now."

4 May 2003

Defence Secretary Donald Rumsfeld tells the Council on Foreign Relations: "Now what happened? Why weren't they [the Wads] used? I don't know. There are several possible reasons for that…it may very well be that they didn't have time to…use chemical weapons. It is also possible that they decided that they would destroy them prior to a conflict."

27th May 2003

"U.S. officials never expected that "we were going to open garages and find" weapons of mass destruction".

(Condoleeza Rice May 12, 2003)

I just don't know whether it was all destroyed years ago—I mean; there's no question that there were chemical weapons years ago—whether they were destroyed right before the war, (or) whether they're still hidden.

Maj. Gen. David Petraeus,

Commander 101st Airborne May 13, 2003

Given time, given the number of prisoners now that we're interrogating, I'm confident that we're going to find weapons of mass destruction.

Gen. Richard Myers,

Chairman Joint Chiefs of Staff May 26, 2003

They may have had time to destroy them, and I don't know the answer.

(Donald Rumsfeld May 27, 2003)

And then time to confess

For bureaucratic reasons, we settled on one issue, weapons of mass destruction (as justification for invading Iraq) because it was the one reason everyone could agree on. (Paul Wolfowitz May 28, 2003)

When President Bush claimed that the WMD hunt had turned up something. It later turned out that the equipment was used to generate hydrogen gas for artillery balloons.

22 Aug 2003

Former U.N. chief weapons inspector Richard Butler hypothesizes: "I'm a bit shaken, as everyone is, by the fact that the country, now under occupation, hasn't yielded this treasure trove of WMDs."

4 Sep 2003

At the US Embassy in Paris, Undersecretary of State John Bolton declares that whether Saddam actually possessed WMDs "isn't really the issue…The issue, I think, has been the capability that Iraq sought to have…WMD programs

David Kay's interim report on the Iraqi WMD hunt, regarding the threat of chemical weapons, the Iraq Survey Group reluctantly admitted:

Information found to date suggests that Iraq's large-scale capability to develop, produce and fill new CW munitions was reduced—if not entirely destroyed—during Operation Desert Storm and Desert Fox, 13 years of UN sanctions and UN inspections.

And as for nuclear projects:

Despite evidence of Saddam's continued ambition to acquire nuclear weapons, to date we have not uncovered evidence that Iraq undertook significant post-1998 steps to actually build nuclear weapons or produce fissile material; Oct 2003

During a speech in Denver, Dick Cheney declares: "In Iraq, a ruthless dictator cultivated weapons of mass destruction and the means to deliver them. He gave support to terrorists, had an established relationship with al Qaeda, and his regime is no more."

21 Jan 2004

And then David Kay resigned his post as head of the Iraq Survey Group and promptly reported that Saddam neither had any of those horrible WMDs, *nor could he have ever developed any.*

In an interview with Reuters, former weapons inspector David Kay is asked about the WMDs; his answer was "I don't think they existed. I think there were stockpiles at the end of the first Gulf War and those were a combination of U.N. inspectors and unilateral Iraqi action got rid of them. I think the best evidence is that they did not resume large-scale production, and that's what we're really talking about, is large stockpiles, not the small. Large stockpiles of chemical and biological weapons in the period after 95." 23 Jan 2004

David Kay tells CNN that since Saddam was unlikely to have ever succeeded in developing WMDs: "If the administration had laid out a case based solely on the intentions of the Iraqi regime, I doubt you would have had massive public support or any international support for that. The argument last year was one not only of intentions but of capability and actual possession of weapons of mass destruction." 28 Mar 2004

Collin Powel defensive

Colin Powell spoke to meet the Press: "When I made that presentation in February 2003, it was based on the best information that the Central Intelligence Agency made available to me. We studied it carefully; we looked at the sourcing in the case of the mobile trucks and trains. There was multiple sourcing for that. Unfortunately, that multiple sourcing over time has turned out to be not accurate. And so I'm deeply disappointed…it turned out that the sourcing was inaccurate and wrong and in some cases, deliberately misleading. And for that, I am disappointed and I regret it."

17 May 2004

Secretary of Defence Donald Rumsfeld tells an audience at the Heritage Foundation that he fully expects to find those WMDs, eventually: "I can't guess how much longer it will take to get what we will finally look and say was ground truth—certainly months, maybe a year-plus. I just don't know how long it will take. We certainly won't just discover anything. I mean, we did not just discover Saddam Hussein, and he was hiding in a hole that was big enough to put chemical weapons in it that would kill tens of thousands of people."

17 Jun 2004

President Bush attempts to deflect the WMD issue: "I always said that Saddam Hussein was a threat. He was a threat because he had used weapons of mass destruction against his own people. He was a threat because he was a sworn enemy to the United States of America, just like al Qaeda. He was a threat because he had terrorist connections—not only al Qaeda connections, but other connections to terrorist organizations; Abu Nidal was one. He was a threat because he provided safe-haven for a terrorist like Zarqawi, who is still killing innocent inside of Iraq. No, he was a threat, and the world is better off and America is more secure without Saddam Hussein in power." 17 Jun 2004

As far as we know, AlZarqawi was not heard of before the American invasion, certainly he was not in Iraq, and the chaos after the occupation made Iraq a safe haven for terrorists, smugglers of drugs, fundamentalists from neighbouring countries, thieves of museums and oils pirates.

In summary the invasion was based on the alleged presence of WMD, which did not exist, to rationalize that the American officials tried to link Saddam to terrorist organization, which was never proved. Saddam is terrible man who ruined a nation in its entirety, but Iraq was a safe place to live at least.

The United States evidently had chose not to kill the Abu Musab al-Zarqawi, before the March 2003 US-led invasion of that country.The claimwas made a oprevious CIA agent Mike Scheuer in a aninterview with ABC television..

Scheuer worked for CIA for 22 years, he was head of the CIA Osama bin Laden unit; he resigned in 2004.

During 2002, the Bush Administration received full information about Zarqawi's training camp in the northern part of Iraq, that was UN protected zone."*Mr Bush had Zarqawi in his sights almost every day for a year before the invasion of Iraq and he didn't shoot because they were wining and dining the French in an effort to get them to assist us in the invasion of Iraq,*". Accorfing to Mr. "*Scheurer-During the lead-up to the invasion of Iraq, Zarqawi's presence in the north of the country was used by US officials to link Saddam Hussein to terrorism*".

Reference

Chris Evans (The Age)US 'allowed Zarqawi to escape'May 1, 2006

13

Dr. David Kelly

He was an employee of the British Ministry of Defence an expert in biological warfare, and a former United Nations weapons inspector in Iraq. His talk with a journalist about the British government's dossier on weapons of mass destruction (WMD) in Iraq inadvertently caused a major political scandal, and he was found dead days after appearing before a Parliamentary committee investigating it. The Hutton Inquiry, a public inquiry into his death, ruled that he had committed suicide. In 1984, he started as head of the Defence Microbiology Division, he was advisor for the ministry. He was selected as a United Nations weapons inspector in Iraq following the end of the Gulf War, he was s member of the UNSCOM, and his success in uncovering Iraq's biological weapons programme caused Rolf Ekéus to nominate him for the Nobel Peace Prize.

In 2002, he was working for the Defence Intelligence at the time of the compilation of evidence on the weapons of mass destruction in Iraq. Kelly was unhappy with some of the claims that was made by the intelligence that Iraq was capable of firing battlefield biological and chemical weapons within 45 minutes of. Kelly believed Iraq had retained biological weapons after the end of inspections. He made one trip to Iraq after the war 5 June–11 June 2003.

Andrew Gilligan meeting

On May 22, 2003, Kelly met with Andrew Gilligan, a BBC journalist who had spent the war in Baghdad. Kelly told Gilligan of his concerns over the 45-minute claim and ascribed its inclusion in the dossier to Alastair Campbell, the director of communications for Tony Blair.

Gilligan aired his report on May 29, in which he said that the 45-minute claim had been placed in the dossier by Tony Blair government, even though it knew the claim was dubious. In a subsequent article in the (*Mail on Sunday*), Gilligan said that Alastair Campbell was the man who was responsible.

The story caused a political scandal, Tony Blair gevernment denied any involnement in tampering with the evidnece. The government had put pressure on the BBC to reveal the source.

As the political fight ensued, Kelly knew he had talked to the journalist involved but felt that he had not said exactly what was reported. He said "I am convinced that I am not his primary source of information".

Kelly was extremely disturbed by the publicity and arranged with a family friend to leave his home and visit Cornwall with his wife. He was asked to appear as a witness before two committees of the House of Commons that were investigating the situation in Iraq, and was upset that one of the appearances would be in public, The minstry of defence has warned him they might take more action if they find out he had been lying to them.

When he appeared before the Foreign Affairs Select Committee on July 15, Kelly appeared to be under severe stress. His told the committee was that he had not said the things Gilligan had reported his source

His Death

On the morning of July 17, Kelly was working as usual at home in Oxfordshire. At 3:00 p.m, Kelly told his wife that he was going for a walk. He appears to have gone directly to an area of woodlands about a mile away from his home, where he ingested up to 29 tablets of co-proxamol, an analgesic drug. He then apparently cut his left wrist with a knife.

Kelly's wife reported him missing shortly after midnight that night, and he was found early the next morning. The government formed a judicial Hutton Inquiry into his death. The BBC had confirmed that Kelly had indeed been the source for Andrew Gilligan's report. The Hutton Inquiry reported on January 28, 2004 confirming that Kelly had committed suicide.

Lord Hutton wrote:

"I am satisfied that none of the persons whose decisions and actions I later describe ever contemplated that Dr Kelly might take his own life. I am further satisfied that none of those persons was at fault in not contemplating that Dr Kelly might take his own life. Whatever pressures and strains Dr Kelly was subjected to by the decisions and actions taken in the weeks before his death, I am satisfied that no one realised or should have realised that those pressures and strains might drive him to take his own life or contribute to his decision to do so".

References

Our doubts about Kelly's suicide Letter to the Editor, *The Guardian*, January 27, 2004

Kelly death paramedics query verdict by Anthony Barnett, *The Guardian*, December 12, 2004

New Kelly claims splits medical opinion by Vikram Dodd, *The Guardian*, December 13, 2004

The Hutton Inquiry

David Kelly: the interrogator—an account from *The Guardian*, written by Kelly's colleague, of how they set about examining Iraq's biological weapons programme

14

The evidence of WMD

The CIA had provided the evidence, have they got it wrong, or it was sexed up and by whom? Where things went wrong? Regardless it led to destruction of a country, which remains mortally wounded and may not recover?

Everyone knew that Iraq had chemical and biological weapons in the 1980s and 1990s. Saddam Hussein used chemical weapons against Iran and his own people on at least 10 different occasions. He launched missiles against Iran, Saudi Arabia, and Israel. And we couldn't forget that in the early 1990s, we saw that Iraq was just a few years way from a nuclear weapon—this was no theoretical program. It turned out that we and the other intelligence services of the world had significantly underestimated his progress. And, finally, we could not forget that Iraq lied repeatedly about its unconventional weapons.

United Nations could not—and Saddam would not—account for all the weapons the Iraqis had: tons of chemical weapons precursors, hundreds of artillery shells and bombs filled with chemical or biological agents. Over eight years of inspections, Saddam's deceptions—and the increasingly restrictive rules of engagement UN inspectors were forced to negotiate with the regime—undermined efforts to disarm him

The Iraq Survey Group found that two separate groups in Iraq were working on a number of Unmanned Aerial Vehicle designs that were hidden from the UN until Iraq's Declaration of December 2002. Now we know that important design elements were never fully declared.

The question of intent—especially regarding the smaller Unmanned Aerial Vehicles—is still out there. But we should remember that the Iraqis flight-tested an aerial Biological Weapon spray system intended for a large Unmanned Aerial Vehicle.

A senior Iraqi official has now admitted that their two large Unmanned Aerial Vehicles—one developed in the early 90s and the other under development in late 2000—were intended for delivery of biological weapons.

Most agencies believed that Saddam had begun to reconstitute his nuclear program, but they disagreed on a number of issues such as which procurement activities were designed to support his nuclear program. Keep in mind that no intelligence agency thought that Iraq's efforts had progressed to the point of building an enrichment facility or making fissile material. We said that such activities were a few years away. Therefore it is not surprising that the Iraq Survey Group has not yet found evidence of uranium enrichment activities.

We believed that Iraq had lethal Biological Weapon agents, including anthrax, which it could quickly produce and weaponries for delivery by bombs, missiles, aerial sprayers, and covert operatives. But we said we had no specific information on the types or quantities of weapons, agent, or stockpiles at Baghdad's disposal

Before I leave the Biological Weapons story, an important fact you must remember. For years the UN searched unsuccessfully for Saddam's Biological Weapons program. His son-in-law, Hussein Kamil, who controlled the hidden program defected and only then, was the world able to confirm that Iraq indeed had an active and dangerous biological weapons program. Indeed, history matters in dealing with these complicated problems. While many of us want instant answers, this search for Biological Weapons in Iraq will take time and patience.

After the Invasion of Kuwait by Saddam George Bush (senior) decided to liberate Kuwait, between the invasion and the first Gulf war the American administration apparently debated the removal of Saddam from power. However, Bush was going to pursue military removal of Saddam only if the Latter decided to use weapons of mass destruction against the American troops.

By the end of the war Saddam was compelled to agree to an inspection and monitoring program to insure that Iraq was going to dismantle its WMD and did pursue further development of WMD. The UNSCOM was implemented and continued until December 16, 1998.

George W. Bush's wan the election and became the US president in January 2001, he made it clear that he will deny Saddam the opportunity of building WMD even if that means military intervention.

The Security Council had imposed the Inspection Commission (UNMOVIC) and warned Saddam to cooperate or face serious consequences. Iraq agreed to accept the U.N. decision and inspections resumed in late November 2002. Iraq submitted its report to the UN and claimed there is no WMDs. American and British officials dismissed that as "lies and deception"

The American and British forces had invaded Iraq March 2003, no weapons were found and suspicions started over the performance of U.S. (and British) intelligence in collecting and evaluating information about Iraqi weapons of mass destruction. It has been suggested that some intelligence may have been deliberately fabricated by some Iraqis in exile to overthrow Saddam.

Iraq's motives for seeking high-strength aluminium tubes was questioned by the US, and in the United Kingdom Government claimed that Iraq sought to acquire uranium from Africa. Congress members in the US and parliament members in the UK had criticised their corresponding governments of distortion of the intelligence and its selective use.

The only publicly acknowledged evidence for the claim that Iraq had tried to acquire uranium from Africa, which President Bush made in his January 28, 2003 State of the Union address, based on British intelligence information, are these documents that were claimed to have been official correspondence involving officials of the Republic of Niger.

According to the intelligence "Baghdad has begun renewed production of" a variety of chemical weapons—mustard gas, sarin, cyclosarin, and VX. It also stated that all key aspects of Iraq's offensive biological weapons program were active—including R&D, production, and deionization—and that most components were larger and more advanced than they were before the Gulf War". The State Department's Bureau of Intelligence Research was not convinced that Iraq's activities made strong evidence that it was trying to acquire nuclear weapons.

Hans Blix was the head of UNMVOC, he was almost certain that Iraq was free of WMDs; however he was unhappy with the cooperation. Powell's had shown the UN Security Council, February 5, 2003 the content of satellite imagery being. information about which was obtained from human sources (Intelligence sources on the Iraqi program including a chemical engineer, a civil engineer, and a defector from the Iraqi Intelligence Service), on the existence of a "Higher Committee for Monitoring the Inspections Teams" as well as the presence of Al-Qaeda associates in Baghdad. Those were proved to be fabricated by some Iraqis in exile.

Blix said "so far UNMOVIC has not found any WMDs only a small number of chemical materials which should have been declared and destroyed." El-Baradei head of the (IAEA) Similar to Blix, reported that "we have to date found no evidence of nuclear or nuclear related activities in Iraq," but that "a number of issues are still under investigation."."

September and February "dossiers," British government assertions concerning Iraq's chemical and biological weapons and its nuclear weapons program, Iraq's alleged attempt to acquire uranium from Africa and the assertion that Iraqi forces could deploy chemical or biological weapons within 45 minutes. However it was thought that the government genuinely perceived "a real and present danger" from Iraq, in the absence of significant human intelligence Britain was heavily dependent on US technical intelligence, defectors, and exiles "with an agenda of their own," so the accuracy of British assessments could not yet be determined.

Statement by Director of Central Intelligence George J. Tenet on the 2002 National Intelligence Estimate on Iraq's Continuing Programs for Weapons

He characterizes much of the commentary as "misinformed, misleading, and just plain wrong," and goes on to state that "we stand by the judgments in the NIE," and promises that after the Iraq Survey Group completes its work, "but not before," the Intelligence Community, "will stand back to professionally review where were are."

Tenet's statement goes on to defend the consistency of the community's analysis concerning Iraqi programs as well as its collection efforts after the departure of U.N. inspectors in 1998. He then proceeds to examine intelligence performance with each component of Iraqi weapons of mass destruction programs—nuclear, chemical and biological weapons, and delivery systems.

The most extensive part of his statement is a defence of the estimate's judgment that Iraq was seeking to reconstitute its nuclear weapons program. He states that this conclusion was based on six factors, which did not include its reported attempt to acquire uranium from Africa. In addition, he describes the alternative views within the Intelligence Community as to whether Iraq was attempting to obtain high-strength aluminium tubes for use in uranium enrichment or for conventional military uses.

David Kay also noted a number of factors that had hindered the ISG's search—including the compartmentalization of Iraqi WMD programs, deliberate dispersion and destruction of material and documentation related to those programs, post-war looting, and a "far from permissive environment" for search activities.

In addition, Kay summarized some of the Survey Group's discoveries, which included: a clandestine network of laboratories and safe-houses controlled by the Iraqi Intelligence Services containing equipment suitable for CBW research; reference strains of biological organisms concealed in a scientists home; documents and equipment hidden in scientists' homes that could be used for resuming uranium enrichment activities; and a continuing covert capability to manufacture fuel propellant useful only for prohibited SCUD missiles.

Congresswoman Jane Harman, "The Intelligence on Iraq's WMD: Looking Back to Look Forward," January 16, 2004. This speech given by the Jane Harman (D-

CA), the vice chairman of the House Permanent Select Committee on Intelligence, characterized the October 2002 National Intelligence Estimate on Iraqi weapons of mass destruction programs as "significantly flawed." She singled out two specific conclusions—that Iraq possessed chemical and biological weapons, and that it was reconstituting its nuclear weapons program, noting that "these were the centrepieces of the NIE and of the case for war and it appears likely that both were wrong."

Transcript of David Kay testimony before Senate Armed Services Committee, January 28, 2004

David Kay appeared before the Senate Armed Services Committee shortly after he resigned as special advisor to the Iraq Survey Group. Kay states, referring to the expectation that there would be substantial stocks of, and production lines for, chemical and biological weapons in Iraq, that "we were almost all wrong, and I certainly include myself here." He also notes that other foreign intelligence agencies, including the French and the German, also had believed that Iraq possessed such stocks and production lines. In addition, he discusses the issue of whether political pressure had any impact on the content of the October 2002 national intelligence estimate. Kay also notes that "based on the work of the Iraq Survey Group...Iraq was in clear violation of the terms of [U.N.] Resolution 1441. He goes on to note the discovery of hundreds of instances of activities prohibited by U.N. Resolution 687.

Tenet said "As David Kay reminded us, the Iraqis systematically destroyed and looted forensic evidence before, during and after the war. We have been faced with the organized destruction of documentary and computer evidence in a wide range of offices, laboratories, and companies suspected of WMD work. The pattern of these efforts is one of deliberate rather than random acts. Iraqis who have volunteered information to us are still being intimidated and attacked".

While we had voluminous reporting, the major judgments reached were based on a narrower band of data. This is not unusual. There was, by necessity, a strong reliance on technical data, which to be sure was very valuable, particularly in the imagery of military and key dual use facilities, on missile and Unmanned Aerial Vehicle developments—and in particular on the efforts of Iraqi front companies to falsify and deny us the ultimate destination and use of dual use equipment.

References

- The CIA briefing on Iraq and Weapons of Mass Destruction (National Security Archive) February 11, 2004Edited by Jeffrey Richelson

- http://cia.gov/cia/public_affairs/press_release/2003/pr08112003.htm

- http://www.cabinet-office.gov.uk/reports/isc/http://cia.gov/cia/public_affairs/speeches/2003/david_kay_10022003.html

- http://www.house.gov/harman/press/releases/2004/011604_WAC.html

- http://www.ceip.org/files/projects/npp/pdf/Iraq/kaytestimony.pdf

- Remarks as prepared for delivery by Director of Central Intelligence GeorgeJ.Tenet at Georgetown University 5 February, 2004

- Hans Blix. Security Council 7 MARCH 2003

- B Bill Nichols, U.N.: Iraq had no WMD after 1994 USA TODAY; 3.2 2004

15

Illegal weapon sells to Iraq

S. companies listed in the report who gave very substantial support especially to the biological weapons program but also to the missile and nuclear weapons program, Zumach said. Pretty much everything was illegal in the case of nuclear and biological weapons. Every form of cooperation and supplies was outlawed in the 1970s.

The list of U.S. corporations listed in Iraq's report include Hewlett Packard, DuPont, Honeywell, Rockwell, Tectronics, Bechtel, International Computer Systems, Unisys, Sperry and TI Coating.

Zumach also said the U.S. Departments of Energy, Defence, Commerce, and Agriculture quietly helped arm Iraq. U.S. government nuclear weapons laboratories Lawrence Livermore, Los Alamos and Sandia trained travelling Iraqi nuclear scientists and gave non-fissile material for construction of a nuclear bomb.

There has never been this kind of comprehensive layout and listing like we have now in the Iraqi report to the Security Council so this is quite new and this is especially new for the U.S. involvement, which has been even more suppressed in the public domain and the U.S. population, Zumach said.

The names of companies were supposed to be top secret. Two weeks ago Iraq provided two copies of its full 12,000-page report, one to the International Atomic Energy Agency in Geneva, and one to the United Nations in New York. Zumach said the U.S. broke an agreement of the Security Council and blackmailed Colombia, which at the time was presiding over the Council, to take possession of the UN s only copy.

The U.S. then proceeded to make copies of the report for the other four permanent Security Council nations, Britain, France, Russia and China. Only yesterday did the remaining members of the Security Council receive their copies. By then, all references to foreign companies had been removed.

According to Zumach, only Germany had more business ties to Iraq than the U.S.

As many as 80 German companies are also listed in Iraq's report.

The paper reported that some German companies continued to do business with Iraq until last year.

US Corporations named in Iraqi Report :

1. Honeywell

2. Spectra Physics

3. Semetex

4. TI Coating

5. Unisys

6. Sperry Corp.

7. Tektronix

8. Rockwell

9. Leybold Vacuum Systems

10. Finnigan-MAT-US

11. Hewlett-Packard

12. Dupont

13. Eastman Kodak

14. American Type Culture Collection

15. Alcolac International

16. Consarc

17. Carl Zeiss

18. Cerberus

19. Electronic Associates

20. International Computer Systems

21. Bechtel

22. EZ Logic Data Systems, Inc.

23. Canberra Industries Inc.

24. Axel Electronics Inc.

Ref

List of US Firms That Armed Iraq Household Names; truthout.com. 18 December, 2002

A US Media Mystery: The Case of the Missing Information about Iraq's Weapons; Baltimore Chronicles

Jim Croga. A guide to Iraq's weapon of mass destruction, La Weekly. March 20. 2003

16

Tyranny and the Sanctions

Iraq needs after the effects of tyranny and the sanction

The long years of sanction had undermined the quality of human existence in Iraq, which was at best tenuous, life was brought to a standstill, the 1991 war and the sanction had destroyed the livelihood of the more than 20 million people in Iraq and converted the country into a mere large refugees camp. Iraq did not need another war and turmoil it needed international collaboration to enable citizen participation in Iraqi civil and political life and ensure the viability of a vibrant civil society sector that can hold the government accountable, the donor community will need to:

- empower women through education and training and incorporate them into the political process, concurrent with the accelerated creation of women's organizations and centres in southern and central Iraq;

- provide professional training and capacity building to civil society groups with a focus on organizational development (fund-raising and proposal writing, advocacy and coalition building, program development, and information technology), political party building, and media training;

- reach out to educate communities about their constitutional rights and responsibilities, as well as wider issues relating to democracy and civil society;

- give priority to "training the trainer" programs, to empower local actors;

- engage moderate elements in civil society, not just to invigorate civil debate, but to counteract the increasing radicalization of religious groups; and

- Ensure justice for the victims of human rights violations alongside ongoing changes to Iraq's legal, judicial, and penal systems.

One of the main challenges of peace-building in Iraq, in particular, will be addressing the legacy of past violence. The road to reconciliation in post conflict societies is cemented, not just through the establishment of structures and processes for society built on participation, equity, and inclusion, but also through the rehabilitation of the national psyche and the rebuilding of relationships among communities, without which the structures will remain hollow. It is imperative to avert the temptation of ethnic and religious communities to resort to revenge to reverse past victimization. In designing a road toward a peaceful future, donors should therefore seek to foster, as a means for reconstituting social relationships and rebuilding the human infrastructure, a process of reconciliation that combines key ingredients of a lasting democracy: justice, truth, healing, and reparation. Part of this effort should be directed at helping to cope with the past in ways that lead to a peaceful, cooperative future by promoting an understanding of the relationship between trauma, truth, and reconciliation. This includes investigating ways of repairing intercommunal relations and avoiding further segmentation of civil society along communal lines, with a strong emphasis on engaging communities in dialogue, and supporting projects that address the link among trauma, victimization, and legal remedies. The tragedy of Iraq today is the "loss of the ties that bind, not their non-existence," as the Iraqi academic Sami Zubaida has observed, and this is what makes the divisions so threatening. Confidence-building initiatives will help engage communities and restore citizens' relationship of trust, accelerating social reconciliation. Iraqis need to explore ways to hold accountable perpetrators of human rights violations to bring a sense of justice to victims, perhaps by documenting the experiences of torture victims and acts of violence taking place under the Ba'ath regime. Finally, while the inclusion of human rights protections (especially for women and minorities) in the new constitution has been crucial, the realization of rights will take more than legal and institutional reforms. Public discourse and education around human rights are essential to generate a culture of human rights and provide the best protection against future abuses.

Despite the tremendous efforts of international organizations engaged in civil society development, more remains to be done. During the Ba'ath period, citizen participation in decision making was curtailed and Iraqi civilians had little opportunity to shape their lives and destinies. Today, it is crucial that a post-war Iraq be built on solid foundations of social, economic, and political justice and democracy. A viable democracy can only be sustained through the active involvement and support of citizens who are engaged in their communities and able to determine their future

17

The Anglo-American invasion

The bush administration tried hard connect the invasion of Iraq to the events of September 11. Prior to the war, virtually every White House official said that Iraq was responsible for the attacks on the World Trade Centre and the Pentagon. Vice-President Dick Cheney insisted that there is a link despite the evidence to the contrary. The bottom line is that Iraq had nothing to do with September 11, one of the principal reasons for invading Iraq. When the US public wanted proof, the White House created a new battleground against terror and chose Iraq to be the battlefield.

The invasion of Iraq was illegal, against the will of the international community and had been hatched up by the neo-conservatives, those with right-wing ideology and pro-Israel in the Bush administration. Paul Wolfowitz, who was one of the prime instigators of the war and was among the most fierce opponent of Saddam and his alleged weapons of mass destruction, which at the end didn't exist-is, he latter tired to deflect attention from the disaster in Iraq by blaming the media and attacking AL-Jazeera, because it kept showing the American crimes in Iraq.

Ignoring the pleas of millions of people around the world and most of the United Nations members, Bush and Blair had had launched the illegal war. Contrary to their claims, Saddam was never an imminent threat to the United States or Europe. Until Bush and Blair launched their military machine to destroy the country, al Qaeda did not exist there; Iraq had no relation to the terrorists. Yet since the Anglo-American invasion Iraq became the forefront of a war fought between the American and the Jihadis.

Everyone was happy that Saddam was gone, The Iraqis new the challenges were ahead of them, but no one could foresee that the worse was to come. One of the main challenges in Iraq proved to be overcoming the heritage of more than 30 years of tyranny and oppression, which had left deep wounds in the heart of the society. Added to it the effects cultural, religious, and ethnic identity of different parts of the society which proved to have tremendous implication on the country.

All that is needed to get us into war is one clear reason for acting, one that would be generally persuasive. But efforts to link the Iraqis directly to Osama bin Laden have proved inconclusive. Assertions that Iraq threatens its neighbors have also failed to create much resolve; in its present debilitated condition—thanks to United Nations sanctions—Iraq's conventional forces threaten no one.

Perhaps the strongest argument left for taking us to war quickly is that Saddam Hussein has committed human rights atrocities against his people. And the most dramatic case is the accusations about Halabja.

Bush

looking at GW Bush while he is trying to convince the world that Saddam is an eminent danger to the world stability and threat to the international peace, the only conclusion that could be drawn from his demeanour is that he was under intense pressure from the more powerful figures in the white house to invade Iraq.

He had to get convince the world that he should get rid of Saddam, because America had the power and the rationale to do so, whether it was about the weapons, Alaqaeda or human right issues in Iraq under Saddam, he had the best power in the entire world in his disposal and under his control, at some stages he did not seem genuinely convinced that Iraq was a danger to the world peace, it was almost evident he and his administration was telling lies about the weapons of mass destruction. He made every effort to disguise the real intention of the war and wanted the world just have to believe him, Rumsfeld, Negroponte, Wolfwitz and Cheney were working frantically behind the scenes, and they said yes Iraq is the biggest threat for the world peace, they are part of the axis of evil they tortured their own people.

Collin Powel was the reasonable man he was the peace maker, but the Bush administration did not need a peace maker, they wanted someone who support their propaganda. The congress was concerned about the cost of the war, billions of dollars; to the Bush administration; Iraq has all the oil in the world, more than enough to finance the invasion and to maintain the occupation

Blair

While he was trying to be assertive and convince the world to back him up in the war against Iraq.

He seemed convinced that his friend Bush had made up his mind he was going for the war, and he seemed willing to do whatever it takes to back the American plans. Remember that the Americans defended Britain in the Second World War and there is similarity in the interests. He probably knew and was aware that the evidence of WMDs that was put forward was sexed up to suit the motives, but unfortunately Dr Kelly knew and had to bear the consequences and someone had to do it, he seemed under so much pressure to back the Americans and even dared to say that Iraq was a significant danger that they can launch attack on the world within 45 minutes.

18

Baghdad a lawless city

Baghdad a lawless city after the fall of Saddam (National Day)

On the 9th of April of Saddam's statue IN Al—Fardous Square was brought down by American solders and the American flag was wrapped around his face, that scene was aired by many TV channels to the world. Hating Saddam, we were excited to see this(what a day!!), however the disappointment came soon, Baghdad was a city of looters, killers, assassins and those who hurried in across the borders with a vengeance. Soon Baghdad was a city of death and distasters.

Reporter for the BBC's said there are at least 70 cars a day being hijacked in Baghdad alone. Baghdad was not a friendly place any more it is a large jungle, the Iraqi army and police force has just been dissolved, the civil system had had totally collapsed; that was not by natural reasons, it was the occupation that ordered the dissolution, Baghdad was a place of shooting, looting, American tanks rolling the main streets, rape, abductions, and assassinations.

It was just like a large Jungle; where the hungry restrained lions and tigers have been released in the wild, killing any pray the can see. The occupying forces were watching that, indeed everyone thought that people were venting the anger and frustration that had built over many years of oppression, war, deprivation and poverty.

However it seems that overlooking the chaos did send the wrong message to the mob. Criminals, thieves and assassins, who did their crimes and got away with it, no prosecution not even investigations, were carried out by the officials; but where were the officials it was total anarchy. Perhaps the only right thing that Saddam did, he kept the extremists out and the criminals locked in jails with severe punishments.

The morning Baghdad fell the general feeling in Baghdad was solemn, a total 35 years of oppression is gone, some were excited and joyful others were apprehensive at what was going to happen next and sure enough what happened next was the worst ever. People in Baghdad were astonished at what happened.

American tanks were rolling in Baghdad streets, what a dreadful situation; Baghdad was not a place of safe living any more. To most people that I spoke to, there feeling of that occupation had injured the pride of a city that once in the history was the capital of the world. The first few days of the occupation was a mixture of the delight of getting rid of an oppressive regime and the shame of living under the occupation. There was some armed resistance; however the city was quickly falling in the hands of the occupying army. It was the 9th of April 2003, to most of the mob it was a delightful occasion, to the Iraqi nationalists it was the loss of sovereignty and independence of a pride nation.

for those who came from everywhere on the American and British tanks, who called them selves as "liberators", some of them had hardly seen the country, others were living in luxury while the average Iraqis were grieving for their lost ones, were crushed by poverty under the sanctions, for those opportunists it was it was a 'National Day'.

The mixture of jubilation and despair on the faces of the young and naïve defeated Iraqi Solders was clearly seen on television screens around the world. People who lived in Baghdad during all this are truly heroes, the city was burning, it had been wrecked by continued bombing for several weeks, the city was dark, it was without running water, shops were all closed, food was scarce, the civil system had collapsed, people were confused, many had left the city earlier, other simply had no where to go or felt they had to stay home to avoid the looting of their belonging. People were inconsolable, they were shocked and horrified.

Skirmishes of fighting were happening in the residential neighbourhoods, in certain parts it was street to street fighting, often the innocents were caught in the middle of those fights, and many had lost their lives, families in their entirety, children and women were killed; yet April 2003 had a "National day" in it.

Baghdad was a grieving city, bodies of the killed people were rotting in the streets, no one clamed them, no one knew who they are, no city council existed anymore to deal with bodies, and streets were empty apart from the homeless people and the stray dogs.

People were looking for shelter and those who would did not leave Baghdad were virtually waiting their inevitable fate, the fait of being shot or bombed or getting their house demolished on their heads, by a missile from no where or by American tank that was manned by young and inexperienced solders who would demolish an entire neighbourhood if they get shot at.

Baghdad skies were full of smoke of burnt buildings and Apache helicopters. All what people could hear was the explosions and armed clashes. Baghdad lived weeks of horror, fear, and uncertainty. Around Baghdad the Iraqi tanks shelled and burnt by the Apaches with the bodies of solders who were burnt beyond recognition.

The insurgency started soon after that and the counterinsurgency was issued in Iraq, which was a field manual distributed to each and every soldier and issued by the Pentagon. Counterinsurgency missions must achieve the end state established by the president. All leaders must keep in mind the purpose of their operations and the criteria of success used to assess them. Achieving success in counterinsurgency operations involves accomplishing the elimination of counterinsurgency and building local political authority…

The mostly unheard of tragedy Baghdad was invaded by new armies, there were huge numbers of Iraqis who defected to Iran (those went to Iran mainly after the 1991 war, probably some of them were war prisoners in the Iraq-Iran war) then got recruited in a militia trained by the Iranian revolutionary guard and given the name of Badr Army (Badr originally is a battle between Prophet Mohammed PBUH and the Arab infidels). That militia was headed by Al-Hakim.

In response to that followers of the young cleric Al-Sader instantly formed a militia called the Mahdi Army, composed mainly of young people of impoverished background.

Al-Chalabi who had appeared on the radar screen in the few years before the invasion, had made his appearance in Baghdad, he had some followers who were in less numbers than the militias of the Clerics. However those people had reportedly confiscated documents from various governmental offices (those documents were mainly from intelligence and security offices, with regard to people who were secretly disappeared and executed by Saddam), the Chalbis evidently had sold those documents to the poor people who were trying to find any link to their loved ones who totally vanished 9 most those people were found in mass graves latter).

That militia had continued to dominate the politics for years to coma.

Gangs and armed illegal militia had grown gradually, became more organised and continued to terrorise, abduct and assassinate the people mainly in Baghdad since the fall of the city in the hand of the occupying army, who in turn fail to provide security to an occupied country, which is against the Geneva Convention regulations.

Abductions became a commonplace, organised crimes were something new to Baghdad, gangs raid house, offices and even hospitals and abduct people in demand of huge ransom, doctors became a prim target, their children or wives or they get abducted regularly; if they don't get what they want the answer is to kill their hostage.

University professors did not have much money, in fact they were impoverished in Saddam time, they were the target of politically motivated assassinations, hundreds of them lost their lives at the hands of obscure militiamen who killed and got away with it, neither the Iraqi government nor the occupying force took the initiative to investigate or pursue any kind of justice.

So was the 9th of April 2003 a "National Day" or a Day of National Mourning

19

Cluster Bombs

Cluster bombs had killed thousands of Vietnamese, Cambodian and Laotian civilians during and after the Vietnam War. The Russian forces in Chechnya, but their use in urban areas of Iraq and the casualties they caused has given a new momentum to anti war movements to restrict their use.

In 2003 when the invasion of Iraq was imminent, humanitarian groups warned the Pentagon against using cluster bombs, in urban areas. New York-based Human Rights Watch predicted on March 18 2003: "The use of cluster munitions in Iraq will result in grave dangers to civilians and friendly combatants." Cluster bombs are especially dangerous because they spray large areas with hundreds of bomblets, and many of the bomblets don't explode on the immediate impact. Experts in clearing conflict zones of unexploded bombs say that millions of Iraqi adults and children are at risk

As they moved from Kuwait toward Baghdad late March and early April 2003, U.S. forces fired rockets and artillery shells loaded with bomblets in Hillah, in Baghdad and in other cities. U.S. aircraft sometimes dropped cluster bombs.

Although U.S. forces sought to limit the danger civilian lives in the war against Iraq, they defied the united nation rules and used 10,800 cluster weapons; their British allies used almost 2,200

The little canisters dropped onto the Baghdad with attached white ribbons trailing behind them. They looked strange, clattered into streets, landed on the roofs, and settled onto lawns. They are size D batteries. Those deadly objects are the "cluster bomblets", explosives packed by the hundreds into bombs, rockets and artillery shells they are called the cluster weapons.

When these weapons were fired on Baghdad on April 7, 2003, many of the bomblets failed to explode on impact. They were picked up or stumbled on by their victims.

Paul Wiseman of USA today reported that four people died in the al-Dora, south of Baghdad; Rashid Majid, 58, who was nearsighted, stepped on an unex-

ploded bomblet near his home. The explosion ripped his legs off. As he lay bleeding in the street, another bomblet exploded a few yards away, instantly killing
three young men, including two of Majid's sons Arkan, 33, and Ghasan, 28.

The deaths occurred because the world's most powerful military machine
decided to minimize civilian casualties; however they invaded Iraq with predeter-
mined use of banned weapons known to endanger civilians…The weapons
claimed victims in the initial explosions and continued to kill afterward, as Iraqis
accidentally detonated bomblets lying like land mines. The occupation forces
have a responsibility to protect those Iraqi civilians who now live with this lethal
legacy.

A four-month examination by USA TODAY about cluster bombs use in Iraq
found dozens of deaths from cluster bombs among civilians that were predictable.
One anti-war group calculates that cluster weapons killed as many as 372 Iraqi
civilians and many Iraqi families buried their dead without reporting their deaths.
Forty civilians were killed in one neighbourhood in Hillah, 60 miles south of
Baghdad, according to local hospital staff. These unintentional deaths added to
the hostility that has complicated the U.S. occupation.

USA TODAY visited Iraqi neighbourhoods and interviewed dozens of Iraqi
families, U.S. troops, teams clearing unexploded ordnance in Iraq, military analysts and humanitarian groups. They found

The Pentagon presented a misleading picture during the war of the extent to
which cluster weapons were being used and of the civilian casualties they were
causing.

The attacks left behind thousands of unexploded bomblets that continued to
kill and injure Iraqi civilian's weeks after the end of the invasion.

Unexploded U.S. cluster bomblets have killed or injured at least eight U.S.
troops.

The U.S. Air Force, criticized for using cluster bombs that killed civilians during the wars in Vietnam, Kosovo and Afghanistan, has improved its cluster
bombs. But U.S. ground forces relied on cluster munitions known to cause a high
number of civilian casualties.

Ref

- Paul Wiseman, Cluster bombs kill in Iraq, even after shooting ends. USA
  TODAY, 16 Dec 2003

- Kamal Ahmed, Revealed: the cluster bombs that litter Iraq. The Observer

- June 1, 2003.

- http://hrw.org/doc/?t=arms_clusterbombs

- Iraq: Use of cluster bombs; Civilians pay the price Amnesty International. April 2nd. 2003

- Ben Russell, Political Correspondent UK's deadly legacy: the cluster bomb. The Independent 21 November 2005

20

Al-Qaeda

Iraq and Al-Qaeda (was there a link?)
Donald Rumsfeld

"I have acknowledged since September 2002 that there were ties between Al Qaeda and Iraq."

But a short time later, Rumsfeld released a statement: "A question I answered today at an appearance before the Council on Foreign Relations regarding ties between Al Qaeda and Iraq regrettably was misunderstood.

When asked about any connection between Saddam Hussein and al Qaeda, Rumsfeld said, "To my knowledge, I have not seen any strong, hard evidence that links the two."

"There clearly was a relationship. It's been testified to. The evidence is overwhelming," Cheney said in an interview with CNBC "It goes back to the early '90s. It involves a whole series of contacts, high-level contacts with Osama bin Laden and Iraqi intelligence officials"; he said. Suggesting that the 9/11 commission had reached a contradictory conclusion was "irresponsible,"

Before the war, in a speech in Atlanta in September 2002, Rumsfeld said the CIA provided "bullet-proof" evidence demonstrating "that there is in fact al Qaeda in Iraq."

In Monday's address, Rumsfeld told the Council on Foreign Relations those U.S. intelligence analysts have changed their assessment: "I have seen the answer to that question migrate in the intelligence community over a period of a year in the most amazing way."

The 9/11 commission report, issued in July, concluded there may have been meetings between Iraqi officials and Osama bin Laden or his aides in 1999 but there was "no evidence that these or the earlier contacts ever developed into a collaborative operational relationship."

Nor did the commission find any evidence indicating that Iraq cooperated with al Qaeda in developing or carrying out any attacks against the United States," the commission report said.

In June, President Bush repeated his administration's claim that Iraq was in league with al Qaeda under Saddam Hussein's rule, saying that fugitive Islamic militant Abu Musab al-Zarqawi ties Saddam to the terrorist network.

"Zarqawi's the best evidence of a connection to al Qaeda affiliates and al Qaeda," Bush told reporters at the White House. "He's the person who's still killing."

But Rumsfeld Monday in his address to the CFR questioned whether al-Zarqawi is working with al Qaeda even as he seemed to have a similar agenda.

"In the case of al Qaeda, my impression is most of the senior people have actually sworn an oath to Osama bin Laden, and to my knowledge, even as of this late date, I don't believe Zarqawi, the principal leader of the network in Iraq, has sworn an oath, even though what they're doing—I mean, they're just two peas in a pod in terms of what they're doing," Rumsfeld said.

21

Iraqi museum

Iraq is no doubt the cradle of ancient civilization; it is the home of historically proven early human civilization, cities such as Akad, Sumer, Ur, Babylon, and Nineveh. It is widely believed that cuneiform writing, law, glass, mathematics accounting, astronomy and bureaucracy were invented here.

Nippur in Iraq was an ancient holy city that dates to 5000 B.C, one fragment with cuneiform writing on it found earlier at Nippur helped to explain the flood mentioned in the Bible. It is situated in the desert around hundred miles south of Baghdad, currently is great mound of man-made debris sixty feet high and a mile across. Nippur, for thousands of years was the religious centre of Mesopotamia, where Enlil, the supreme god of the Sumerian pantheon, created mankind.

The collections of Mesopotamian artefacts in the Iraq Museum are UN outstanding heritage of humanity and an unrivalled treasure for all mankind. The Items Span a time period from probably before 9,000 B.C. into the era of Islamic Civilization and world dominance. The museum in Baghdad had some of the earliest tools man had ever made, examples are

Painted polychrome ceramics from the 6th millennium B.C.,

Decorated cult vase from Uruk,

Gold treasures from the Royal Cemetery at Ur,

Sumerian votive statues from Tell Asmar,

Assyrian artefacts and bull figures from the Assyrian capitals of Nimrud, Nineveh Khorsabad, and Islamic pottery and coins

It was established after the first world war by the British traveller and author Gertrude Bell (who was widely regarded as the mother and founder of the twentieth century Iraq) and opened in 1926. Georgina Herrmann (Institute of Archaeology, London/British School of Archaeology) have images of Nimrud ivories from the Iraq Museum.

It was called by then the Baghdad Archaeological Museum. Due to the archaeological fortunes of Mesopotamia (old Iraq), it had one of the most important collections of artefacts (170,000 piece) in the world displayed in 28 galleries. Due to the British connections with the museum all exhibits have been displayed both in English and Arabic. It contains artefacts that date back to more than 5,000 years of civilization in Mesopotamia.

The Baghdad museum had been targeted since 1991 war by armed gangs who bribed guards on occasions and or shot guards to get at ancient treasures. Looting had never been a problem in Iraq before 1991 because of tough laws protecting antiquities.

Before the invasion of Iraq world archaeological experts had warned about the dangers that face the tens of thousands of archaeological sites in Iraq. In an interview with CNN University of Chicago archaeologist McGuire Gibson, who has been leading archaeological digs in Iraq since 1964 "War and archaeology are not a good mix," said. He added "When you have a war, armies tend to occupy higher ground. When they take higher ground, they tend to dig in. And when they dig in, they are digging in to ancient sites," The American Council for Cultural Policy wanted US officials and army to be aware of those precious sites. Its president, they evidently had offered maps and expertise to the US administration. That council regarded the cultural sites and monuments in Iraq are part of the world's heritage.

The American Association of Museum Art Directors, the Archaeological Institute of America and American Schools of Oriental Research had voiced similar concerns to the Bush administration to protect Iraq's museums, cultural centres and archaeological sites. British archaeologists had similar plea to the Blair government.

In the same documentary by CNN Harriett Crawford, president of the British School of Archaeology in Iraq said "Trying to get the message across is a very slow business. It's like trying to push a dinosaur out of the way," Crawford said the U.S. and its allies need to realize Iraq's heritage is a unifying factor in a country with no natural boundaries, made up of diverse groups with varying loyalties: Kurds, Shiites Muslims, Sunni Muslims and Christians".

Immediately before the 2003 Iraq war, various archaeological experts in the world, with representatives from the American Council for Cultural Policy asked The Pentagon and the British governments to ensure safety of the museum from both air strikes and looting. The theft of Baghdad museum was at least in part the work of well-organized antiques thieves from outside Iraq who planned the biggest cultural theft in history.

Immediately after the fall of Baghdad in April 2003 the museum was systematically looted and damage, the museum had lost unknown number of its

170,000 pieces. The looting had happened at professional hands, with the most valuable pieces removed. It has not been possible to assess the degree of looting or the number of lost pieces, officials has claimed there was no database for the collections!

The Museum corridors, galleries and its floor was ransacked, broken glass from smashed, display boxes as well as ancient statues were knocked down from their stands; the scene was shocking and devastating.

A well-developed black market for stolen antiquities does exist, it is estimated to be multibillion dollars market, it spans from the Middle East to Europe, North America and Japan. The collapse of the Iraqi police and legal system and the absence of check-points border controls provided a golden opportunity to those thieves.

Experts worldwide said that details of the museum theft was not just amateurs and likely to be an organized gang. Replica items were left untouched. Records of the museum that would make it hard to sell the priceless items were systematically destroyed; evidently the thieves had keys to the vaults. "It looks like part of the theft was a very deliberate action," said University of Chicago Prof. McGuire Gibson. "They were able to take out the very best material. It really looks like a very professional job."

The Bush administration was criticised by the archaeological community for doing nothing to protect the museum after the fall of Baghdad. Evidently the looting was predicted and the US officials were warned, the looting could have easily prevented, yet did nothing to protect the museum.

Martin Sullivan (chairman of the U.S. President's Advisory Committee on Cultural Property), and State Department cultural advisor Gary Vikan had resigned in protest to the looting of the museum and the American indecisiveness toward that. There is a large black market for stolen antiquities; it is a market of billions of dollars. Stolen items often end in private collection all over the world.

Richard Myers (chairman of the Joint Chiefs of Staff in the pentagon), was asked why the U.S. military did not try to protect the museum after the fall of Baghdad, He said *"If you remember, when some of that looting was going on, people were being killed, people were being wounded, It's as much as anything else a matter of priorities."*. However, the occupying army did not protect people from being killed, the let go with the security of Baghdad and released the criminals in the wild

Donald Rumsfeld had described the period of looting and chaos as "untidiness", said of the museum's looting, "To try to pass off the fact of that unfortunate activity to a deficit in the war plan strikes me as a stretch." Stretch, yet was able to get enough tanks to protect oil fields and the Oil Ministry and valuable Saddam Palaces and let the mob and the professional alike to loot other ministries and the museum.

Colin Powell said, "The United States understands its obligations and will be taking a leading role with respect to antiquities in general but this museum in particular."

The occupying army had not complied with Geneva Conventions that require the occupying army to protect cultural facilities such as museums from damage.

However, they had an excuse; Geneva Conventions also ban fighting from buildings such as museums. Eric Schwartz, Lt Colonel of the U.S. Army's Third Infantry Division said he was unable to protect the museum because there were fighters shooting at the American who were based in the museum building! That would have made it almost impossible for looters to get in and loot the museum; I think this is just a politically correct remark of being defensive,

Danny George, General Director Research Studies for the Board of Antiquities in Iraq, said about the looting, *"It's the crime of the century, because it affects the heritage of all mankind"*.

Dr George went to the headquarters of the occupying army and pleads for protection of the museum; there was a delay of three days before any guard as sent. The American Army had no comments on that. Few days latter the Bush administration had sent FBI agents to investigate and search for the looted artefacts; team of about two dozen agents were sent to help and liaise with the Interpol and art experts from around the world. That followed an outcry by much cultural organization to do something about the museum.

McGuire Gibson, professor of Mesopotamian archaeology at the University of Chicago (who is also head of the American Association for Research in Baghdad) was appointed to investigate the looting he reportedly said "We have dodged a bullet," he said. "Through some luck and some real preparations by the museum staff, we have saved a lot," Gibson said. "The museum authorities didn't have much time, but they got some very important stuff in storage and they completely trusted that the U.S. would secure the museum. They were inside waiting to surrender it, but the U.S. never came," said Gibson,

Dr George and his staff had moved hundred of boxes of museum treasure to safe storage in a safe shelter at a distant place from the museum. Luck saved many priceless pieces that were there but was overlooked by thieves, for example a basalt stele, or carved frieze, that dates to the third millennium B.C. was left alone. "This chunk of rock is extremely important. We were very worried about it," said Gibson, patting the black stone fondly.

"It shows a guy killing a lion with a bow and arrow. It is important because it is one of the earliest examples of someone acting like a king. All through history, this is what kings do. They hunt," he said.

The UNESCO organized an emergency meeting April the 17th, 2003 in Paris to deal with the aftermath of the looting of Baghdad Museum. On April 18, 2003, the Baghdad Museum Project was established in the United States to try to return whatever possible to that museum. The project aimed to establish a database for all the collections of the museum, it also aimed at establishing a website for the museum with picture of all the antiquities to be available to the public. Since April 2003 scholars at the Oriental Institute have made a tremendous effort to establish a database of objects from the Iraq Museum; with the hope of trying to recover the stolen antiquities. The UNESCO experts urged nations to adopt emergency measures to bar the import of archaeological artefacts and establish a "heritage police" in Iraq to protect the ancient sites.

Gibson's report of the looting had raised important question s: why did some of the looters have keys to display cases and? Why did they take some items of great value but overlook others precious items in the same area?

Among the stolen Antiquities two of the most famous pieces, the Sumerian Warka alabaster vase, circa 3200 B.C., and a large bronze Acadian statue called the Basiqi. Those items were probably specifically targeted by art thieves.

Eventually many items believed to be looted from the museum were seized in Jordan, Switzerland, the United States and Japan; some even appeared on e-bay for sale. One television reporter was arrested with connection to the seized items.

Evidently some treasures were returned Iraqi citizens who told authorities that they entered the museum with the looters and took some items to protect them from the theft. "They said that if we don't take it, the looters will. They came later and told us that they would return these things when the situation settled down," said Donny George, director of research at the museum. The offer was accepted on some occasions there was reward for those who turned in some items. Among the items returned was a stone slab containing cuneiform inscriptions from Nimrud, a city in northern Iraq.

Latter on US officials announced that nearly 40,000 manuscripts and 700 artefacts that belong to the Iraq Museum in Baghdad were recovered. Some looters had returned items after promises of rewards, and many items previously reported missing were found hidden in secret storage in the underground of the museum before the beginning of the war.

On June 2003 U.S. authorities announced that world famous treasures of Nimrud were found hidden in the Central Bank in Baghdad. Officials said that of the 170,000 items initially believed missing, just 3,000 remained unaccounted for. And, of those, 47 were main exhibition artefacts.

In November, 2003 Coalition Provisional Authority (CPA) officials reported that few dozens of the important items remained missing from, along with another 10,000 items, most of them tiny and some of them were very fragile.

Even two years after the fall of Baghdad a complete assessment of the extent of the damage is still missing. A complete list of all losses can only be finalized after a complete inventory of all remaining items has been complied, the efforts for the experts work was hampered by the fact that the museum's archive had been devastated during the looting. About15, 000 items are now confirmed to be still missing. It does seem that the damage is les severe than what initially was estimated.

Many other important pieces, including the museum's collection of 4,800 cylinder seals are still missing. Regardless of the numbers the loss is a tragedy to humanity.

The university of Chicago has a large database for pictures of antiquities, the website has the following statement to the public :

(The objects shown here are known to have been in the Iraq Museum in Baghdad or in one of Iraq's provincial museums before the war. Their appearance on this site does not necessarily imply that they have been stolen. If you encounter any of these items outside of Iraq, contact law enforcement authorities immediately!)

Ref

- Tom Hundley, Chicago tribune, May 16, 2003

- The loot time (Museum, Chicago sun-times *June 11, 20030*

- http://oi.uchicago.edu/OI/IRAQ/dbfiles/objects/33.htm

- Job for Indiana Jones& G-men. Helen Kennedy

- daily news Washington bureau April 18, 2003, Oriental institute's Iraq museum project.

22

Ambassador Paul Bremer

Ambassador L. Paul Bremer became a special envoy and Administrator of the Coalition Provisional Authority, the temporary authority that ruled Iraq after the fall of Baghdad, in May 2003.

Ambassador Bremer received his BA from Yale University, a CEP from the Institute D'Etudes Politiques of the University of Paris, and an MBA from Harvard Graduate School of Business Administration. L. Paul Bremer was appointed as Presidential Envoy to Iraq May the 6th, 2003 he was the chief of the doomed to fail Coalition Provisional Authority (CPA). He had a long 23-year career at the State Department; Ambassador Bremer served as Special Assistant or Executive Assistant to six Secretaries of State. His overseas assignments included service at the Embassies in Afghanistan and Malawi and service as Deputy Chief of Mission at the American Embassy in Norway. He was appointed by President Reagan as Ambassador to the Netherlands in 1983 for three years. Ambassador Bremer was Executive Secretary of the State Department and was President Reagan's special Ambassador for what was called Counter Terrorism.

President Ronald Reagan's Secretary of State Alexander Haig appointed him as his special assistant in charge of the department's "crisis management" centre

Ambassador Bremer is one of the world's prominent experts on crisis management, terrorism and security. In September 1999, the Speaker of the House of Representatives, Dennis Hastert, appointed him Chairman of the National Commission on Terrorism. In June 2002, President Bush appointed Ambassador Bremer to the President's Homeland Security Advisory Council. He has also served on the National Academy of Science Commission examining the role of Science and technology in countering terrorism and chaired a Heritage Foundation study, "Defending the Homeland".

Two days after September 11, Bremer wrote: "Our retribution must move beyond the limp-wrested attacks of the past decade, actions that seemed designed to "signal" our seriousness to the terrorists without inflicting real damage. Naturally, their feebleness demonstrated the opposite. This time the terrorists and their supporters must be crushed. But we must avoid a mindless search for an international 'consensus' for our actions. Tomorrow, we will know who our true friends are."

Intentions and rules

Bush administration had ensured that the economy in Iraq get dominated by American firms for tens of years to come, look at the following samples

Order No. 39 allows for: (1) privatization of Iraq's 200 state-owned enterprises; (2) 100% foreign ownership of Iraqi businesses; (3) "national treatment"—which means no preferences for local over foreign businesses; (4) unrestricted, tax-free remittance of all profits and other funds; (5) 40-year ownership licenses.

Thus, it forbids Iraqis from receiving preference in the reconstruction while allowing foreign corporations—Halliburton and Bechtel, for example—to buy up Iraqi businesses, do all of the work and sends all of their money home. They cannot be required to hire Iraqis or to reinvest their money in the Iraqi economy.

Orders No. 57 and No. 77 ensure the implementation of the orders by placing U.S.-appointed auditors and inspector generals in every government ministry, with five-year terms and with superior authority over contracts, programs, employees and regulations.

Order No. 17 grants foreign contractors, including private security firms, full immunity from Iraq's laws. Even if they, say, kill someone or cause an environmental disaster, the injured party cannot turn to the Iraqi legal system. Rather, the charges must be brought to U.S. courts.

Order No. 40 allows foreign banks to purchase up to 50% of Iraqi banks.

Order No. 49 drops the tax rate on corporations from a high of 40% to a flat 15%. The income tax rate is also capped at 15%.

Order No. 12 (renewed on Feb. 24) suspends "all tariffs, customs duties, import taxes, licensing fees and similar surcharges for goods entering or leaving Iraq." This led to an immediate and dramatic inflow of cheap foreign consumer products—devastating local producers and sellers who were thoroughly unprepared to meet the challenge of their mammoth global competitors.

Clearly, the Bremer orders fundamentally altered Iraq's existing laws. For this reason, they are also illegal. Transformation of an occupied country's laws violates the Hague regulations of 1907 (ratified by the United States) and the U.S. Army's Law of Land Warfare. Indeed, in a leaked memo, the British attorney general, Lord Goldsmith, warned Prime Minister Tony Blair that "major structural economic reforms would not be authorized by international law."

With few reconstruction projects underway and with Bremer's rules favouring U.S. corporations, there has been little opportunity for Iraqis to go back to work, leaving nearly 2 million unemployed 1 ½ years after the invasion and, many believe, greatly fuelling the resistance.

The Bremer orders are immoral and illegal and must be repealed to allow Iraqis to govern their own economic and political future

Ref

Antonia Juhasz (a project director at the International Forum on Globalization in San Francisco and a Foreign Policy in Focus scholar). Los Angeles times August 5. 2004

Bremer Misuse in Iraq

The September 2003 CPA (under Bremer) draft request to rehabilitate and reconstruct Iraq $5.136 billion for security, $14.868 billion for infrastructure,$300 million for democracy, civil society, human rights, and refugees. Of the total $20.304 billion requested, CPA eventually received $18.6 billion through the Emergency Supplemental Appropriations Act for Defence and for the Reconstruction of Iraq and Afghanistan, 2004.

CPA officials reported that approximately $730 million have been allocated for democracy programming, which involves several area; anticorruption, government transparency; political parties development; elections; strengthening governmental institutions; civil society building; women's programs; and media infrastructure development.

Iraq is truly the most unfortunate place on this plant. Saddam during his 35 years of oppressive rule had abused and squandered the wealth of the nation, during the Iran war the US had a tremendous benefit from the weapons sale and the cheap Iraqi Oil; most of Iraq's oil went to American refineries in California provided cheap petrol for American voters. Many American companies particularly those who were favoured by Saddam had made enormous wealth. We were crushed under the sanction, the world turned its back on us; our country was ruined by the wars that not only took the lives of our young men but ruined our economy. Now it is history repeating itself, the system is the oil goes to California, and the new Iraqi Ministers squandering the national wealth to profit themselves, their friends and to finance their own militia.

When Paul Bremer went to Baghdad June 2003, he arrived in Iraq soon after the official end of the war, there was $6bn left over from the UN Oil for Food Programme, as well as the frozen assets that was pu on hold for long time during the long years of the economic sanctions, the oil exports were resumed soon after the war and during 2003 there was also at least $10bn from Iraqi oil revenues. Under Security Council Resolution 1483, passed on May 22 2003, all these funds were transferred into a new account held at the Federal Reserve Bank in New York, called the Development Fund for Iraq (DFI), and intended to be spent by the Coalition Provisional Authority (CPA) "in a transparent manner for the reconstruction projects and for the benefit of the Iraqi people".

The "reconstruction" of Iraq is the largest American-led occupation programme since the Marshall Plan; However the US government funded the Marshall Plan. Defence secretary Donald Rumsfeld and Paul Bremer have made sure that the reconstruction of Iraq is paid for by the Iraqis themselves, from oil revenues and frozen assets.

The US Congress had agreed to spend $18.4bn on the reconstruction of Iraq. By June 28 2004, however, when Bremer left Baghdad the CPA had spent up to $300m of US funds.

The "financial irregularities" described in audit reports carried out by agencies of the American government and auditors working for the international community collectively give a detailed insight into the mentality of the American occupation authorities and the way they operated. Truckloads of dollars were handed out for which neither they nor the recipients felt they had to be accountable.

The auditors have so far referred more than a hundred contracts, involving billions of dollars paid to American corporations, for investigation and possible criminal prosecution. The auditors had also found also discovered that $8.8bn that passed through the new Iraqi government ministries in Baghdad while Bremer was in charge is unaccounted for, with little prospect of finding out where it has gone. A further $3.4bn appropriated by Congress for Iraqi development has since been siphoned off to finance "security".

Although Bremer was expected to manage Iraqi funds in a transparent manner, it was only in October 2003, six months after the fall of Saddam, that an International Advisory and Monitoring Board (IAMB) was established to provide independent, international financial oversight of CPA spending. (This board includes representatives from the United Nations, the World Bank, the IMF and the Arab Fund for Economic and Social Development.)

The IAMB spent months trying to find auditors acceptable to the US. The Bahrain office of KPMG was agreed upon and appointed in April 2004.

"KPMG had encountered stiff resistance from CPA staff with regard to the submission of information required to complete their tasks," they wrote in an interim report. "Staff has indicated that cooperation with KPMG's undertakings is given a low priority." KPMG had one meeting at the Iraqi Ministry of Finance; meetings at all the other ministries were repeatedly postponed. The auditors even had trouble getting passes to enter the Green Zone.

At the end of June 2004, the CPA had handed the power ti interim Iraqi authority (still under the occupation control, which had "advisors" in every ministry) and ambassador Bremer left Iraq. There Bush administration did not want independent auditors to investigate the financial spending and its appropriateness of the CPA under Bremer leadership

The report of the audit was published in July 2004.The auditors found that the CPA could not account of the hundreds of millions of dollars that they had spent, they had agreed and signed contracts that values billions of dollars to American contractors without prior tenders. The CPA had no idea what eventually happened to the money of the Iraq reconstruction project (Development Fund for Iraq (DFI)), the money was spent by the ministries of the interim Iraqi government. After "election" of new authority following Bremer, many of those ministers and their high ranking officials had disappeared, mostly went abroad, and likely with large sums of embezzled money from the reconstruction projects. Iraqi contractors had complained repeatedly that they had to bribe bribes to Iraqi officials in order to get CPA contracts. Iraqi or only to bid for a contract ministers' relatives had high ranking official jobs in their ministries and obviously their friend and relatives wan the flawed reconstruction contracts.

Certainly there was no transparency in Bremer time for the spending of the money, which has led to allegations many accounts of corruption. An Iraqi hospital administrator who told Ed Harriman of the Guardian newspaper that when he came to sign a contract, *"the American army officer representing the CPA had crossed out the original price and doubled it"* The Iraqi protested that the original price was enough. *The American officer explained that the increase (more than $1m) was his retirement package!* How about the poor Iraqis who had no electricity of running water? Iraqis who were close to the Americans were mainly those who were in exile and came with them during the invasion, had installed themselves into the Green Zone were the ministers and high officials in the new government were also in a personally profiting from the corruption.

When the Iraqi Governing Council asked Bremer why a contract to repair the Samar'a cement factory would cost US $60m, they had agreed on $20m earlier, the American representative reportedly told them that they should be grateful the coalition had saved them from Saddam.

Further evidence of lack of transparency comes from a series of audits conducted by the Coalition Provisional Authority's inspector general's office. It was established in January 2004 and reported their findings to the Congress. It seems that those audit people were unwelcome in the Green Zone, not only by the Iraqis but also by their American fellow-men. Their audit was published in July 2004 and reported that the American contracts officers in the CPA and the ministries "*did not ensure that...contract files contained all the required documents, a fair and reasonable price was paid for the services received, contractors were capable of meeting delivery schedules, or that contractors were paid in accordance with contract requirements*".

Millions of dollars was reported missing from the Iraqi Central Bank. Between US$11m and $26m worth of Iraqi properties confiscated by the CPA was unaccounted for. The payroll had hundreds of ghost employees who never existed. Millions of dollars were paid to contractors for contracts that did not exist. Some $3,379,505 was billed, for "*personnel not in the field performing work*" and ".Thousands of contracts to repair pipeline or renovate a school for example was allocated large and improper sums of money.

And then there are the mobile phones. Many local companies from the middle east had bided for contracts to open centres for mobile phones, one of those companies where from Bahrain, however, the Americans ordered the system shut down because the Bahrain operating company, by opening its service so early, was supposedly not giving other bidders a fair chance at the contract. Those other companies are largely American.

The Committee had filed 69 criminal investigations related to theft, fraud, waste, assault and extortion, in appropriate use of expenses...It also investigated "*a number of other cases that, because of their sensitivity, could not be included in this report*". One of those may have been the scandal when 19 billion new Iraqi Dinar (about US $12 million US dollars) was found on a plane in Lebanon that was smuggled then by the Iraqi minister of internal affairs.

The IAMB also discovered that Iraqi oil exports were not measured by any mean and could not be audited. Neither the American authorities the Iraqi State Oil Marketing Organisation nor was able to give a reasonable answer to that or could even explain it. It was obviously an unprecedented opportunity for corruption, whether it was deliberate acts or untidy mess, the responsibility falls on the shoulders of the CPA. However those officials proved to be immune from prosecution.

Iraq had exported $10bn worth of oil in the year 2003 under the American occupation. Christian Aid has estimated that up to $4bn more may have been exported and was unaccounted for. That had created an off-the-record sums of money that both the Americans and their Iraqi allies could use with impunity to cover illegal expenditures they would rather keep secret.

One explanation possibly the cost of the invasion and occupation was high, and to cover it up the bush administration may had siphoned the Iraqi oil money to cover the cost; possibly to maintain the backing of the congress of the war in Iraq.

Just before Bremer left Baghdad, the CPA had agreed on and signed $3bn in new contracts to be paid for from the Oil revenues and managed by the US embassy in Baghdad. The CPA inspector general, renamed as Special Inspector General for Iraq Reconstruction (SIGIR), who latter released an audit report on the way the embassy had dealt with the reconstruction money. They audited of 225 contracts worth $327m to see if the embassy "could identify the current value of paid and unpaid contract obligations". It couldn't.

The report of the SIGRI said "Our review showed that financial records, understated payments made by $108,255,875" and "overstated unpaid obligations by $119,361,286". The auditors also reviewed the paperwork of a further 300 contracts worth $332.9m: "Of 198 contract files reviewed, 154 did not contain evidence that goods and services were received, 169 did not contain invoices, and 14 did not contain evidence of payment."

It is obvious the American administration in Iraq did not care to make any effort to rationalize the financial spending of the country's revenues on construction, probably part of that was to be able to finance the military machine in Iraq. The Excuse was always the security difficulties.

In January 2005, the SIGIRI reported clear and detailed evidence of fraud and corruption by the Iraqi Interim Government when Bremer was in charge. They found that US$8.8bn (the whole Iraqi Interim Government budget from October 2003 through June 2004) was not accounted for. Iraq appointed by the occupation and their senior officials (usually relatives and friends) were handing out hundreds of millions of dollars in cash at their discretion, mostly on fraudulent projects, the American advisors of the ministers did not intervene which raises serious concerns.

Auditors say "CPA personnel did not review and compare financial, budgetary and operational performance to planned or expected results". Some of the ministries had spent hundreds of millions of dollars without knowledge of the CPA personnel. One ministry for example spent $430m in mostly fraud contracts without American advisers verifying their documents. Another minister claimed he was paying 8,206 guards, but only 602 were verified to exist. There no system and no way of knowing how much of the $8.8bn went into private pockets.

The fraud and lack of accountability was ripping the nations wealth in the name of reconstruction, it is Iraqi revenues, a country in total anarchy and easy pray for American contractors, security companies and the Iraqi officials. Little money goes into the construction and mostly goes to do simple jobs that had proved to cost much less than what they were contracted for. It is all going to ministers, their families and cronies

In reply to the SIGIRI report "At liberation, the Iraqi economy was dead in the water. So Cap's top priority was to get the economy going."

The SIGIR released another report in April 2005; an investigation into the way Bremer's CPA managed cash payments from Iraqi funds in just one part of Iraq, the region around Hillah:

"During the course of the audit, we identified deficiencies in the control of cash of such magnitude as to require prompt attention. Those deficiencies were so significant that we were precluded from accomplishing our stated objectives.

CPA headquarters in Baghdad "did not maintain full control and accountability for approximately $119.9m

Agents in the field cannot properly account for or support over $96.6m in cash and receipts. The agents were mostly Americans. Many of the them submitted their documentations only hours before they left Iraq

One agent's account balance was "overstated by $2,825,755, and the error went undetected.

Another agent was given $25m cash for which Bremer's office

"Acknowledged not having any supporting documentation".

Of more than $23m given to another agent, there are only records for $6,306,836 paid to contractors.

Two agents left Iraq without accounting for $750,000 each, which has never been found.

CPA office cleared several agents' balances of between $250,000 and $12m without any receipts. One agent who did submit receipts, on being told that he still owed $1,878,870, turned up three days later with exactly that amount.

The auditors said "this suggests that the agent had a reserve of cash", pointing out that if his original figures had been correct, he would have accounted to the CPA for

approximately $3.8m more than he had been given in the first place, which "suggests that the receipt documents provided to the DFI account manager were unreliable".

The schools, hospitals, water supply and electricity, all of which were supposed to benefit from these funds, are in ruins, no renovations, no new facilities were built in Hilla. In conclusion, it sounds that most contracts were fraudulent, American agents grabbed most of the money and gave some of the Iraqi officials what they wanted for their retirement.

The IAMB's during 2005 (three years after the invasion) had reported

lack of documented justification for limited competition for contracts at the Iraqi ministries

Possible misappropriation of oil revenues

Significant difficulties in ensuring completeness and accuracy of Iraqi budgets and controls over expenditures

Non-deposit of proceeds of export sales of petroleum products into the appropriate accounts in contravention of UN Security Council Resolution 1483

Bremer kept nearly $600m in cash for which there is no paperwork: $200m of that sum was kept in one of Saddam's palaces.

One ministry claimed to be paying 8,206 guards, but only 602 could be found

One American agent was given $23m to spend on reconstructions; only $6m is accounted for

Paul Bremer then wrote a book; My Year in Iraq: "The Struggle to Build a Future of Hope." You wonder what kind of future and hope will it be; is it going to be a future of civil war, a corrupt state with no borders or moral obligations; or a state where the Iraqis are busy killing each other while the oil companies and other contractors are growing fat from fraudulent deals and cheap oil? Only time will tell.

Bremer disbanded the army, and abolished the entire civil system in Iraq, that made the country truly belongs to the pre-industrial era. Since then Iraq has been torn apart by the civil conflict. Bremer admitted to Brian Williams of NBC news that, "…we really didn't see the insurgency coming," Bremer had pointed out the faults of his superiors in the pentagon and blamed them for not having enough troops in Iraq. Trying to doge responsibility from the mess in Iraq he said "I believe I did everything I could do. My view is in government, you have an obligation to tell the President what you think. You should do that in private through appropriate channels, as I tried to do. *The President, in the end, is responsible for making decisions.*"

He says about his decision to disband the army *"a force comprised of Shiite draftees who had deserted and refused to serve under their former Sunni officers"*. This in my views either a deep misunderstanding of the Iraqi community, or an evil remark that aims to deepen the ethnic division in Iraq.

Bremer describes his meetings with President Bush in his book and outlines his admiration for the president's "firm wartime leadership". But realistically you wonder how much of that is just political correctness, to try to say the "right thing". He says he had a vision to democratic Iraq, three years since the fall of Baghdad and if anything it is going from bad to worse.

In an effort to diffuse the responsibility of what went wrong Bremer outlined his struggle with Rumsfeld, the defence secretary, and military leaders who were determined to reduce the US troop presence despite the escalating violence.

There is wide misconception about Iraq as "The Shiite Arabs are the country's long-repressed majority, who deeply distrusted the Sunni Arab minority who had held power for centuries". This was emphasized on and on again, by politicians, military leaders and the media. The truth of the matter is that Iraq is made up of Arabs, Kurds, Turkmen's and other few minorities, the Arabs traditionally are either Sunnis or Shiites (the two main religious schools in Islam), that mixture is not unique to Iraq; as far as the Iraqi community was concerned no one really cared whether you are Sunni or Shiites, they are intermarried, have strong tiers with ach other, no hatred. As about the leadership; the very First Iraq Leader after the fall of the monarchy 1n 1957 was Shiites (A. Kassim), he was favoured by most Iraqis regardless of their loyalties. It is often stated that Saddam had persecuted the Shiites; however, the truth Saddam was a vicious villain who distributed equally his oppression on all Iraqi regardless of their ethnicity. The American policy makers had put to much emphasis of the persecution of the Shiites and used it in their propaganda in part to justify the invasion.

Bremer was evidently responsible for most of the mistake that took place in Iraq. He had harsh criticism from white House officials and Congressmen.

Ref

The Guardian 7th of July 2005

The exclusive interview "Dateline NBC," Sunday, and on "Nightly News with Brian Williams," Monday, Jan. 9. 2005

Criticism of Bremer

Bremer is impressive person, who dresses well and talk convincingly, evidently Bush had seen Jay Garner wearing casuals after the fall of Baghdad and asked his advisors to replace him for someone that "the Iraqi people to look-up to".

Bremer's criticism of the white house had angered officials and evidently he was asked to explain his remarks. According to The Washington Post story he said we never had enough troops on the ground." He added: "We paid a big price for not stopping it because it established an atmosphere of lawlessness."

The hearty of criticism to Bremer was his decision to disband the army, which is widely seen as the problem that had instigated violence in Iraq. Bush administration had insisted that this decision was made on the ground in Iraq, rather than in Washington. The plan in Washington before the war (according to the Washington post) was to get rid of the officers and use the solders in reconstruction and security. Bremer had changed that to total disintegration of the army. The White House officials say that when Bremer arrived in Baghdad may 2003 they warned him there will be chaos if he disband the army; he was told by CIA chief "That's another 350,000 Iraqis you're pissing off, and they've got guns." When ex-Iraqi soldiers demonstrated outside Bremer's office at the former Presidential Palace, US troops shot two of them dead.

This quote is taken from the Washington post

"According to one source who was at the meeting, Garner then asked if they could discuss the matter further in a smaller meeting. Garner then said: "Before you announce this thing let's do all the pros and cons of this, because we are going to have a hell of a lot of problems with it. There is a hell of a lot more cons than there are pros. Let's line them all up then get on the phone to [Defence Secretary Donald] Rumsfeld." Bremer replied: "I don't have any choice. I have to do this." Garner then protested further, but Bremer cut him off. "The president told me that de-Baathification comes before the immediate needs of the Iraqi people."

Bremer had been harshly criticised for his policy, he is i to blame about the historical disaster in Fallujah that remained the spearhead of the insurgency and the symbol of instability. By his iron fist policy he did undermine the democratic process in Iraq, by all accounts there was hope before Bremer time, and certainly there is no hope after his radical view that derailed the freedom and democracy in the country. He was looking for a quick victory; he was described successful politician, terror expert and foreign relations master yet did not realizing the dangers ahead. World Socialist Web Site, in 1981 described Bremer's bread and butter issue was terrorism.

Was he the right person in Iraq, he always adopted tough policy against terrorism; he extended his field by regarding the Iraqi resistance and labelling them as terrorist. This mistake had angered the average Iraqis who are proud of their nation and who they are, they wanted to defend their nation regardless of what Bremer thought.

Bremer had consistently adopted a tough stance towards terrorists. In August 5, 1996, in an article in the Wall Street Journal he said "*Terrorists' Friends Must Pay a Price*" Bremer urged the Clinton administration to "get serious about the fight against terrorism." Bremer advised Clinton to deliver ultimatums to Libya, Syria, Iran and Sudan telling them to close down terrorist bases or they will "receive the full weight of American might." Ironically, Iraq was not one of those countries. which in fact highlights the well known fact that Iraq and the Iraqis ha nothing to do with terrorism.

Bremer past experience is mostly dealing with the terrorists, in Iraq, however, he delivered ten of thousands of terrorists who brought the fight to Iraq, the borders were very porous, no check points and for a significant while in his time the borders were free for any one who wants to get in there.

What special expertise about Iraq or the Middle East is Bremer bringing to Iraq? None, a former senior State Department official who has worked with Bremer said to News Day. He is a "voracious opportunist with voracious ambitions," the official told Newsday. "What he knows about Iraq could not quite fill a thimble. What he knows about any part of the world would not fill a thimble. But what he knows about Washington infighting could fill three or four bushel baskets."

Ref

Washington post 5. October 2004

The post. IE; August 31.2003

The situation in Bremer time

But he is a famous "anti-terrorism" expert who is supposed to be rebuilding the country with a vast army of international companies-most of them American, of course-and creating the first democracy in the Arab world. Since he seems to be a total failure at the "anti-terrorist" game; Bremer made a real mess (to say the least) of the "reconstruction" in Iraq, to the Iraqis he was just another leader with radical policies, he cared about nothing but his own fame, whether he made a big fortune for himself or not the auditors had stopped short of accusing him of embezzlement, may be he was one of the embarrassing details that was not released.

In his year the American propaganda had glorified its achievement in Iraq, they talked about the schools they opened, the universities that started to function, the economy that started to recover and the health system that was being modernised. No few years down the track, were all that? Where is the security, how about the jobs, the health system is ailing, the universities are targets of radicals with almost daily assassinations, were are the oil revenues going, the country is simply ruined and had disintegrated to an extent that is beyond any description. The average Iraqi as ever is thinking that the only way is out, that is to look for new life abroad, it is just more than what any one can put up with, thanks to the occupation.

The oil industry was supposedly up and going, exports had reached to almost a million barrel a day; the lack of electricity during 2003 that stayed the same had affected the oil exports, smugglers of oil had been reportedly caught, but probably the business was booming. Iraq, with the world's second most abundant oil reserves, was importing fuel from other oil producing countries to meet domestic demands. Prices of petrol had risen many times during and after the CPA time, it became hardly affordable. Crisis in petrol availability in the country is the worst in the world, long line and long time of waiting.

He was planning the opening of Baghdad airport. The Airport and the way to it is the most dangerous place in the world, the airport still has huge American military base and it was made the official prison for former regime members, it is under daily mortar attacks, road-side bombs and grenades. The airplanes had been attacked by hand held rockets; it is so dangerous no airline would risk travelling to Baghdad. Mayhill Aviation" made some advertisements in the local press saying that it was intending to fly a Boeing 747 once a week from Gatwick to Basra (south of Iraq), that route was eventually for British solders and their families transportation.

Another big criticism for Bremer was his policy of eradicating all Baathist from university staff which result and firing 436 professors. In the same vein, the CPA annulled the academic system whereby student party members would automatically receive higher grades. This de-Baathification policy resulted in acute shortage of teaching staff. Many of the 436 were party men in name only and received their degrees at British and American universities. At Al-Mustansiriyah University, for example, the same professors who were sacked by Bremer were re-hired after filling out forms denouncing the Ba'ath party. Obviously he regretted his decision and rehired them.

Health services

Bremer and his interim provisional authority did put some effort and money to rehabilitate the hospitals and the health service.

. But a mysterious American company called ABT Associates they describe themselves as

"ABT Associates applies rigorous research and consulting techniques to a wide range of issues in social and economic policy, international development, business research and consulting, and clinical trials and registries. One of the largest for-profit government and business research and consulting firms in the world, ABT Associates delivers practical, measurable, high-value-added results. Our staff of more than 1,000 employee-owners includes national and international experts who are recognized for their knowledge, innovative research techniques, and insightful analyses and recommendations"

It all sound like they know how to "talk the talk"

They turned up in Baghdad to give "Ministry of Health Technical Assistance" support to the US Agency for International Development (USAID) and "rapid response grants to address health needs in-country".

They recommended that all medical equipments should match the US technical standards; it simply means that all equipments would have to come from the US, not from other countries.

Of course, Iraqis protest at much of this. They protest in the streets, especially against the aggressive American military raids, and they protest in the press.

Democracy (American style)

When Falujah residents staged a protest April 2003, the American military shot 16 dead. Another 11 were later gunned down in Mosul in anti-American protest. During two demonstrations against the presence of US forces near the shrine of Imam Al-Hussein in Karbala August 2003, US soldiers shot dead three people. It was no different to Saddam time, if you express your opinions against the authorities you get shot down. That was the democracy in the "New Iraq"

Under the Bremer rule US troops were losing hearts and minds of the average Iraqis, military raids to Iraqi house, which frightened the ordinary families had helped to build the hatred against the Americans.

Paul Wolfewitz was constantly attacking al-jazeera for airing scenes of American abuse and crimes in Iraq. The media in Iraq had actually flourished in Bremer time, with as many as 150 papers were publishing, but was it democratic, well most of them were financed by the occupation and those who criticised the occupation were shut down, newspapers that offended the Americans were raided by US troops

Deteriorations under Bremer.

Sciri or Supreme Council of Islamic revolution in Iraq was founded in Iran by AL—Hakim, who was killed by a suicide bomb in AL—Najaf. The recruits are Shiites Arab who fled to Iran after the war in 1991. The Council came under attack as it chose to operate from one of former Saddam palaces and reportedly bought new cars for its members, in a fashion similar to Saddam time.

Violence that mounts to anarchy had emerged and became well entrenched in the Iraqi society during Bremer time; large numbers of Iraqi were being killed by the Americans daily and for the most simple of reasons, such as driving your car at a near distance from an American armoured vehicle. Mysterious militia had appeared, mostly radicals who were outside Iraq and came back with hatred and grudge thirsty for blood and determined for revenge, young people were getting abducted and disappear to be found killed after gruesome tortures, mainly drilling the bones or the head; fingers were pointed to different political factions and the crack in the society got deeper and deeper and ripped into the nation for years to come.

Those abductions and assassinations were some phenomenon the Iraqis are not used to see, it was mainly politically motivated or done in the name of the religion. The Murders, thefts became the daily norm of Baghdad, and to lesser extent in the rest of the country.

Christians who were the only people in the country could get licence to sell alcohol were receiving constant threats from various factions, several places of alcohol stores were raided and ravaged and some people were killed in Baghdad and Basra for selling alcohol.

The CPA officials had failed to report the extent of the trouble the country was in, or at times underestimated the seriousness of it.

Women abduction and rapes became a new phenomenon in the "New Iraq"

The Independent (British newspaper), had in August 2003 discovered the identity of a young woman who had been kidnapped, raped and then freed, only to attempt suicide three times at her home. Another family gave the paper a photograph of their abducted daughter in the hope that it might be printed in the Iraqi press to help finding their daughter. Incidents like that were happening on daily basis. The irony of it all is that bush in contempt to Saddam said immediately before the invasion. "There will be no more torture and rape chambers"

For the people of Iraq, a new era of misery was coming, more lives lost, more Diasporas, more poverty and humiliation. Even though another $100 million is "missing" in so-called "reconstruction" funds, it may never be known how much Paul Bremer's Coalition Provisional Authority (CPA) actually skimmed in Iraq War Fraud. "There was no assurance that fraud, waste, and abuse did not occur in the management and administration of cash assets," the May 2005 audit concluded.

Bremer Quotes

About Saddam Bremer said *"We've thrown out Saddam and Saddam, dead or alive, is finished in Iraq"*. And "While it's very hard to know exactly how to measure public opinion there, because there's no really good polling, the fact of the matter is that in all the polls I've seen the vast majority of the Iraqis prefer to be free and are pleased that the coalition freed them"; there is in fact some truth in this as people believed the promises the bush administration made.

About "terrorists" 'I hope they're going to learn, and as a result of our response, that it isn't going to work. They're not going to change our life, they're not going to have us throw out our Constitution, and they're not going to chase us out of the Middle East.

"Iraq has become, for better or for worse, the front on the war on terrorism, and so we've got to do this, and I can understand why congressmen and senators would take their responsibility seriously, but I think in the end we'll get the money". The problem here is it is very hard for us to swallow this fabricated lie, since when Iraq had terrorists, we should remember the statement made by Bush after September 11 "We will take the war on terror to their own land". Although it will seem like a conspiracy theory, but the only conclusion that could be drawn is that Bremer and his superiors in the White House wanted Iraq to be the place for that war; by abolishing a full system in the country it was almost an open invitation to the terrorists to get into Iraq; a plan that may very well had happened.

Democracy "I think the Iraqi people have shown extraordinary patience and courage in the last few months. They have really put a political system on the way to success, to a real democracy here".

"I think what we've learned is that the terrorist threat is serious, but it shifts. You cannot make a single person the sole focus of your counterterrorism".

"Saddam spent 35 years stealing and wasting money, and all of these systems are very fragile and brittle, and you try to fix one thing and something else gets in trouble". But how about the sanctions that tore the country apart for almost 14 years.

Then it gets more confusing, who was derailing the democratic process, is it terrorist or some disgruntled Saddam followers. In this respect he said *"The fact of the matter is that we are facing a small group of bitter-enders who are basically trying turning the tide of history"*.

"These people hate the United States, not for what we do, but for who we are and what we are".

23

Refugees Again

According to the UN and Jordanian authorities, the count of Iraqis seeking refuge in Jordan is more than half a million, who overwhelmed Jordan, a country of less than 5 million people and limited resources. Admittedly some of those people had left during Saddam time, but those are small numbers that are registered with UNHCR as refugees. According the UNHCR the resources are limited and it would not be possible to support such huge numbers if they decide to seek a refugee's status.

Many Iraqis had a job opportunities by joining the new police force, however police stations and forces became the prime target for terrorists who are suicide bombers, mostly radicals who fought in Afghanistan against the Russians, the Americans put them out of work by throwing the Taliban; now they are in Iraq, new recruits had joined and wrecked the country under the name of Jihad. Even before becoming a policeman recruits had been massacred while in line waiting to fill some routine forms for police enrolment. Many occasions happened when they were gunned down before they even make to the waiting lines of recruitments. This and other trouble had led hundreds of thousands to leave Iraq, many left for their lives.

John Elmer of the Dominion newspaper had visited Amman, Jordan to assess the conditions of the Iraqi who fled across the borders to Jordan; they ran away fro the hellish situation in Iraq, from lack of security, violence, miserable living conditions and lack of adequate medical care. He described an Iraqi family who really was an example of the true hardship that all most of the 26 million Iraqi had suffered under the occupation and Saddam before that. A lady by the Name Susan Shaker was employed by a local bank, one day her employer sent her in a van for some form of work along with many other employees, on the way to work the had to stop at a police check point, suddenly a suicidal bomb went off. The suicide bomber was planning to detonate the bomb at the bank, however he was stopped by a police at a checkpoint and decided to detonate the bomb, few people got killed and other injured; Susan was very unlucky, a shrapnel hit her in the spine and damaged the spinal cord and another one penetrated the skull. She got paralysed instantly, lost her sight and was unable to speak.

At a hospital in Baghdad her condition was stabilized but there were little facilities of any specialized treatment to look after such a incapacitating injuries, the health system was not capable in fact to treat or deal with the size of the disasters that system had disintegrated under the sanctions. Susana and her husband sold every thing they had including the source of their livelihood which a book store they bought during the sanctions time; they sold it for a quarter of the price they bought it for due to the failing economy of the country.

Susan and her husband had spent more than $25,000 US dollars for treatment in Amman, Jordan. According to the author of the article (her Husband said "We have lost everything: our future, our families' future. His voice trailed off as he choked-back tears". Eventually when they go back to Baghdad, she will have no medical care appropriate to her condition, the family livelihood is gone, and they truly lost everything.

What they said to John Elmer "Please, I ask that you put more pressure on the American government—on the Western governments—to pull out of Iraq, immediately,"

Tens of thousands of Iraqis were in Amman escaping the crushing disaster of every day life, which is haunted by poverty, lack of security, abduction assassinations and road side bombs. They eyes remain on Iraq, hoping that one day they will be able to go back to Iraq, a friendly and perhaps a peaceful Iraq. For Iraqis who left to Jordan it is virtually impossible for Iraqis to obtain work in the public sector unless their employers recommend them, most of them live illegally in Jordan, facing the possibility of deportation when their permit expires.

many Iraqis are leaving every day across the borders to Syria and Jordan, some are lucky enough to have family members somewhere else in the world and were able to join their families and got better life; but the majority are hanging around in neighbouring countries, roaming the streets, living on their savings; what the holds for them is anyone guess. Indeed after long periods of waiting with no job and no opportunity to go somewhere else, large numbers have to go back and face their fate in a country where there is no hope.

Life is simply not possible in Baghdad now few years under the occupation, people had given up any hope, they are demoralised from a long-lasting suffering for the last 35 or so years; first under a terrorist regime then 14 years of the international siege and wars and occupations and local opportunistic politicians who came from no where full of hatred to their fellow citizens only because they belong to different form of Islam to lit the fire of the civil conflict, which may never end. Indeed it does look so bleak that it will go on for eternity.

People are fleeing their homeland leaving behind families because of the violence that had taken the entire country and strangled the nation since the March 2003 US-led invasion of their country. That is only one aspect the had ruined the life of millions; other troubles are lack of electric power, no fresh water for human consumption, and most of the basic human needs are not met; yet the politicians are fighting a ferocious battle to gain a seat in the government and they haggle for months and months for that, and the purpose is not the nation it is rather an opportunity to get their hands on some thing they can to ensure their financial well being, it does seem that the country is actually gone for sell! Everyone wants to take a piece of it. The violence is to Iraqi people is clearly seen as a direct result of the foreign occupation.

Most of us thought that the curse of sanctions and Saddam for decades is gone when we saw his statue being pulled down in the heart of Baghdad. We were promised there will be no more rapes and torture chambers, reconstructions, freedom and better life but here it is few years and the violence and the battle is even more ferocious, it had engulfed the lives or tens of thousands of young people in Iraq, and ruined the life of the millions who remained alive, no freedom, no basic necessities no security; it does seem that the country is doomed for ever. It is not only the lack of jobs that force many to leave, the problem is complicated by lack of security, suicidal bombs, assassinations, American attacks on suspected resistance place made every single task fraught with dangers, innocent get killed by hundreds each day simply it happened they were at the wrong place in the wrong time.

Iraqis are generally struggling to make ends meet whether they are in Iraq or they fled to Syria or Jordan, still some had managed to gain refuge in one of the European countries, who restarted to accept the Iraqis as refuges gain after a short while of suspending that in the time immediately after the occupation. Most people in the neighbouring counties do simple and sometimes only occasional jobs, often at low salaries, which is much less than the local workers wages, their situation and living standards are terrible and yet they got taken advantage of by local employers. There is stiff competition for jobs because the neighbouring countries are poor, Iraqi are regarded as illegal immigrants and mostly are not allowed to hold Government jobs, there is growing resentment of those illegal Iraqi immigrants, there looked upon with eyes of suspicion, the general popular idea is they had driven the prices up, taken jobs from local workers. This discrimination is the reality for most Iraqis who are lucky enough to find work in Jordan. Women are sitting in the streets of Amman and other places as street vendors selling different things that they can retail with a small profit. That phenomenon was common during the sanction years and now it is back again. Central park (Medan al-Hussein and the Roman Theatre) is the place for Iraqis to meet each other, everyday larges numbers of them as unemployed people, from different parts of Iraq, sit, smoke and chat. Most of them can't work because they can't afford to pay the $200US fees of the work permit, yet it is not easy to get a work permit. It is apparently the official's policy of the local governments to protect their own workers. Iraqi workers are allowed to stay in Jordan only for three months unless they have a work permit if the were caught in violation of that visas or work permits; they get detained in police custody for a week and then deported to a third country. Most Iraqis will chose to go to Yemen which does not require a visa for the Iraqis. It seems that they are not allowed to deport the m back to Iraq due to the volatile situation there.

Many Iraqi with a university degree are unable to get a job opportunity in the volatile current situation, the economy had grown slightly after the fall of Saddam but its growth is hampered by the lack of security. Most Iraqi families are extended with large numbers living under one roof, often 10 or 15 people and usually supported by one or two employed or working men, which made life difficult to sustain.

Syria

Syrian officials reported 700,000 Iraqis fled the country since the 2003 invasions; they are from various sectarian, religious and economic backgrounds. The number is far more than in any other country in the region. The flow is ever increasing as there is no sign of improvement. According to the UN statement in 2005 doctors, professors, university graduates, business people and other professionals are leaving the country increasingly, the constitute the elite of the Iraqi society that would form the main section of the community which would rebuild the country. The situation is similar to the flood of immigration of professional that followed the Kuwait war and during the years of sanction.

There are efforts from the UN to try to find a solution for the terrible situation in Syria for Iraqi who suffer from shortages of medical care, crowding and rising rate of crimes which is increasing the burden on the Syrian community. There is ongoing effort to help the fleeing Iraqis without encouraging them to flee, the U.N. had arranged with the Syrian officials a "temporary protection status" that that allows them to stay without facing deportation, however the Syrians are not obliged to provide any financial assistance to them. The UN had expected exodus of Iraqi at the war time and had arranged for camps in Syria for refugees, however there was no immediate exodus, but people gradually started to move in increasing numbers. The stamina of the Iraqis is truly remarkable, they endured the tough sanctions, went through the wars and got used to the most hostile circumstances, their needs are not sophisticated and they know how to live on meagre resources.

Ref

Violence, Poverty Underscore Story of Iraqi Refugees in Jordan

John Elmer Dominion July 2005. http://dominionpaper.ca"

24

Sergio Vieira De Mello

Born in Rio de Janeiro in 1948, Sergio De Mello joined the United Nations in 1969 while studying philosophy and humanities at the University of Paris (Panthéon-Sorbonne). He spent the majority of his career working for the United Nations High Commissioner for Refugees in Geneva, and served in humanitarian and peace-keeping operations in different countries.

Sergio Vieira de Mello was requested to go to Iraq after the war by the U.N. Secretary General Kofi Annan for a four-month humanitarian commitment. He spent three months in Baghdad, one month before f his scheduled return to Geneva, Mr. de Mello was killed in Baghdad (buried alive) under the rubble of the UN building in Baghdad which was targeted by a suicide bomber. Sergio Vieira de Mello was the United Nations High Commissioner for Human Rights. Mr. de Mello devoted most of his life to the U.N.'s mission to protect human rights and achieve international peace and security. He served in some of the toughest trouble spots in the world, including East Timor, Mozambique, Bosnia, Peru, Sudan, and Cambodia.

Saudi Arabian Islamists were blamed as the suicide bombers; they may have crossed the border into Iraq at the time of lawlessness to prepare for a holy war against the foreign occupying power. The A satellite television channel Al-Arabiya aired a statement presumably from al Qaeda, which urged Muslims around the world to volunteer to fight the U.S. occupation of Iraq, and claimed that attacks on U.S. forces had been carried out throughout the country by Mujahidin.

In addition to Mr. de Mello The blast that killed 19 other people who worked for the United Nations, it also wounded more than 100 in the U.N. compound in Baghdad. It was believed to be the work of Islamic radical Jihadis; the same group that bombed the Jordanian embassy killing 11 people in Baghdad 12 days prior to that. Alaqaeda chiefs had always condemned the role of the United States and the UN for the economic sanctions against Iraq; they also decried the United

Nations support to the United State in the invasion of Afghanistan and the removal of the Taliban from power.

Bush's invasion of Iraq was not supported by the United Nations; however to most radicals the two are seen as linked to each other. The war was In fact was seen by the UN as a clear violation of the U.N. Charter. The UN was accused by Bush to be irrelevant when the Security Council refused to back the US and Britain in the war against Iraq, despite the intense pressure from the US.

This stance of the UN and the latter bombing of the UN headquarter in Baghdad had led many people to question the Al-Qaeda role in that bombing. De Mello was shocking loss to the World and to the Iraqi people in that critical time.

When Sergio de Mello's was sent to Baghdad, he was on a mission to help the Iraqi people, his dream was to see the people of Iraq to build a country that can build a true democracy example in the middle east. He was going to help the Iraqi people to over one of the most difficult time in the history of the nation, whose pride was injured by foreign occupation. For De Mello the interest of the Iraqi people was first.

Sergio De Mello's death was a tragic loss to the entire world Salim Lone, Mr. de Mello's spokesman in Baghdad, said in an interview with CNN "He was a wonderful guy. He was the U.N. in a way." He added, "I grieve most of all for the people of Iraq because he was really the man who could have helped bring about an end to the occupation. An end to the trauma the people of Iraq have suffered for so long."

After his death many scholars an peace activist such as Professor Marjorie Cohn (Thomas Jefferson School of Law) had called upon Bush and his administration to relinquish power in Iraq to the United Nations. To Sergio the occupation was the most terrible tragedy to the Iraqi people, he was strong opponent of the occupation, and he always wanted the Iraqi people to take control of their future in their own country.

Sergio was a remarkably effective international civil servant. He was asked by the United Nations to tackle the most complicated humanitarian and peacekeeping missions. His record of success was extraordinary, whether it was fashioning a refugee protection and resettlement scheme for Vietnamese refugees, overseeing the repatriation of 300,000 Cambodian refugees from Thailand, setting up a UN civil administration in Kosovo, or managing the political transition in East Timor. He was the obvious choice to lead the UN effort in Iraq, unfortunately that had cost him his life.

Marjorie Cohn, a professor of law at Thomas Jefferson School of Law in San Diego, is executive vice president of the National Lawyers Guild. August 20, 2003

25

Reconstruction Plans

The rebuilding of Iraq was supposed to be the most far-reaching reconstruction plan since the American efforts in Europe and Japan after the at the conclusion of the Second World War (The Marshall plan). The largest sum of money was going to be spent on rehabilitation of the country's infrastructure, building of democracy, civilian projects, and human rights. Most of the emphasis has been on the reconstruction of premises and infrastructure of civil society organizations. The women's organizations are to be aiming to income generation rather than at programs that aim to enhance their ability to protect their rights.

Essential aspects of civil society development needed enormous international attention and funding. In addition to that Iraq was in urgent need for funds devoted to society development, such as building democracy, civic programs, human rights, and education. Several organisation including the American Peace Institute had studied the conditions of Iraq and put together plans for rehabilitation of the country. Few conferences were held to urge wealthy countries to funnel money into the civil reconstruction projects. The statement that came from the AIP in 2004 was "In fact, in financial terms, the first two years of civilian reconstruction in Iraq are proving more ambitious than the first two years of civilian reconstruction of post-war Germany, Japan, Haiti, Bosnia, Kosovo, and Afghanistan combined (though it should be noted that the Marshall Plan did not begin until 1947)". It is hard not to think about that with some Sinicism, given the situation that is discussed elsewhere.

At the Madrid conference held on October 2003, some $32–$36 billion in grants and loans were appropriated or otherwise pledged for the reconstruction of Iraq. However most donors either did not honour their commitment or left it hanging and did not deliver. There is no comprehensive statistics to find how much was really donated. In Madrid, Japan pledged $3.5 billion in non-grant money and $1.5 billion in grant. Japan, in particular, was assisting in reconstruction of public life relating to power generation, health, water supply, sanitation, education, employment, as well as security improvement. United Kingdom pledged $603 million toward Iraq's reconstruction, including its 13 percent share of currently planned European Community spending of $358 million.

The American officials say since April 2003, the United States had mobilized national and international resources to finance reconstruction plan in Iraq. Additional funds came from seized assets of Saddam's family (3% billion, move to Syria, Lebanon, and Jordan are estimated at around $3 billion. All three countries have indicated that they will return the funds), the Oil-for-Food Program had about $3.2 in uncommitted funds and another $10.1 billion that had been committed, although unpaid, for goods not yet delivered to Iraq. The funds was going to be channelled to Iraq through the Development Fund for Iraq (DFI), established under the UN Security Council Resolution 1483 and administrated by the Coalition Provisional Authority (CPA). (Please refer to the corruption in the Bremer section).

The reconstruction so far has been all but failure and the sectarian violence that had resulted in a country of chaos with no rule for the law, was blamed for that failure.

Financial Management of Reconstruction under the CPA was very untidy job, it was claimed the US. Government appropriated $18.6 billion for Iraq's reconstruction in cash by June 2004. The U.S. Army Corps of Engineers and U.S. Navy were the primary agencies issuing contracts on behalf of CPA, in 2006 most of the country still has no power, no water, a failing education system and a shameful health system, and you wonder where all the money went.

Most of the reconstruction funds, particularly U.S. Congress—allocated funds, were directed toward the rebuilding of Iraq's security and infrastructure. The civil society sector has received little attention in comparison.

Funding for Civil Society Development

Several institutions have been visibly active in the civil society and community-building arena. Such as USAID: Community Action Program (CAP), USAID/ Civil Society, CPA/Governance and Partners in addition to The United States Institute of Peace. The Institute has received $10 million from Congress to use for programs to prevent sectarian violence, promote the rule of law, train and educate a new generation of Iraqi leaders, and prepare American civilians for assignment in Iraq.

Excerpt from AIP website:
"Through the Grant Program, the Institute was providing assistance to CSOs and activities aimed at the following:

- promoting intercommunal and inter-religious reconciliation, such as the newly formed Iraq Council for Dialogue, Reconciliation, and Peace;

- training officials and civil society leaders in conflict management techniques and strategies;

- designing educational activities and programs to help the transition to democracy and reduce conflict;

- creation of Iraqi institutions committed to religious and ethnic coexistence; and

- Support for projects promoting the rule of law.

- The Institute is also actively seeking to support Iraqi women through targeted programs that will provide conflict resolution training and support their participation in civil society and the public arena."

Plans of the American peace institute

The $87 billion Emergency Supplemental Appropriations Act for Defence and for the Reconstruction of Iraq and Afghanistan, 2004, signed by President Bush on November 6, 2003 made available to the United States Institute of Peace $10 million for "activities supporting peace enforcement, peacekeeping and post-conflict peace-building" in Iraq. Aiming at identifying areas in which the Institute might provide added value, the Institute undertook a preliminary mapping of donor activities, focused primarily on the civil society and governmental sectors.

Indeed the Institute had its visible role in Iraq during the occupation years. It was also sponsoring seminars for high-ranking Iraqis to help in the set-up of an Iraqi Special Tribunal to prosecute the perpetrators of atrocities under the former regime, including Saddam Hussein himself. The seminars bring a broad range of international experts with Iraqi lawyers and judges, and focus on the legal and practical aspects of establishing a tribunal. That was impressive effort, however, the atrocities that was perpetrated by the occupation armies and the sectarian violence does rendered that relatively irrelevant latter on.

International NGOs and Others

A wide variety of international NGOs have been active in Iraq. Some of the most prominent were:

* *Women for Women International (WWI),* an NGO based in Washington, gives direct financial and emotional support to vulnerable women; develops awareness and understanding of women's rights and offers vocational skills training.

Civil Pillar (CP), a Danish NGO, was training Iraqis on establishing successful, non-violent, and democratic civil associations. In late 2003, CP began to engage moderate Islamists in southern Iraq.

Reconstruction Frauds

the money that was allocated to reconstruction was part of "Development Fund of Iraq," (DFI), handed to the CPA under the rule of former Iraqi transitional governor Paul Bremer's CPA. However the frauds committed by then had crippled the reconstruction process. Yet CPA fraud did not gross as much as Halliburton frauds, According to the US Government Accountability Office.

Hundreds of millions were spent with no accounting records, for example, the $24.7 million that was supposedly given for the process of printing a new Iraq's currency was not recorded. According to the audit by Stuart Bowen, money were spent with no receipts or any mechanism of checks or balances. Stuart W. Bowen (the CPA inspector) reported in June 2004 that his office was investigating 27 criminal cases and had referred for prosecution 42 other fraud cases.

Brig. Gen. Stephen Seay of the occupation army tried to cover up the fraud and wrote to the Inspector General that "we believe the contracts awarded with Iraqi funds were for the sole benefit of the Iraqi people, without exception." Reportedly his bank account swelled up with millions of dollars.

American companies had controlled most of the contracts and future work in the country, example of this corporate control, it was announced early 2005 that Iraqi farmers could no longer save wheat or rice. Instead they must buy them from the multi-national, agricultural business-giant Monsanto, a company which has been at the working actively on the attempts to growing genetically modified foods. Their seeds are genetically modified to withstand large doses of pesticides, specifically the brand manufactured by Monsanto.

We have already seen what happened when the occupying powers gave the most lucrative reconstruction contracts to companies close to the US government. Halliburton massively overcharged for meals it never provided to soldiers and contractors. Bechtel charged a fortune to do nothing at all apart from sub-contract jobs to other foreign and local smaller companies, and the resulting work, much of it on schools, was of poorly done. Companies with no genuine interest in Iraq's future simply suck out what they can and leave the people to suf-fer. It means small wages, high unemployment rates, poor working conditions, and no trade union rights.

In June 2004 Paul Bremer interim authority "handed over" the to Iraqi offi-cials, however on the grounds the occupying army continued to rule the country with 138000 fighters who patrol the streets; it essentially continued to be a mili-tary rule. Added to that the fact that the defunct Coalition Provisional Authority (CPA) had put in place the rules to govern the economic and civil life, which continues to be valid. Those roles had unjustly favoured the American firms, over the local entrepreneurial abilities o9f the Iraqis in order to ensure long-term US economic advantage with only few if any, advantages to the Iraqi people.

Bremer laws continued to control every aspect of life in Iraqi, from traffics to the privatization of public enterprises, in a country that had every aspect of life run by the public sector until the fall of Saddam. A fast transition was guaranteed not to work.

The interim constitution of Iraq, written by the U.S appointed Iraqi Govern-ing Council, which was a group of Iraqis who lived most their lives outside the country and had connections to the CIA, British Intelligence and ties with Iran. This mixture of people was a lethal mistake as it turned that everyone of those had their own agenda and they couldn't work together, could not negotiate any agreement and they had their fundamental differences. This and the American interest of course led the US to fashion an intern law and then a constitution that imposed the rules made by Bremer Authority and made of them a permanent rule.

Ref

Hector Duarte Jr Headline News May 5, 2005

Jo Wilding, activist and freelance writer 2005

http://www.usip.org/pubs/specialreports/sr124.html. July 2004 | Special Report No. 124

Antonia Juhasz is a project director at the International Forum on Globalization in San Francisco and a Foreign Policy in Focus scholar. Los Angeles times. August 5. 2004

26

Fallujah tragedies

April 28 when the Americans shot and killed over a dozen kids and teenagers in Fallujah. The American troops had taken over a local school and the kids and parents went to stand in front of the school in a peaceful demonstration. Some kids started throwing rocks at the troops, and the troops opened fire on the crowd. That incident was the beginning of the massacre in Fallujah.

In April 2003, U.S. troops opened fire on civilian protesters in Fallujah, killing 13 and injuring 75. That marked the beginning of a bitter and long conflict in Fallujah. Fallujah is populated by citizens of tribal descent, very conservative and proud people. The attack on protesters had seized the city by anger and grief. Attacks against the occupying army had continued and Fallujah became a symbol of national resistance and a monument of defence against the occupation. Subsequent U.S. attempts to install their control on the city and put in place an effective government was met by fierce local resistance and continued conflict.

In March 2004 four U.S. "security contractors" who were seen obviously as the villains were ambushed and killed while driving through the city. The bodies of two of the men were hung from a local bridge on the Euphrates River by an angry mob. By that date hundreds of Iraqi were killed each day for different reasons, and the occupying army couldn't care less, however the killing of fellow American citizens had instigated a revenge attack of the civilians in Fallujah. Fallujah has been a hot spot since the occupation in 2003; for an American to travel through the city is a dangerous plan. Four Western men slaughtered in Fallujah yesterday—all contractors for the Americans, some apparently armed—and they had been dragged from their cars, mutilated, stoned, and burnt, beaten with iron pipes. The mujahedin, "holy warriors", had thrown two grenades at each car before dragging the occupants onto the road. Brigadier General Mark Kimmitt, (American deputy director of military operations in Iraq), was boasting that the US Marines in Fallujah were encountering fewer security problems and were "quite pleased with how they are moving progressively forward." Prior to that attacks on foreigners were happening on daily basis. Two Finns were been killed; a British and Canadian contractor, two American aid workers—one a woman—and two US missionaries, including another woman.

One of them was decapitated, and then dragged through the streets behind a car. What the Anglo-American occupation power later called a "particularly brutal" crime. "The bodies were hanging upside down on each side of the bridge. They had no hands, no feet, one had no head." Reportedly those men were dragged from their car, begging for their lives. "They had gasoline splashed on them and were set alight," he said.

The headquarters of the US occupation, Paul Bremer was by then surrounded by massive walls of concrete with several checkpoints in the surrounding area with and iron gates and surrounded by heavily armed US forces. Yet his compound is hit by rockets every day, which symbolised the lack of control on Iraq and the strength of the resistance.

By then the words "insurgents"; and terrorists were used by the American army to discriminate between "former regime elements" who attacked the American army and the Fallujah police station; and "terrorists" who were conducting "suicidal attacks" which targeted the Iraqi army, hotels, mosques and religious festivals in Karbala and Baghdad. Those may have involved Abu Mussab al-Zarkawi who was portrayed as the leader of the radicals. The truth was that "foreign fighters" were never convicted beyond doubt despite the claims to the contrary; the US military by then was convinced that the increasing attacks in Iraq were being carried out by local Iraqi resistance to the occupying force.

The American officials had always claimed that fallujah had turned into a refuge for "terrorists" and the headquarters of a faction led by Abu Musab al-Zarqawi, who may or may not exist. Instead of reconciliation the occupying army had launched repeated revenge attacks on the city and hundreds of civilians including women and children. 90% of the civilian were driven outside their hometown by fierce battles that had ruined the civilian life in Fallujah, not only by killing but also by detentions of civilians and destruction of their houses in an indiscriminate fashion. After all Fallujah is a small town, whether it mattered to the American to control the city or not is debatable, probably they wanted the town to be an example and scapegoat for all Iraqi people should they decide to fight the occupation. What happened on the ground in Fallujah was an atrocity and a war crime, whether the decisions to the armed assault was in Washington or on the ground in Iraq is not clear, regardless of who was responsible, war crimes were committed against civilians.

It was estimated that 90% of the city's 250,000 residents, had been forced to vacate their residence and most of them can't move back due to the destructions of their homes. Elections in 2004-2005 were so important to the policy makers and that had partly driven the occupying power to control the city and try to give some legitimacy of the elections. Fallujah was mostly empty in 2005 and the U.S. military tried to get people back to their town with promises of up to $10,000 per house for rebuilding. The town was totally devastated with no power of water and was a constantly a war zone, to most people the elections did not matter. Many of them were angry and bitter and they resented the occupying army and saw the elections as a part of the occupation rather than a true democratic process.

The Association of Muslim Scholars had demanded a timetable for U.S. withdrawal before it will participate. Clearly that did not suite the U.S officials. This indicates their intention of keeping Iraq under the tight grip of the occupation until they are certain the American interests are assured for generations to come.

Clearly the authorities did not think well when the Iraqi election commission has set up special procedures, allowing residents in Anbar province. People of Fallujah could vote in the refugee camps!! That was still operating two months after the end of the American attacks on Fallujah. So it was a mixture of war, protests and election process for the refugees, which did not make any sense.

There was a controversy and claims of the use of banned weapons that raged for a long time since the US forces attacked in November 2004 to clear Fallujah of resistance. There have been claims that the occupying army used "unconventional" weapons in the assault that all but flattened the city. Specifically the use white phosphorus shells (WP), which is regarded as an offensive weapon banned by international treaties and conventions.

In April 2004 an Italian documentary **"Fallujah: the Hidden Massacre"** claimed Iraqi civilians including women and children had been killed by terrible burns caused by white phosphorus. The documentary was broadcast by state run channel, cited a Fallujah human-rights campaigner who reported that *"a rain of fire fell on the city"*. That was followed by waves of protests in Italy against the American occupation.

Independent 1.4. 2004

Steven Komarow, use today, 1.11.2005

History

Fallujah is a city in the province of Al Anbar, located 70km west of Baghdad on the Euphrates river. The city dates from Babylonian times and was host to important Jewish academies for many centuries. the Pumbedita Academy, which from 258 AD to 1038 AD was one of the two most important centers of Jewish learning worldwide.

The region has been inhabited for many millennia. The origin of the town's name is in some doubt, but one theory is that its Syriac name, Pallugtha, is derived from the word *division* because the uphrates dibvide the city into two sections. The city's name in Aramaic is Pumbedita.

Under the Ottoman Empire Fallujah was a small town on the Euphrates. In the spring of 1920 the British gained control of Iraq after the collapse of the Ottoman Empire after the first world war. Lt. Col. Gerard Leachman a senior colonial officer was sent to quell a rebellion in Fallujah. Leachman was killed in the city in a fight Shaykh Dhari, an influential local leader. The British sent an army to crush the rebellion, the battle took the lives of more than 10,000 Iraqis and 1,000 British soldiers.

During the brief Anglo-Iraqi War of 1941, the Iraqi army was defeated by the British in a battle near Fallujah. In 1947 the town had only about 10,000 inhabitants. It grew rapidly into a city after Iraqi independencein1957.

The city was heavily industrialised during the Saddam era with the construction of several large factories, including one closed down by United Nations Special Commission (UNSCOM) in the 1990s that was suspected to be used for chemical weapons production

During the Gulf War, Fallujah was one of the cities in Iraq with the most civilian casualties. Two separate failed bombing attempts on Fallujah's bridge across the Euphrates River hit crowded markets, killing an estimated 200 civilians, enraging city residents.

The first bombing occurred early in the Gulf War when a British jet intending to bomb the bridge dropped two laser guided bombs on city's crowded main market. Between 50 and 150 civilians died and many more were injured. In the second incident, Coalition forces attacked Fallujah's bridge over the Euphrates River with four laser-guided bombs. At least one struck the bridge while one or two bombs fell short in the river. The fourth bomb hit another market elsewhere in the city, reportedly due to failure of its laser guidance system. Within Iraq, it is known as the "city of mosques" for the more than 200 mosques found in the city and surrounding villages. The war had damaged 60% of its buildings, with 20% totally destroyed including 60 mosques.

Fallujah was one of the least affected areas of Iraq immediately after the 2003 invasion by the U.S. led Coalition. There was no major fighting as Iraqi Army stationed in Fallujah abandoned their weapons.

The damage the city had avoided during the initial invasion, was negated by damage from looting. After the collapse of Saddam's regime looters targeted government sites and strippedpublic buildings of anything of value including floor tiles, window frames, and door frames (this phenomenon had in fact happened allover the country). Citizens of Al Fallujah had to defend their own homes and property from these looters and criminals in the absence of peace-keeping authorities.

Local tribal leader had negotiated an agreement with the U.S. Army to stay outside of the relatively calm city. A Fallujah Protection Force composed of local Iraqis was set up, however the American army soon started patroling the twon with its tanks, and the local resentment started..

On the evening of April 28, 2003, a crowd of 200 people defied a curfew imposed by the Americans and gathered outside an occupied secondary school to protest the presence of Coalition forces in the city and demand vacating the city and opening the school. Following that some demonstrators fired shots into the air, Amwerican soldiers at the roof of the building opened fire upon the crowd and killed 13 civilians. A protest against the killings two days later was also fired upon by US troops resulting in two more deaths.

The situation continued to be tense and the fighting continued, that led many people to leave their town. In November 2004 Residents were allowed to return to the city in mid-December after undergoing biometric identification, provided they wear their ID cards all the time. US officials report that "more than half of Fallujah's 39,000 homes were damaged, and about 10,000 of those were destroyed" while compensation amounts to 20 percent of the value of damaged houses, with an estimated 32,000 homeowners eligible, 9,000 homes were destroyed, thousands more were damaged and of the 32,000 compensation claims only 2,500 have been paid as of April 14, 2005.

On 8 Nov 2004, after more than two months of air strikes, the US—with British support—began its second attack on Fallujah, devastating it and killing hundreds of civilians. UK forces supported the attack, with hundreds of troops redeployed their bases in Basra to form part of what was called "ring of steel" around the city.

The scale of the attack—and its effect on civilians—was unprecedented in the bloody history of the occupation, yet the crimes committed in Fallujah received little attention here and have quickly been forgotten.

Half of the estimated 200,000 Iraqis who fled the assault have yet to return to their homes—and those who have been subjected to a draconian regime of curfews, iris scans and checkpoints. Moreover, recent US military offensives in

Ramadi, Haditha, Qaim, Tal Afar and elsewhere, have many more civilians and created thousands more refugees.

According to M. Marqusee of "*Iraq Occupation Focus* writing in the *Guardian*" "Falluja's compensation commissioner has reported that 36,000 of the city's 50,000 homes were destroyed, along with 60 schools and 65 mosques and shrines". Reconstruction did only consist of clearing rubble from heavily-damaged areas and reestablishing basic utility services.

Over 150,000 individuals were still living as internally displaced people in harsh conditions in tents outside Fallujah or elsewhere in the country.

In the aftermath of the offensive calm was restored. However, the number of insurgent attacks had gradually increased in and around the city. By the end of 2005 several US soldiers had been killed by snipers and roadside bombs in and around Falluja and in January 2006 the US army base located outside Fallujah has come under heavy mortar fire of the resistance.

Dahr Jamail (journalist) reported "Despite persistent rumours of injuries among Iraqis consistent with the use of incendiary weapons such as napalm" the Pentagon insisted that "US forces had not used a new generation of incendiary weapons, codenamed MK77, in Iraq."

Atrocities in Fallujah

Fallujah (Napalm)

During the U.S. offensive of Fallujah in October 2004, residents reported that they saw "melted" bodies in the streets of the town, which suggests that the American army had used napalm gas (lethal mixture of polystyrene and jet fuel that makes the human body melt, it turn victims into human fireballs as the gel sticks flames to flesh). In November, furious Labour members of the parliament in the UK demanded Tony Blair (the British prime minister) to answer questions about the American use of Napalm. There was pressure on Tony Blair to pull the British troops from Iraq unless the American stop using banned weapons.

In 1980 after pictures of a naked wounded girl injured with Napalm in Vietnam shocked the world. Following that the United Nations banned the use of Napalm. The United States didn't endorse the UN convention; it is the only country in the world still using the Napalm. American officials lied to British ministers over the use of "internationally reviled" napalm-type weapon in Iraq.

The Mirror (British newspaper) had reported that napalm was used in the siege of Fallujah (November 2004), Reports claimed that civilians had died in napalm attacks. Since the American assault on Fallujah there have been reports of corpse, which appeared to have injuries suggestive of napalm use.

Despite the evidence of injuries among people from Fallujah consistent with the use of banned weapons such as napalm, British Defence minister, assured Labour MPs in January 2005 that US forces had not used a new generation of the napalm weapons that was called MK77, in Iraq.

But Adam Ingram (British defence secretary) admitted to Harry Cohen (Labour MP) in a private letter obtained by British newspaper (The Independent) that he had misled Parliament because he had been misinformed by the US.

Here is the statement published by The Independent Mr Ingram said "The US confirmed to my officials that they had not used MK77 in Iraq at any time and this was the basis of my response to you," he told Mr Cohen. "I regret to say that I have since discovered that this is not the case and must now correct the position."

Then Mr Ingram said "30 MK77s bombs were used by the 1st Marine Expeditionary Force in the invasion of Iraq between 31 March and 2 April 2003" (from the independent). American officials did not admit to using that against resistance in Fallujah and it was said that they were used against military targets "away from civilian targets"; again it depends on the definition of military targets.

The confirmation that US officials and the admitting that napalm was used had led to spreading rumours about the use of napalm against the insurgents in Falujah, US officials denied those claims. It is relevant here to say that the Americans only admitted the use of the napalm after strong and condemning and irrefutable evidence of their use in Fallujah. Following that the US State Department admitted that US forces had used MK77s in Iraq.

Mike Lewis (a spokesman for group called Iraq analysis, which is anti war), said to The independent: "The US has used internationally reviled weapons that the UK refuses to use, and has then apparently lied to UK officials, showing how little weight the UK carries in influencing American policy."

The problem is so serious that it is not known how much and against who those weapons were used and what was the scale of the crime, no independent source could evaluate the extent of the use of napalm against civilians. Dr. Khalid ash-Shaykhli (Iraqi health ministry envoy in Fallujah), reported to Al Jazeera that the US forces used internationally prohibited substances, that may include mustard gas, nerve gas, and other burning chemicals in attacks on Fallujah.

He added "all forms of nature were wiped out in Fallujah such as hundreds, of stray dogs, and birds that had perished as a result of lethal materials used in the attack."

As journalist Dahr Jamail reported later in his article

"What is the US trying to Hide?"; "At least two kilometres of soil were removed. Exactly as they did at Baghdad Airport after the heavy battles there during the invasion and the Americans used their special weapons."

Napalm (The evidence)

UK Independent ran an article on (06-17-05) which confirmed that the US had *"lied to Britain over the use of napalm in Iraq"*.

No American newspaper or TV channel had picked up the story; the Pentagon however, verified the claims. Downing Street had reluctantly published a report about treasure after the media reports; the American media had always ignored any story that was not in favour of the American troops the war. The prospect that the US military is using "universally reviled" weapons runs counter to the media-generated narrative that the war was motivated by humanitarian concerns (to topple a brutal dictator) as well as to eliminate the elusive WMDs. We can now say with certainty that the only WMDs in Iraq were those that were introduced by foreign invaders from the US who have used them to subjugate the indigenous people.

The use of napalm firebombs puts the US in breach of the 1980 Convention on Certain Chemical Weapons (and is a clear violation the Geneva Protocol against the use of white phosphorous, it causes indiscriminate and extreme injuries especially when used in civilian areas.

Regrettably the American terror in Iraq continued to be well-coordinated strategy designed to spread fear by random acts of violence. It's clear that the military never needed to use napalm or depleted uranium Iraq. Their conventional weapons and laser-guided bombs were more than enough to dominate and control Iraq with minimal resistance.

Napalm was used to terrorize the Iraqi people; to pacify through intimidation. Cheney, Rumsfeld, Wolfwitz and Negroponte are experts on terrorism. Their history date back to their counterinsurgency projects in Nicaragua and El Salvador. They know that the threat of immolation serves as a powerful deterrent and fits seamlessly into their overarching scheme of rule through fear. Terror and deception are the rotating parts of the same axis; the two imperatives of the Bush-Cheney foreign policy strategy.

Alzarqawi

Fallujah by now was regarded as part of Iraq's Sunni Triangle, and has been out-side the control of Iraqi authorities and U.S. military forces since April 2004, when a siege by U.S. army was lifted and Iraqi army was given responsibility. Local and foreign fighters gradually gained control. Fallujah had become a main source of instability in the country.

BAGHDAD, Oct. 12. 2004—U.S. aircraft targeted foreign fighters; however that often led to blanket bombing of the neighbourhood and massive destruction of residences and casualties.

According to Fallujah resident's insurgent leaders and Iraqi and U S officials' Local resistance in the city of Fallujah turned against the "foreign fighters". Relations between the two groups deteriorated as local fighters were negotiating to avoid a U.S. military attack against Fallujah, while the foreign fighters wanted to attack the Americans army and their Iraqi counterparts. Fallujans had killed at least five foreign Arabs prior to that.

U.S authorities had insisted that if Fallujah is to avoid military assault, foreign fighters must be ejected. Several local leaders of Fallujah wanted to expel the for-eigners, whom they regard as terrorists. They had particular contempt and resent-ment on Abu Musab Zarqawi, the Jordanian whose group had claimed responsibility for many attacks on police and suicide bombs that had terrorised people across Iraq, including beheadings that were videotaped and broadcasted.

Fallujah residents by then thought that foreign fighters were attracting attacks on Fallujah and denied shelter in residential neighbourhoods. The air strikes and the fierce conflict in the streets had driven half of the city's 300,000 residents to flee.

Indeed most people in Iraq believed that he had distorted the image of Islam and the resistance and defamed it by their ruthless attacks on police recruits and other innocents. One of the foreign fighters was killed by local fighters called "Abu Abdullah Al-Suri", a Syrian and a leading man of Zarqawi's group. Al-Suri's body was found shot in the head and chest by local people who chased him outside the town.

People from Fallujah and witnesses said that local opinions about the foreign fighters have changed dramatically since they poured into Fallujah after the siege ended in April 2004. Fallujah people had welcomed them first because they thought those fighters came to support them against the American Army.

Among the tensions dividing the locals and the foreigners is religion. The non-Iraqi Arabs had attacked women who did not cover themselves head-to-toe, very rare in Iraqi culture, and violently opposed local customs of the town's more mystical religious tradition. Residents said the majority of Fallujah people have been repulsed by the atrocities that Zarqawi and other extremists have made commonplace in Iraq. The foreign militants are thought to produce the car bombs that ravaged the country and killed large numbers of civilians. Zarqawi's organization had also claimed responsibility for the beheading of several foreigners who were initially taken hostages. some of which were shown in videos posted on the Internet.

The Iraqi resistance was a different group of fighters with different ideology from the foreign fighters who had caused revolting atrocities in the country more so against the Iraqis who cooperated with the occupation than the Americans, since the Iraqis where a softer target.

It is obvious these people are desolate and poor; however the American Army is searching their house

Ref

Robert Fisk "The Independent" April 01, 2004

(Washington Post Foreign Service
Wednesday, October 13, 2004; Page A01)

Napalm in Fallujah (independent 17.6.2005)
("Fallujah Napalmed" UK Mirror, 11-28-04
Daher Jamail, Antiwar.com

The Media

The American press has been as skilful at painting the non existing heroics of Jessica Lynch and Pat Tillman as they have been in concealing the damning details of the Downing Street report of the napalm or the lack of evidence concerning the alleged WMDs. Bu we are not surprised that the media has remained silent about the melting bodies in Fallujah by the napalm.

The American press seemed like an integral part of the state-information system. Its meticulously managed message has been the most successful part of the entire Iraqi debacle. By diversions and omissions, the media had shown itself to be an invaluable asset to the men in power; perpetuating the deceptions that keep the public quiet during a savage and brutal war. Given the scope of the media's culpability for the violence in Iraq, it's unlikely that the use of napalm will cause any great crisis of conscience. Their deft coverage has already facilitated the deaths of tens of thousands of innocent people; a few more charred Iraqis shouldn't matter.

Fifteen years before Fallujah, Halabja—when Washington was a friend of Saddam and main source supplier of chemical weapons to Saddam Hussein, thousands of Kurds were killed in a historical atrocity. Even the US Central Intelligence Agency has disputed Saddam's responsibility, blaming Iranians instead. Assuming Saddam did it, and did it deliberately, the US may have done the same thing in Fallujah.

Asia Times Online had reported; Fallujah doctors have identified either swollen and yellowish dead people without any sign of external injury, or "melted bodies"—victims of napalm, the lethal cocktail of polystyrene and jet fuel. Asia times via sources of the new agency had confirmed testimonies by residents of Fallujah who managed to escape the Jolan neighbourhood of bombing by "poisonous gases".

Residents reported to Asia Times "weird bombs that smoke something like a mushroom cloud, and then small pieces fall from the air with long tails of smoke behind them. The pieces of those bombs explode into large flame that burns the skin even when you throw water over them". This happens to people bombed with napalm or white phosphorus.

Sunnis simply don't trust US-trained security forces; they were identified as collaborationists, similar in Nazi-occupied France, or in Algeria fighting French colonialism in the early 1960s. The resistance has widely infiltrated the US-trained Iraqi forces, added to it hundreds deserted the police force and joined the resistance immediately before the attacks on Fallujah.

A long-term US combat had undermined the legitimacy of the interim government and converted the conflict into a US war against Iraqis. That combat also further alienated the Muslim cultures that are hostile to the US. On the occasion when the threat to US interests is great, pre-emptive US combat were launched. Direct use of US combat forces in counterinsurgency operations remains a policy option for the president, and army forces provide it when required.

The majority of Iraqis know this has always been a US-only war; they have been "alienated" for a long time now. Fallujah was indeed a "pre-emptive US operation", so this means an indigenous resistance was a "great" threat to US interests; and also means, that the responsibility for the Fallujah massacre is ultimately Bush's.

Fallujah was reduced to mere grieve over the dead and the rubble of destroyed buildings. Not a single government agency, be it American or Iraqi, offered any assistance to the more than 200,000 Fallujans who were turned into refugees, instead the occupying army turned off the water and electricity supply in the city. And the UN High Commissioner for Refugees (UNHCR) was nowhere to be seen and there was not any representative of the "international community". The real story of what happened to Fallujah is being told by those 200,000 refugees, and a few hundreds who managed to escape during the attack on the city…Saul Landau (of counter punch) wrote "They are the Picassos who will paint the new Guernica for future historians".

As soon as these thousands of refugees return home, so will the bulk of the resistance: after all they are residents of Fallujah themselves, enjoying total local support; and they will certainly attack any US-trained kind of force left behind to protect whatever US-installed puppet government is put in place. So the Americans may leave the "house of Satan", and then the Fallujah mujahideen Shura (council) that was running the city since last April inevitably will be back to power; or the Americans may stay in Fallujah, and the resistance will continue to wreak havoc in a string of other cities in the Sunni heartland. The result will be the same: the new Guernica sacrificed for nothing.

The iron-clad, not-so-hidden neo-conservative agenda for the Middle East is balkanization of the Arab world—serving the interests of their allies, the Likud Party in Israel. The neo-cons want the Middle East to fracture along ethnic and tribal lines. They want Sunni against Shiite. They want civil war in Iraq. They want chaos, as in "the empire of chaos" as formulated by stellar French scholar Alain Joxe. Israel Shahak's *The Zionist Plan for the Middle East* details that to survive; Israel must become an imperial regional power by Balkanizing all existing Arab states. In this scenario, a major counterinsurgency operation like Fallujah, the new Guernica, may have been the first. It certainly won't be the last

Stories of the people

Stories will continue to emerge from Fallujah for generations. Refugees and displaced people from Fallujah spoke about what they had experienced in Fallujah.

Dahr Jamail spoke to a doctor who ran away to Jordan. He spoke about what he saw and witnessed as a doctor working inside Fallujah, he had had shown him videos and photographs that prove all what he said, he spoke as an anonymous source.

"I entered Fallujah with a British medical and humanitarian convoy at the end of December 2004, and stayed until the end of January," he explains, "But I was in Fallujah before that to work with people and see what their needs were, so I was in there since the beginning of December." About what happened in Fallujah he said "it was like a tsunami struck the city".

Fallujah was surrounded by refugee's camps; people of Fallujah had left the city and lived in tents and makeshift caravans like any refugees. They had no medical care; many children were suffering from chest infections. Almost everyone left their house with nothing, and no money, people lived on humanitarian aids they got from charities and other organizations. It was reported that in one refugee north of Fallujah there were 1,200 students living in seven tents, very crowded with no facilities. Fallujah had previous siege in November 2004 but according to the doctor "The disaster caused by this siege is so much worse than the first one, which I witnessed first hand," and here is an example; the testimonies he video taped recently "a young girl who is 16 years old, stayed for three days with the bodies of her family who were killed in their home. When the soldiers entered she was in her home with her father, mother, 12 year-old brother and two sisters. She watched the soldiers enter and shoot her mother and father directly, without saying anything". The girl managed to hide behind the refrigerator with her brother and witnessed the crimes first-hand. "They beat her two sisters, and then shot them in the head," he said. After this her brother was enraged and ran at the soldiers while shouting at them, so they shot him dead.

"She continued hiding after the soldiers left and stayed with her sisters because they were bleeding, but still alive. She was too afraid to call for help because she feared the soldiers would come back and kill her as well. She stayed for three days, with no water and no food. Eventually one of the American snipers saw her and took her to the hospital,"

Another story he documented of a mother who was in her home during the siege. "On the fifth day of the siege her home was bombed, and the roof fell on her son, cutting his legs off," "For hours she couldn't go outside because of the strict curfew and anyone goes out would get shot. "So all she could do was wrapping his legs and watch him die before her eyes."

There weren't many families in there after the siege, but they had absolutely nothing. The suffering was beyond any description. He continued "One of my colleagues, Dr. Saleh Alsawi, he was speaking so angrily about them. He was in the main hospital when they raided it at the beginning of the siege. They entered the theatre room when they were working on a patient…he was there because he's an anaesthesiologist. They entered with their boots on, beat the doctors and took them out, leaving the patient on the table to die. "This story has already been reported earlier in the Arab media, that what made the Americans to ban some of those media from working in Iraq. Hay Nazal clinic (one of Fallujah suburbs) "This contained all the foreign aid and medical instruments we had. All the US military commanders knew this, because we told them about it so they wouldn't bomb it. But this was one of the clinics bombed, and in the first week of the siege they bombed it two times." He then adds, "Of course they targeted all our ambulances and doctors. Everyone knows this." The doctor told Dahr Jamail he and some other doctors are trying to sue the US military for the following incident, for which he has the testimonial evidence on tape. About a story that was verified by other refugees from Fallujah in Baghdad as well…at the end of last November while the siege was still in progress.

During the siege of Fallujah the American army had asked people to leave the city within 72hours else they will be considered as combatants and will be targeted as such. About that he says "We documented this story with video-a family of 12, including a relative and his oldest child who was 7 years old. They heard this instruction, so they left with all their food and money they could carry, and white flags. When they reached the intersection where the families were accumulating, they heard someone shouting 'Now!' in English, and shooting started everywhere."

"The family was all carrying white flags, as instructed, according to the young man who gave his testimony. Yet he watched his mother and father shot by snipers-his mother in the head and his father shot in the heart. His two aunts were shot, and then his brother was shot in the neck. The man stated that when he raised himself from the ground to shout for help, he was shot in the side".

"After some hours he raised his arm for help and they shot his arm," continues the doctor, "So after awhile he raised his hand and they shot his hand."

A six year-old boy of the family was standing over the bodies of his parents, crying, and he too was then shot.

"Anyone who rose up was shot," adds the doctor, and then he showed the photographs of the dead as well as photos of the gunshot wounds of the survivors. Although the siege had ended but only minority of people returned and the city was remains haunted by the bodies of the dead; no water or electricity; and people are kept waiting at the check points for hours. The animosity against the

Americans had increased and the hatred on both sides will never settle. At one of the windows of destroyed houses there was a statement written by an American solder that summarize it all *"Fuck Iraq and every Iraqi in it"*

The doctor in his story told Dahr "I've been there, and I saw that anyone who even turns their head is threatened and hit by both American and Iraqi soldiers alike…one man did this, and when the Iraqi soldier tried to humiliate him, the man took a gun of a nearby soldier and killed two ING, so then of course he was shot."

After the end of the siege the Americans were trying to make propaganda for their "good intentions". They were reportedly giving people $200 per family to return to Fallujah and they filmed that, when actually, at that time, no one was returning to Fallujah.

The doctor told old stories in Fallujah "My cousin was a poor man in Fallujah," he explains, "He walked from his house to work and back, while living with his wife and five daughters. In July of 2003, American soldiers entered his house and woke them all up. They drug them into the main room of the house, and executed my cousin in front of his family. Then they simply left." In fact these stories were told on countless accounts of Iraqi been killed like that, no explanations no apologies nothing.

Ref

Dahr Jamail; dar al-jamahir, feb 8.2005)

Peace Talks, October 2004

People of Fallujah were torn apart between their ambitions for peace, their hatred to the U.S and its occupation of the country and their disgust for the tactics of terrorist led by Abu Musab al-Zarqawi, which include suicide bombings, attacks, and kidnappings of foreigners that have ended in gruesome videotaped beheadings of foreigners on many occasions. Almost 80 percent of the city's population of 300,000 had left their town in preparation for the attack on Fallujah,

Iraq's interim government (Under the prim minister Ayad Alawi) has vowed to "smash" the resistance before January 2006 elections. The U.S as well was determined to conquer Fallujah, root out the local resistance, and eject Zarqawi and his band of foreign militants. The Americans had arrested a local tribal leader Khalid Al—Jumaily, when he was released he decided that he will not resume the peace talks. "I think the residents of Fallujah don't want this sort of peace,"Khalid Al—Jumaily said. "They want a real peace, not a peace that stabs in the back and strikes and destroys homes and kills women." Allawi told Iraq's National

Council that an "olive branch" was offered to Fallujah representatives, he added "We shall not be lenient in regard to the question of maintaining security and granting security to every Iraqi."

An important issue by then was the problem of AL-Zarqawi on whom the interim government demanded a handover from the locals who insisted they had nothing to do with Zarqawi, that request was evidently unrealistic; if the mighty American Military machine could not deal with him, you wonder how the local civilians of Fallujah could do that. By them Fallujah people had realized that a military assault on Fallujah was imminent and most people had left their houses.

Prior to that Fallujah had been for several weeks targeted by nightly air strikes and people were threatened with imminent American assault and a U.S.-led siege, people knew this will cost them the life of thousands of Fallujans. Their lives have been shattered by the continued conflict, schools were interrupted by the conflict, and people could hardly sleep because of the continued explosions and air strikes.

Al Jazeera channel had been very active and they constantly showed the Iraqi casualties, one of them was several wounded children in a Fallujah hospital. Media reports had shown witnesses that said the American army had targeted a family of five people who were leaving the city and shot and killed all of them including a child. The policy of the occupying army was unfortunately "*shot first and ask questions latter*"

I an interview with local Iraqis from Fallujah with Scot Peterson they said "What did this teach us about the Americans?" asks Mrs. Salim. "First we thought the Americans came to liberate our country, but now our conclusion is the opposite. We know they came to destroy our country."

Indeed the air strikes had killed so many civilians including women and children to an extent that what was done is beyond any reasonable justification.

Still the US army commanders were insisting that their attacks were very precise and targeted at AL-Zarqawi network of terrorists, yet many civilian were killed.

Salim told Scot Peterson about a strike that targeted his house "I held all my family together and said: 'We die just once in this life, not twice. Thank God, [the bombing] was far from us.'" Salim added the bombing had targeted another house and he "Most of them were children, all of them dead," Salim says, of the families he helped dig out of the rubble with bare hands. "When something happens, everybody runs there to help rescue, like an ambulance—maybe a friend will be the victim there."

The city had shortages of medical supplies and medicines and anaesthetics and treatment of the large number of casualties was something the local hospital was not equipped to deal with, which resulted in more lives lost. People wear fearful for their lives and mostly were forced to leave.

Joe Carr met a Sunni Cleric in May 2005. He was a young man and a quite eloquent speaker. He told Joe about some horror stories he'd witnessed. "During the first invasion, several families near his Mosque took cover in a home. US troops used megaphones to order all them out into the street and told them to carry a white flag. They did this, but when they all got out, the soldiers opened fire into the group, killing five. He said one boy had run to his mother who'd been shot, and Americans shot him in the head. He said he saw a US commander cry as this happened, "but what good were his tears?" he asked, "He didn't do anything to stop it."

Ref

Scott Peterson, Christian Science Monitor. October 20, 2004.

Analysis of what happened in Fallujah (the 21st Century Guernica)

November 12, 2004 as US fighters bombed Fallujah non stop for about 10days, the media had not given that a good cover. On November 15 the BBC that the unofficial death toll was estimated at well over 2000 many of them civilians.

An eye witnesses told BBC reporters they had seen bombs striking residential targets. One photographer captured a Fallujah man holding his dead son, one of two kids he lost to US air strikes. He could not get medical help to stop the bleeding so his son died. Even clinics were targeted; witnesses had seen the bombing killing doctors, nurses and patients. The US military denied the reports. Such stories did not make headlines. Civilian casualties in aggressive US wars don't sell media space; the American media probably had avoided that deliberately, in the claim of "reports that are not supportive to the American army".

Fallujah was said to be the new Guernica of the Second World War. The residents of Guernica were resisting the Spanish dictator Francisco Franco, Franco asked Nazi Germany—which supported him—to bomb Guernica. Fallujah in 2004 was resisting the dictator Iyad Allawi, the US-installed interim premier, Allawi "asked" the Americans to bomb Fallujah. Both towns were defending themselves against the occupation and both had civilians and guerrillas were bombed alike. the order was to "kill them all". The Americans said 'Fuck Iraq and every Iraqi in it", and "the letter could be read from its title" as we say in the Arab world.

The November 12 Los Angeles Times ran a front page shot of a soldier with mud smeared face and cigarette dangling from his lips. This image captured the "suffering" of Fallujah. The GI complained he was out of "smokes."

The young man doing his "duty to free Fallujah," stands in stark contrast to the nightmare of Fallujah. "Smoke is everywhere," an Iraqi told the BBC (Nov 11). "The house some doors from mine was hit during the bombardment. A 13-year-old boy was killed. A row of palm trees used to run along the street outside my house—now only the trunks are left there are more and more dead bodies on the streets and the stench was unbearable."

An eye witness told Reuters (November 12. 2004) that "a 9-year-old boy was hit in the stomach by a piece of shrapnel. His parents said they couldn't get him to hospital because of the fighting, so they wrapped sheets around his stomach to try to stem the bleeding. He died hours later of blood loss and was buried in the garden."

US media's embedded reporters who where hired by the pentagon to serve the Washington policy had reported thousands of Iraqi "insurgents," including the foreign Muslim fighters (Abu Musab al-Zarqawi group of jihadists), had dug in to defend their base in Fallujah. After the armoured and air attack began and the marines advanced, reports filtered out that the marines and the new Iraqi army that trailed behind them had faced only light resistance. Uprisings broke out in Mosul and other cities. For the combatants, however, Fallujah was the hardest spot of resistance.

Retired Marine Corps general Bernard Trainor declared that: "militarily Fallujah is not going to be much of a plus at all." He said that "we've knocked the hell out of this city, and the only insurgents we really got were the nut-cases and zealots, the smart ones left behind—the guys who really want to die for Allah." American officials declared the attack as victory; however "terrorists remain at large." After all the inhumane treatment of the city civilians and thousands of dead people, the attack had not rooted out the "Foreign Fighters".

So the truth of the matter in this war that the American did not have to invade and destroy a small town for no acceptable purpose from the point of view of the "Logically, the media should call Iraqi "militants" patriots who resisted illegal occupation". Instead, the reporter on the counter punch say "the press implied that the "insurgents" even fought dirty, using improvised explosive devices and booby traps to kill our innocent soldiers, who use clean weapons like F16s, helicopter gun ships, tanks and artillery"!!. Bush was kind to offer the "reconstruction" of Fallujah which was followed by corruption that had risen from the evil of this war, one that has involved massive civilian death and the destruction of peaceful cities.

There is similarity between this war and the Nazi wars. In 1935, Nazi General Erich Luderndorff said. ""The Fascist Italian General Giulio Douhet responded "By targeting civilians an army could advance more rapidly. Air-delivered terror effectively removes civilian obstacles". That what effectively happened and made as a regular practice in the unjust war on the Iraqi people.

April 1937. Nazi pilots dropped their deadly bombs on Guernica, the ancient Basque capital, that what exactly US pilots recently did to Fallujah. In 1936, the Spanish Civil War began under the leadership of General Francisco Franco, who was supported by fascist governments in Italy and the Nazis in Germany, led a rebellion against the Republic. The residents of Guernica resisted; Franco asked the help of his Nazi allies to punish the stubborn people of Guernica who resisted his armed attacks on their city. The citizens of Guernica had no anti-aircraft missiles, few fighter aircrafts to defend their city. The Nazis knew that at 4:30 in the afternoon of market day, the city's centre would be crowded with people from all around the city.

The German and the Spanish allies bombed the city with no distinction between civilians and fighting. The target is everyone in the city.

Approximately 1700 people were killed in the barbaric massacre and some 900 were wounded. Franco denied that the raid had ever happened and blamed the citizens of the city on the destruction of Guernica on those who defended it. The Americans in Fallujah had insisted that that the "insurgents' forced the brutal attacks by daring to defend their own city and then hid inside their mosques.

'Where is the new Picasso who will offer a dramatic painting to help the 21st Century public understand that what the US Air Force just did to the people of Fallujah resembles what the Nazis did to Guernica?' the reporter of counter punch says.

Instead of feeling for the devastated citizen of Fallujah, the US media focused on the difficulties encountered by the US marines and how one of them complained he ran out of smoke and shown with his face smeared with mud. It is expected that those marines will not be criticized by the American media; however the devastation of Fallujah should not be overlooked. The American marines were so brutal; they were bullies who looked at the citizens of Iraq as subhuman.

The marines in truth were bullies who were killing patriots (who were defending their town) with superior technology to kill civilians and destroy their homes and mosques. On November 15, a NBC cameraman captured a US soldier murdering a wounded Iraqi prisoner in cold blood (he shot him while he was lying on the floor wounded and not fighting). CNN was defending the solder and fiercely trying to convince the world it was not a murder, the excuse was that the marine was not sure if that injured had a booby trap attached to him. Marine commanders reported that Fallujah was the "house of Satan". And here is the similarity. Franco denied the Guernica massacre and blamed the people of Guernica, Allawi and the Americans deny any civilian deaths and insist "insurgents" are to blame: after all they were instigating the fighting and hiding in the mosques.

The summary execution of that wounded, defenceless Iraqi man inside a mosque by a marine was the defining image of Fallujah for Iraqis, the Arab world and1.3 billion Muslims. The execution was caught on tape. Marine commanders have been on the record telling their soldiers to "shoot everything that moves and everything that doesn't move"; to fire "two bullets in every body"; in case of seeing any military-aged men in the streets of Fallujah, to "drop 'em"; and to spray every home with machine-gun and tank fire before entering them. These "rules" are all confirmed by residents of Fallujah who managed to escape as well as people of other towns who had similar stance like fallujah.

Andrew Greely wrote in November 12, 2004, in the Chicago Sun Times. "The United States has fought unjust wars before—Mexican American, the Indian Wars, Spanish American, the Filipino Insurrection, and Vietnam. Our hands are not clean. They are covered with blood, and there'll be more blood this time" he adds." Fallujah should serve as the symbol of this war of atrocity against the Iraqi people".

More than 250,000 Fallujans had the chance to escape, they became Fallujah refugees. Practically not a single report was made about the Fallujah in US corporate media. By anyone standards, the Fallujah were a humanitarian disaster, Fallujah's citizens were not protected: it was bombed out of the city and turned into a mass of thousands of refugees. Political institutions that were in place (the Fallujah Shura) was running the city before that and now no local government could run a town of rubble. Insurgent were not eliminated; instead the resistance had spread to other 22 cities, which was out of control by the occupation; and the Americans remain without intelligence "from local sources" because they antagonized every possible heart and mind. The local resistance had grown more fiercely and more determined. Those 'insurgents" were an armed young people representing the widespread Iraqi struggle against the occupation. Whole cities are mobilized against the occupation. Whole sectors of Baghdad are totally out of the Americans' control. Many in the Sunni triangle told Asia Times correspondent one year ago they were at the tipping point of joining the armed resistance, they crossed the line long time ago.

Who was responsible

United Nations had been rebuffed by the Defence Department in calling for an independent investigation into what really took place in Fallujah.

It was assumed that the order to use napalm (as well as the other, unidentified substances) came from the office of Donald Rumsfeld. No one else could have issued that order, nor would they have risked their job by using banned weapons. Rumsfeld's directive is consistent with other decisions attributed to the Defence Secretary; like the authorizing of torture at Guantanamo and Abu Ghraib. Rumsfeld's office has been the deciding point for most of the administration's treachery. Napalm simply adds depth to the list of war crimes on Rumsfeld's history.

The aftermath

after the second siege Fallujah was completely surrounded by American Forces, the only way in or out the city is through one of the very restrictive checkpoints that have a long waiting queue and thorough checking. People normally have to wait for hours. Soldiers held-up traffic and slowly checked identifications of people. Like Palestine, these checkpoints had little to do with security and more to do with harassment and intimidation.

Fallujah was devastating to drive through. There is more destruction and rubble than in Rafah, Gaza. The US strikes had levelled entire neighbourhoods, and about every third building is destroyed from US artillery. Rubble and bullet holes are everywhere, the city is indescribably ravaged. To an extent it looks like it's been hit by a series of tornados.

US troops, Iraqi military, and Iraqi police have an overwhelming presence in the city. "Dirty looks directed at the passing forces". In most places people got used to the occupying army, but in Fallujah, the hate is still very alive. 16,000 Fallujan police lost their jobs after the US attacks and were replaced by recruits from other parts of the country. "The US intentionally sends Shiite to patrol Sunni strongholds to breed resentment and abuse, and it works". American Soldiers shoot anyone who drives too close to their convoys, no questions asked, which made driving anywhere in the country and particularly in Fallujah extremely dangerous. It is very easy to accidentally turn a corner and find yourself in the midst of a convoy. The hospital said that around 1-2 people a week die from the indiscriminate shooting by US occupation forces.

Horror stories are everywhere. Joe Carr visited a family's home in a neighbour-hood where every building is damaged. Their home was full of holes and com-pletely charred from inside from fire. They said that they'd left during the strikes on the town with their home intact, and returned to find their house and all their possessions had burned. Three families of their relatives (Over 25 people includ-ing four infants) are now living in this burned 3-room house because their homes were completely destroyed. Some of them tried to get compensation from the US and Iraqi officials but were denied.

Around 25% of families who suffered damaged property have gotten some small compensation from the US military; however it covers less than half of the cost for building materials for a new home. Particularly because the compensa-tion rates are based on the price of building materials before the attacks, and now supplies cost nearly double because of the ongoing dangers of the conflict and restrictive checkpoints.

Food prices had also increased rapidly because of the checkpoints and the ongo-ing conflict. Farmers from around Fallujah could no longer deliver their produce to town unless they have a US-issued Fallujah ID. The shopkeepers now have to go out and pick up the produce each day, which takes several hours because of the checkpoint delays. "They mistreat us," one man said to Joe Carr and added, "they point guns at us and insult us, even the women". He said that "both US and Iraqi troops search through the vegetables roughly, even dumping them on the ground and sometimes smashing them. As soon as he's finished with one checkpoint and cleaned up the mess, another will ransack his load all over again. This can happen as many as four times he said. Sometimes, much of the produce rots from sitting in the hot sun". For all these reasons, the prices have gone up and more people are going hungry.

Fallujah has only one hospital that provides an inpatients' care. Other clinics and treatment centres were damaged by US air strikes.

Even after the fighting, the US troops kept the bridges closed which resulted in the death of several people from heart attacks when they couldn't get to the hospital fast enough. People from the rural areas surrounding Fallujah were also dying of treatable illnesses because they can't get through the checkpoints to the hospital. One hospital employee told Joe that many patients die when they try to transfer them to hospitals outside Fallujah. "It's better to take them in a civilian car than in an ambulance" he said, "because the troops delay and search ambu-lances more."

According to Joe Carr During the first attack the hospital became a main source of information for the outside world. So when the US attacked the second time, they took over the hospital area first and controlled what information got out". Media was operating from the hospital and showing the atrocities in Fallujah to the entire world; so during the second attack the American troops chose to control that and perhaps to keep the world in the dark for known reasons.

A man told Joe some of his horror stories. "The Americans shot and killed my 15-year-old daughter" he said, "Was she a terrorist?" He said the US military denied killing her and refused to give him even minimal compensation. The US gave him only half the compensation for his house that they destroyed. "With all respect to you," he said to Joe, "I hate Americans, they killed my family. My children cannot play in the street, they shot and killed my sister-in-law while she was washing clothes, and my other brother's hands and feet were blown off." He apologized to Joe for interrupting, but he said that "I have to tell you because I am in so much pain".

People fled Fallujah from the first Attack in 2004 to Baghdad to stay with family members, friends or strangers, in mosques, abandoned buildings, empty bomb shelters, or the Red Crescent tent camp. The second attack, in November 2005, was apparently even worse. It appears there were many more civilians killed, homes destroyed, and people driven out of the town. A huge proportion of the population is still unable to go home, either because home is totally destroyed or because they haven't been allowed back in.

Joe Carr said "I felt incredibly safe in Fallujah; the people I spoke with were kind and gentle. They are rightfully angry and indignant at what the US has done to them, but they seemed to understand that it wasn't me or all American's that did it". The cleric told Joe, "We are grateful that you come here and share in our suffering and agony, it shows that there are good and human Americans."

An Iraqi doctor was wounded April 2005 by US bullets while driving an ambulance in Fallujah. What we found there were civilians trapped in their homes in US-held areas of the town because marine snipers were firing at anyone who came outdoors, even children. People were trapped without food or water. The only hospital left open was cut off because the access road was controlled by US snipers and it was almost out of supplies. US forces were firing at ambulances, because previously fighters used the ambulances. Civilians reportedly came under fire from marine snipers while they were trying to reach a woman giving birth prematurely without electricity or medical help.

Fallujah will remain the face of US occupation. It showed the world the brutality of the US military campaign toward those who resist its agenda. But Fallujah has not stopped resisting. It is said that "you can't bomb a resistance out of existence, but you can bomb one into it."

Ref

Joe Carr, Electronic Iraq, 30 May 2005

Saul Landau. Counter punch, 28.November 2004

Pepe Escobar, Asia Times, 2nd Dec 2004

Jo Wilding, free lance writer. April 2004

Joe Carr is a 24-year-old anti-oppression activist and performance artist from Kansas City, Missouri. He attended the Evergreen State College in Olympia, Washington and spent January-April 2003 coordinating for the International Solidarity Movement in Rafah, Palestine, where he witnessed Israeli soldiers murder US peace activist Rachel Corrie and British peace activist Tom Hurndall. Joe is now a full-time activist with the Christian Peacemaker Teams in Palestine. He is currently working with CPT in Baghdad, Iraq, having been denied entry to Israel. He'll be back in the states in June

27

Dealing with the Iraqi resistance

The American way of war has been to substitute firepower for manpower. The extent of bombing Baghdad prior to the military invasion had ruined the infrastructure of the city to an extent that nothing was repairable. As a result, US forces have frequently resorted to firepower in the form of artillery or air force against the growing resistance of the occupation…This created negative impact in the counterinsurgency strikes. The massive air strikes caused massive collateral damage, with many civilians being the victim thereby frequently driving the locals to support the insurgents.

The "American way of war" once again messed up in Fallujah, whatever the method. "Massive firepower" indeed caused widespread "collateral damage"; that had fuelled the local resistance and prompted them to fight. The resistance was fierce in what is called "Sunni triangle" as well as in Mosul.

The successful conduct of counterinsurgency operations relies on the cooperation of the populations involved. The Americans did not make any effort to understand the motivations of the resistance in the conflict and the population as a whole. This requires a detailed understanding of the cultural environment and the human terrain in which the US forces relied before on human intelligence. In most parts of the country those spies "human intelligence" had been targeted by assassinations and treated as collaborators with the occupation. In Fallujah the Americans had lost that type of support.

Human intelligence was the first casualty in Fallujah. When you have marine commanders justifying an attack on a whole city because it is the house of Satan, any "detailed understanding of the cultural environment" had already been buried in the desert sands.

The American army had failed to recognize, respect and incorporate an understanding of the cultural and religious aspects of the Iraqi society in Fallujah and other towns in which US army was fighting the same people that they were supposed to help which lead erosion of the credibility and legitimacy of the American mission. After what happened in many towns in Iraq and the policy of arrogance; no one could trust the occupiers. In fact, this whole scenario started playing out as early as April 2003, when the resistance movement was born at the Abu Hanifa Mosque in (Al-Aadamyah) section in Baghdad and when marines opened fire on a peaceful demonstration in Fallujah.

The American mission was known to the world by the propaganda that was made about their mission in Iraq aimed at; they used the tactic of "starve the water and the fish will die". The majority of Sunnis (the "water") keep supporting the resistance (the "fish") with weapons, cash and shelter, and are not willing to support the elections.

Deny insurgents access to the population and resources.
  Deny the enemy the ability to live.
  Cut them off from food, water, clothing—everything.
  Identify and prioritize population sectors and resources to be secured and protected.
  Unify and coordinate all civil and security forces and assets within the community with special attention given to around-the-clock security, intelligence collection
  Mobilize, arm, and train the local population to provide their own local community security.
  Structure security force activity and actions to lead to the populace overtly picking a side
  Establish leverage. Use advice, equipment, and money to attempt to change people's attitudes and behaviour positively.
  Sever any relationship between the population and insurgents
  Identify and destroy insurgent support activities within the community.
  Identify and destroy insurgent organizational infrastructure
  Identify and eliminate the insurgent political apparatus (communications).
  Institute harsh penalties for those caught supporting the insurgents.
  Create a secure physical and psychological environment for the population, one in which people are free to go about their business and prosper without worrying about insurgents taking their freedom and prosperity from them.
  Counteract enemy propaganda.
  Conduct a national campaign strategy that distributes its message and is responsive to current events to ensure relevancy.

The occupying army had dealt with every Iraqi in the "Sunni Triangle" as the enemy, and targeted every single civilian as such; no one could see any benefit from living under the occupation; so why would they cooperate with the occupiers. They very well know and have seen that fear and terror is not the right tactic to win hearts and minds. This attitude of ignorance, arrogance and inhumane treatment had converted an entire population to be against the occupation, whether by armed or peaceful means. An American marine can call an air strike with a satellite phone the resistance would reply by setting up ambushes, roadside bombs and suicidal attacks.

A new phenomenon, which instigated violence from both sides and went into a vicious cycle of insurgency and counterinsurgency. In addition to that it gave the occupiers, Wright or wrong, the chance to stop any effort of reconstruction and blame it on the ongoing conflict. Americans corporate media made a big propaganda about the effects of the insurgency on the American mission in Iraq; however, they don't acknowledge that it is not enough to break the back of wars of national liberation.

The cumulative effect of the American mistakes was failure due to: cultural insensitivity and because "hearts and minds have been alienated" by a vicious circle of violence; and the inability to secure physical and psychological environment for the population. People capture and detained on the basis of being involved somehow in the resistance got sent to prisons or otherwise held in custody by US soldiers, they received inhumane and disgusting abuse as what happened in Abu Ghraib prison, where abuses took place. The whole city of Fallujah was levelled down by blanket bombing in order to "save it". The failure of US counterinsurgency efforts can be assessed and measured by the occupation statistics.

Killed Iraqi civilians are estimated to be anywhere from 15,000 to 100,000 (the British medical journal Lancet report). Johns Hopkins University is 90% certain there are more than 40,000 dead civilians.

The resistance was around 5,000 strong in late 2003. Now it is at least 20,000 strong. Some British generals put them at 50,000

Of the US$18.4 billion in Iraqi reconstruction funds, Washington/Baghdad has spent only $1.7 billion.

Baghdad had degenerated into a giant, hyper-violent slum, getting worse by the day. There's 25% less electricity now compared with Saddam times in early 2003—66% less in Baghdad.

At least 400,000 Iraqi children suffer from chronic diarrhoea and have almost no protein,

According to a UN development report. Sixty percent of rural Iraqis and 20% of urban Iraqis are forced to drink contaminated water.

According to a Gallup poll—taken before the Fallujah massacre—only 33% of respondents thought their lives were better than before the war. Ninety-four percent said Baghdad was more dangerous. Sixty-six percent believed the occupation could degenerate into a civil war. And 80% wanted the occupation over right after the January 30 elections.

The Bush administration in the face of continued resistance to the occupation had repeatedly suggested that the violence of resistance in Iraq is not home grown but is invasion of Iraq by foreign fighters that belong to extremist Islamic organisations. They had repeatedly explained that the violence in Iraq is due to foreign fighters, or *Jihadis*, as labelled by some American military officials. Prior to that and immediately after the fall of Saddam's regime the blamed some disgruntled Baathists and Saddam loyalists from the Fedaeen and Republican Guards. In fact after the invasion every time an explosion is heard in Baghdad or an Iraqi civilian dies, members of the CPA and the Interim Governing Council quickly point out to Saddam loyalists. The Jihadis are considered to be extremist Muslims who see Iraq as a forefront for Jihad against their American enemy; they claimed they either are loyal to Al-Qaeda or those who sympathize with its cause.

After a Chinook helicopter was brought down in Fallujah, which killed 16 US soldiers, the CPA and the Pentagon were at a loss for words. Had blamed Izzat Ibrahim Al-Douri, former Iraqi Vice-President who is thought to be hiding in Mosul. Attacks on the occupation army become more often and more deadly; US military commanders had started to admit that they face an invisible enemy. Latter the situation became more complex, both Syria and Iran were blamed for meddling in the Iraqi issue. That claim had "matured" and the picture n became clearer. The US is fighting Iraqi terrorists and the foreign Islamic terrorists; those are the same people responsible for the September 11; this rationalisation is being used to support the continued occupation of Iraq. Suddenly, the reasons for invading and occupying Iraq are no longer about weapons of mass destruction, or liberating the Iraqi people. It is the war on terror.

The true resistance in Iraq are ordinary Iraqis who chose to fight the new age Mongol invaders; they are people with pride and dignity who chose to fight and for a cause; the cause is defending their country and keeping it unified.

Ref

Firas Al-Atraqchi Freelance Columnist. 04/11/2003

Saul Landau. Counter punch, 28.November 2004

Pepe Escobar, Asia Times, 2nd Dec 2004

Andrew Greely, November 12,2004, Chicago Sun Times

28

Life under the War and occupation

He starts with A young man who told her on the 20.3 2003 "They are coming. I am sorry."

"Planes had left my country to drop bombs on his and he was sorry". In the early hours of March 20th 2003 Iraqis had woken up to the bombs and the roaring sounds of fighter jets that dropped enormous quantities of explosives on the buildings and establishments, military and otherwise in Baghdad. People had stored food and water, even some of them had dug wells to produce water; they braced them self to a coming disaster that no doubt was even worse than what happened in 1991 after the invasion of Kuwait. Their windows were crossed with parcel tapes to stop them shattering from the vibrations created by nearby bombs dropped in their neighbourhood. People had as much water as they could get, no one knew how long it would go on, and the price of water at the beginning of the offensive was five times that of petrol.

The air strike started just after 4am on he morning of the 20th of March 2003, the bombs and rockets in the sky were "flashing with yellow sparkles as if the stars were burning out", forty cruise missiles roaring through the sky that morning, people in Baghdad new it is the start of the American attack on the country. It was hard to believe they were dropping all this huge amount of explosives at a city full of families, shops and schools.

The war carried on. Jo wrote "For the next twelve days, until I was told to leave by the nervous Iraqi foreign ministry, I stayed in Baghdad, interviewing civilian casualties in the hospitals. Fear and suspicion were intense and it took time to negotiate our way into the hospitals. The first day I was allowed in was March 24th".

The bombing had caused so many casualties among the civilians, the hospitals could not cope with volume of the disaster, it was total chaos, injured and grieving people were screaming, still bleeding, Jo said *"Fatima cradling one child after another, Nada with an open skull fracture and her leg torn apart, Rana deeply concussed, struggling to breathe, Mohammed a patchwork of shrapnel cuts, eyes wide with panic, eight year old Zahra dead in the rubble along with her aunt (Fatima's sister, Hana, who was due to graduate with a teaching degree in the summer)"*. She added

"It was the seventh day after the wedding of Hana's brother, Khalid, to Nahda. They brought Nahda to the house at 4pm, exactly the time when the rocket (one of three fired from a plane which had been circling overhead) hit. It took off the entire upper storey. Khalid collapsed when given the news, as if his breath were entwined with that of his new wife, crushed to death".

Jo wrote "We found Fatima's family in the end, though she and her children are back in the city now. "Their family is broken," Khalid said. "They are too sad. Their house is near the air force centre; so they came here because they were afraid it would be bombed. It was bombed, of course, but her home was not so badly damaged as ours."

The American officials kept telling the world about the precision weapons and how they hit their targets, that was true to certain extent; and on the ground almost every building was a target, even communications centre, electricity station, were all targeted. Fourteen-year-old Nabil told Jo. "I came back at noon from my uncle's house and the house was destroyed. My mother and father and my five brothers and sisters were all dead. I am the only one left," She described his demeanour as "unable to look at another face" from the sorrow and the pain.

The devastation was not limited to Baghdad, many cities were targeted and destroyed in the bombing at another place "a rocket struck one of the houses at midnight, killing sixteen, maybe seventeen people and demolishing three houses"

Houses near any military base were part of the target and many people lost their lives and/or their houses just because it happened they lived near another target whatever it was.

After the fall of Saddam the resistance started and the militia came into play and the situation got so complicated. Many civilians were killed in the crossfire between US soldiers and Iraqi militiamen. People were afraid: "If someone sees us with foreigners, they will tell the Americans we are with the resistance or tell the militias we are working for the Americans. They will come and say, 'How did you communicate with these foreigners, how did they know about you, why did they come here?' We are more afraid now than we were before the war,"

People have learned over the months and years of fighting and chaos. Women were mostly reduced to stay at home and if they have to go out for any purpose, they learned to walk along the road with no expression on their face and not respond to any comment from either side. Schools, hospitals and public buildings were looted after the war; no school had windows or any running water or electricity. There weren't enough schools for all the children and they've been segregated since 1999 so the classrooms, boys in the mornings and girls in the afternoons, or vice versa. The situation after the war was even worse.

Explosion became a common place that causes sudden fullness of the air, with huge bursting and tremor through the ground; the targets are usually the American convoys, and some times the fighting would break from no where, and civilian suddenly find themselves in the middle of a battle.

The consequence of targeting the American is a sudden and immediate eradication of any person or vehicle in that vicinity. Many unlucky civilians faced their fate that way; just because it happened they were at the wrong place in the wrong time.

Dr. Ali Hameed is one of Iraq's few authorities on post-traumatic stress disorder, he spoke to Jo and said "there is not a single child in Iraq without some degree of post-traumatic stress, and that play therapy is the best, perhaps the only means of diagnosing and rehabilitating the children in a country where mental illness is heavily stigmatized". Ironically the funding from the ministry of health for this program was withdrawn by its "American advisors". The funds were reallocated to a centre for torture victims of Saddam regime, which is politically much more valuable for the American and their newly appointed interim government than a program that could criticizes the harm done by the war and occupation.

Thousands of people have been arrested and detained in house raids, at checkpoints or from workplaces, imprisoned without charges, no trials, without access to lawyers or visits from their families, sometimes for many months. Released detainees were the only source of information for most prisoners' families, which was the only reassurance that the detained person is still alive. House raids became a phenomenon during the occupation, conducted by Americans sometimes on the basis of suspicions of involvement with the armed resistance, and at most times by the Iraqi police and other unidentified militiamen. Those raids had terrorised the Sunni population throw ought Baghdad and other cities in the so called "Sunni triangle". Nothing has changed," Iraqi people say. "The Americans are the same as Saddam."

Abu-Graib became a monument of abuse and a symbol of hatred to the occupation. Detainees were abused and people who were arrested had no access to family visits or lawyers, and without any charges. And worse of all the tactics that was used by the Americans who built and emphasized the religious division of the

Iraqis in a manner of "divide and conquer" a tactic that was used by the Saddam regime who made an informant of almost every Iraqi. A former detainee Abdul Rahman spoke to Jo and said "the US administration has continued the old regime's practice of paying for information and acting on it without verification so that a grudge can be profitably exercised by accusing a neighbour of working for the resistance then watching US forces arrest him".

Every move in the occupation process was fraught with abuse and fear. Even the change of the currency to new notes had led to some tragedies, corruption became a phenomenon. Hundreds of bank tellers, usually women, had been threatened with arrest, sixteen actually imprisoned, and forced to pay for the discrepancy between the genuine value received and that given out in the exchange of the old Saddam notes for the new currency. There is no suspicion of any fraud or theft by the clerks. They were instructed by other bank officials to pay out new notes for old ones, even if they appeared to be forged, as there was no way of verifying which forgeries were. Now the shortfall will be taken from their wages in instalments.

Jo spoke to their lawyer, Faleh Maktuf, he said "there's no legal basis for the arrests, nor the coerced payments, but in the absence of a legal framework, power is unchecked in the hands of ministers, police and judges. "Nothing has changed," he added", in reference to the old regime.

The US government-linked corporation Bechtel was involved with schools rehabilitation. Bechtel worked in Nasariyah: she is one example of their work; they have a contract for $40,000 to rehabilitate a school and they immediately subcontracted the work for $28,000, keeping $12,000 for doing nothing. They just paint the walls, with bad brushes and paint, so there are bristles on the walls, nothing else was done, the $40,000 is gone, a testimony of the failed Bremer reconstruction project. Most Iraqis felt that the yesterday of Saddam has not changed the same corruptions and the same issues with prisons and more than that with lack of security.

Unemployment has risen to 60-70% throughout Iraq. Workers in many industries have been unhappy about the newly appointed US managers and against the unfair and non-sufficient wages set by the Coalition Provisional Authority (CPA). Attempts to set up trade unions have been suppressed in several places, including the port of Um Qasr. And so on, stories continue to emerge, but we offer only examples.

The control of food ration is just a part of that control of Iraq's economy. It was to be replaced with a financial assistance to the poor families; however approximately 70% of Iraq's young employable people, which is the bulk of the workforce remain unemployed; the majority are still desperate for financial help.

The imminent problem is this financial assistance instead of food ration package permits the government to manipulate market prices and wages, forcing families and small businesses to surrender and accept slave wages for the profit of the big corporations which really control Iraq.

Little has been done for women's rights, in fact women situation had got worse under the occupation in a country that used to be a secular nation, the CPA has been setting up "women's centres" and other hollow establishments dedicated to emphasize the fact that Saddam's was terrible, in fact the crimes under the occupation had rendered Saddam and his atrocities irrelevant. While some really positive women's projects coming from the Iraqi women themselves are attacked by militia and groups opposed to them (unprotected by the coalition). Women frequently say that before the war had few rights, at least they had security.

Of course it's not quite true to say nothing has changed. Some people are out of prisons. The Kurds are celebrating the establishment of a federal state of Iraqi Kurdistan. Dissatisfaction with the occupation does not really mean that people want Saddam back. Iraqis think they would rather have been given the opportunity to get rid of Saddam themselves. It is fair to say that

- Human rights are not being respected,

- The Iraqi people are still being crushed between other people's agendas,

- Financial gain and cronyism are still dictating the policy,

- There is no security,

- Inadequate electricity

- Petrol rationing in a country that have huge oil reserve.

- And Iraq is not free.

- Torture chambers assassinations and abductions are haunting the lives of

Ref

Jo Wilding (*British Activist*) visited Iraq 20.3 2003

Jo Wilding is an Iraq-based British human rights campaigner, writer and trainee lawyer from Bristol, UK. 29-year old Wilding first came to Iraq in August 2001 with Voices in the Wilderness. Then he returned to Iraq as an independent observer in February 2003 and stayed for the month before the war and the first 11 days of the bombing as a human shield, before being expelled by the Iraqi foreign ministry as part of a purge of independent foreigners.

Currently inside Iraq, Wilding is taking part in Circus 2 Iraq, "a small group of circus performers—fools, clowns, jugglers, stilt walkers and magicians—set up to…perform and give circus skills workshops to children [in Iraq] traumatized by sanctions, war and its aftermath."

His writings about Iraq and ordinary Iraqis were published in the Guardian, the New Zealand Herald, Counterpunch, Australian radio, and in Japan, Korea and Pakistan.

29

Democracy, Law, Freedom and constitution and Lies

April 9, 2003, US soldiers wrapped the US flag around the head of the Saddam statue in AL-Fardous square and were then told to remove it because it sent out the wrong message. "The right message was that Iraq was liberated, not conquered".

Iraq's American-appointed government, no matter what its intentions or loyalties, is not really sovereign. It nominally represented Iraq's Kurds and Shiites and included other ethnicities, but is still is like the rest of the population lacking any control over the government. The hollow promises of the democracy became obvious soon after the occupation. The occupying force had appointed advisers and minders in every public institution, those advisers are the actual managers, and basically no decision is taken without their prior approval.

On October 15, 2005, millions of Iraqis headed to the ballot box to vote on the referendum for the adoption of the new national constitution. Iraqis from all groups were busy wrangling and bickering between them on the wording of the document that was going to shape up the new political system in the country. It was promising seen from outside, the alliance between the Kurds and the south did not seem to come out of affection to each other, it rather comes from the hatred of Saddam regime, the irony of that not only comes from the fact that Saddam time was terrible to every Iraq, but also, the fact that the Kurds are Sunnis who made alliance with the Shiites south against the Sunni Arabs. That shows how fragile the fabric of the society became under the occupation.

As for the rule of law, successive scandals and the scandals of what events happened in Iraq's prison; the thousands who have been detained indefinitely without charge or trial, the torture, the assassination for any one who opposed the Americans, the abductions and impunity for the vast majority of those who were responsible. General Ricardo Sanchez, although officially denied, he in fact

185

signed his approval of at least three of torture techniques, including use of dogs to intimidate prisoners.

American corporations have been involved in some f those scandals, employees of private security contractors were blamed for the worst crimes in Abu Ghraib. And the worse was they got away with it with impunity. Because they were not military personnel, they were not subjected to military prosecution. Because there was no effective civil legal system, they were not subjected to civilian law either.

Early in 2005 the United Nations at last had authorised the International Criminal Court to begin investigating and prosecuting crimes. However the United States had big time opposition to the court and they demand exemption for US citizens; which is disturbing, because many of the fraud crimes were committed by American citizens and American corporate organizations, which effectively means the armed and the powerful are exempt from the rule of law, on the other hand there is the Iraqi population, who have no legal rights whatsoever.

One of the fundamental foundations and essentials of democracy that people should not be punished without a fair and public trial. Another essential rule is that a person must be presumed innocent until proven otherwise. Those basic principles should be applicable regardless of the culture or other political consideration.

Again an important example is Fallujah. Because several civilians had been shot dead by US forces a few days earlier, and four foreign fighters were killed by local people. Instead of exerting political pressure on local authorities in Fallujah to identify the individuals responsible for the killings of the mercenaries (let alone identifying those responsible for killing the Fallujans beforehand), US forces besieged the town, cut off electricity and water supply, closed down the main hospital, and largely prevented access of medical supplies.

There were thousands of criminal acts committed by US forces which amount to war crimes; and command-level war crimes were perpetrated throughout the US military hierarchy, but the only individual prosecuted for actions in Fallujah was the one caught on television shooting dead an unarmed man in a mosque.

So there is no rule of law in the new Iraq or "liberated Iraq". Iraqis are not able to exercise legal rights, crimes are not investigated or prosecuted, even the right to a fair trial does not exist, while the occupying forces, unless they were stupid enough to be caught on camera, had escaped prosecution with complete impunity. Non-military employees, apparently, are safe even when they are caught on camera.

Iraq's economy and its politics is still wrapped up by the "US Flag", the International and the Pentagon favoured corporations. It seems the right message is liberation of Iraq from the $120 billion debt and liberation of the market to free market economy and enslave the Iraqis. Freedom/, it are for the market, and freedom for American giant companies, but still no democracy and no freedom for the poor people Iraq. People

Where once it was impossible to publicly criticize Saddam, and risky even privately, now there is freedom to condemn him and criticised what he did; something the Iraqi authorities dwelled on and yet did or allowed to occur some of the most heinous crimes that he did. Various media outlets have found that it was not advisable to criticize American appointed prime-minister or his government. Reports tended to be in favour of the government's point of view. Al-Jazeera, Al-Arabiya, and perhaps other media outlets dared to criticise them and were closed down or expelled from the country.

The constitution

The draft of the constitution was scheduled to be completed by August 15, 2005. When that deadline is breached, the national assembly was by law meant to dissolve itself. This was to be followed by other definitive elections for Iraqi government. This part of the law was not implemented because. The national assembly was comprised of Shiite and Kurdish legislators. The Sunnis had only small representation because of a nation-wide boycott of the elections January 2005. Since then Sunnis, including the Association of Muslim Scholars, have called on all Sunnis to participate in the January 2005 elections.

The debate over how to word the constitution continued between the various groups. The Sunnis complained that the current wording emphasized federalism, which was seen as pretext for divided Iraq, Al-Hakim was particularly adamant to have federal state on the south and his group had emphasized repeatedly over the years for their federal demands. The Kurds were also for federal state in the north, with particularly contentious issue of Kirkuk, which has on third of the Iraqi Oil reserve. That was to adopt an autonomous form of governance similar to what has existed in Iraqi Kurdistan since 1991. However, the Sunnis seem to have reluctantly accepted the status quo of Kurdish autonomy.

The resistance to the federalism goes much more beyond the national aspirations to keep the unity of the country. At the heart of this dilemma is the location of Iraq's most of Iraqi oil revenues, which is located in Iraq's south, from Al Nasiriyah and Al-Amarah to the port of Um Qasr, the oil reserve in that area is estimated to be over a billion barrels most of it is yet to be discovered and mined.

Iraq's north, particularly the area surrounding Kirkuk and stretching north east to the Zagros Mountains, is also oil rich. The centre, which could possibly be what the Sunnis are left with, is mostly arid with a few agricultural resources.

The Association of Muslim Scholars remained steadfast to a unified Iraq and would ensure the country not is divided. This division of opinions and aspirations had instigated ethnically based and politically motivated attacks from either side, and continued to be a major national threat and are still pushing the country closer to civil war.

The draft constitutions had a major blow to the Arabic identity of the country; a country with more than 80% Arabic people, the claim was Iraq had many ethnic minorities. This was followed by a sharp criticism from the Arab League, which criticized the draft for not including Iraq's Arabic heritage. By all accounts the efforts to strip Iraq from its Arabic heritage was a conspiracy directed by the occupying force and welcomed by some opportunists who would rather appease the occupiers and perhaps to please other sides to which they had their loyalties.

Furthermore, confusion has been added by the existence of two versions of the same draft, each with a different introduction in Arabic. The first begins, "We the peoples of Iraq…" while the second version starts off with "We the peoples of the valley of two rivers…" While this does not have any impact on the constitution it may get interpreted in different ways. The latter would seem to indicate that people living in Iraq are not constitutionally obliged to call themselves Iraqi and this could potentially open the door for changing the name of the country at some point.

There are also some international concerns about the wording of the constitution which may not only reverse gains for the emancipation of women in Iraq but impose further restrictions. "Reference to Islamic Shari'ah in the constitution has heightened fears that an Iranian-style theocracy lies ahead". Violence against women is not ruled out in the draft; the role of women is attributed to a family and home setting; provisions outlining the role of women in parliament expire within two years. For the referendum to be struck down, a majority in three provinces must say no. Sunnis are a majority in four Iraqi provinces. However it was finally approved by the majority.

There is also secular and nationalistic Shiites, who see Iraq as distinctly an Arab nation and dedicated ti, keep its unity. The referendum passed, and that caused cries of foul play by the Sunnis, which resulted in escalation of violence.

Ref

Alexander Gainem. Freelance Writer Sep 13, 2005 (Alexander Gainem is a freelance journalist who has written extensively on Middle East issues).

Jo Wilding April 7. 2005

30

The abuse (Torture at Abu-Graib Prison)

Abu Ghraib is a name for a region, twenty miles west of Baghdad; it has Abu Ghraib prison, which during Saddam Hussein rule of 34 years was one of the world's most notorious prisons, with daily torture, weekly executions, and very poor living conditions. In the late 1950s the Iraqi government had contracted American company to build a modern prison in Baghdad. It was decided that the agricultural area of "Abu Ghraib" was the best place to build the prison. Iraq had its American designed and built prison in the early 1960's

Approximately fifty thousand men and women—no accurate count is possible—were jammed into Abu Ghraib at one time, in twelve-by-twelve-foot cells that were barely enough for a human body. People used to disappear for years and years, with no charges and no trials, some of them then get summarily executed, in particular those who were political prisoners.

Saddam managed to release the prisoners (most of them were there for civil crimes) just before the war in 2003. The huge prison complex was by then evacuated and all the criminals were released into the community. In the looting that followed the regime's collapse, April 2003, the prison was stripped of everything that could be removed, including doors, windows, and bricks. Most of the actions were in revenge for the bad memories of the notorious jail.

The coalition authorities had renovated the jail, with putting tiles on the floors, and cleaning the prison cells and various repairs; bathrooms, showers, and a medical centre were added. Abu Ghraib became the U.S. military prison.

By September 2003 there were several thousands of detainees. Most of the prisoners were civilians among them were many women and teenagers. Most of them were picked up in random military raids on houses that had not been involved in military combats, others were taken at roads checkpoints usually for no convincing reason, and most of that action was for the purpose of intimidation.

According to the Coalition provisional Authority they fell into three defined categories:

Common civilian criminals

Security detainees suspected of "crimes against the coalition"

Suspected "high-value" leaders of the insurgency

The U.S.'s treatment of detainees in Abu-Ghraib and other occupation prisons was shrouded in secrecy from the beginning of the occupation.

June 2003, brigadier general Janis Karpinski, (Army reserve), was named commander of the Military Police Brigade and was in charge of military prisons in Iraq including Abu-Ghraib. General Karpinski, the only female commander in the war zone, was an experienced operations and intelligence officer who had served with the Special Forces and in the 1991 Gulf War; she had never run a prison system.

Karpinski was enthusiastic about her new job as a Jail commander. In an interview December 2003 with the St. Petersburg *Times*, she said that, "for many of the Iraqi inmates at Abu Ghraib living conditions now are better in prison than at home. At one point we were concerned that they wouldn't want to leave". A month later she was suspended, and a major investigation into the Army's prison system was authorized by Lieutenant General Ricardo Sanchez (the senior commander in Iraq).

In February 2004 report, the ICRC reported that "methods of physical and psychological coercion were used by the military intelligence to get confessions and extract information. Those methods included:

hooding to disorient and prevent detainees from breathing

being forced to remain for prolonged periods in stress positions

being attached repeatedly over several days, for several hours each time to the bars of cell doors naked or in positions causing physical pain

being held naked in dark cells for several days and paraded naked, sometimes hooded or with women's underwear over their heads

sleep, food, and water deprivation

prolonged exposure to the sun during the hottest time of day

A fifty-three-page report, obtained by *The New Yorker*, written by Major General Antonio M. Taguba and not meant for public release, was completed in late February 2004. Its conclusions about the conduct of many of the occupation solders of the Army prison were devastating.

Amnesty international got concerned about the abuse of the detainees by the occupation forces in Iraq, which in some cases were regarded to be "tantamount to torture",

There was a leak of a report on the abuse investigations by Major General Antonio Taguba, which reported "numerous incidents of sadistic, blatant criminal abuses" against detainees in Abu Ghraib prison between October and December 2003. The report goes on to say that US agents in the mentioned prison had hidden a number of detainees from the international Red Cross agents.

During the year 2003, the American authorities initiated criminal investigations and prosecuted several soldiers as well as investigations and reviews of the detention policies and practices of the US Army.

Taguba found that between October and December of 2003 there were numerous instances of "sadistic, blatant, and wanton criminal abuses" at Abu Ghraib, he added. "This systematic and illegal abuse of detainees was perpetrated by soldiers of the 372nd Military Police Company, and also by members of the American intelligence community". Taguba added—"detailed witness statements and the discovery of extremely graphic photographic evidence." Photographs and videos taken by the soldiers as the abuses were happening were not included in his report, Taguba said, because of their "extremely sensitive nature."

Taguba's report listed some of the crimes:

Breaking chemical lights and pouring the phosphoric liquid on detainees

Forcing groups of male detainees to masturbate themselves while being photographed and videotaped;

Beating detainees with a broom handle and a chair

Threatening male detainees with rape

Allowing a military police guard to stitch the wound of a detainee who was injured after being slammed against the wall in his cell

Sodomizing a detainee with a chemical light and perhaps a broom stick,

Using military working dogs to frighten and intimidate detainees with threats of attack, and in one instance actually biting a detainee.

Punching, slapping and kicking detainees; jumping on their naked feet;

Videotaping and photographing naked male and female detainees;

Forcibly arranging detainees in various sexually explicit positions for photographing

Arranging naked detainees in a pile and then jumping on them;

Positioning a naked detainee on a box, with a sandbag on his head, and attaching wires to his fingers, toes and penis to simulate electric torture;

Writing "I am a Rapist" (sic) on the leg of a detainee alleged to have forcibly raped a 15-year-old fellow detainee, and then photographing him naked;

Placing a dog chain or strap around a naked detainee's neck and having a female soldier pose with him for a picture;

A male military police guard having sex with a female detainee

Threatening detainees with a loaded pistol

Pouring cold water on naked detainee

Allowing a military police guard to stitch the wound of a detainee who was injured after being slammed against the wall in his cell;

Sodomizing a detainee with a chemical light and perhaps a broom stick;

Using military working dogs (without muzzles) to frighten and intimidate detainees with threats of attack, and in at least one case biting and severely injuring a detainee;

Forcing detainees to remove their clothing and keeping them naked for several days at a time;

Forcing naked male detainees to wear women's underwear;

Taking pictures of dead Iraqi detainees

There was overwhelming evidence to support these allegations. The photographs—several of which were broadcast on CBS's "60 Minutes 2" showed occupation solders taunting naked Iraqi prisoners who are forced to assume humiliating positions. Six suspects—Staff Sergeant Ivan L. Frederick II, known as Chip, who was the senior enlisted man; Specialist Charles A. Graner; Sergeant Javal Davis; Specialist Megan Ambuhl; Specialist Sabrina Harman; and Private Jeremy Sivits—were prosecuted in Iraq, on charges that include among others: conspiracy, cruelty toward prisoners, maltreatment, assault, and indecent acts. A seventh suspect, Private Lynndie England (was prosecuted latter in the US), was reassigned to Fort Bragg, North Carolina, after becoming pregnant.

The following paragraph is graphic description of the abuse that was caught on camera:

Private England, in one picture was shown with a cigarette dangling from her mouth, is giving thumbs-up sign and pointing at the genitals of a young Iraqi, who is naked except for a sandbag over his head, as he was forced to masturbate. Three other hooded and naked Iraqi prisoners are shown, hands reflexively crossed over their genitals. A fifth prisoner has his hands at his sides. In another, England stands arm in arm with Specialist Graner; both were smiling and giving the thumbs-up behind a cluster of seven naked Iraqi prisoners, piled on top of each other in what looks like a pyramid. There is another photograph of a cluster of naked prisoners, also piled on top of each other in a pyramid. Near them stands Graner, smiling, his arms crossed; a woman soldier stands in front of him, bending over, and she, too, is smiling. Then, there is another cluster of hooded bodies, with a female soldier standing in front, taking photographs. Yet another photograph shows a kneeling, naked, un-hooded male prisoner, head was turned away from the camera, posed to make it appear that he is performing oral sex on another male prisoner.

Such dehumanization is not acceptable in any culture, and it is more so in the Arab world. Homosexual acts are against Islamic law and it is humiliating for men to be naked in front of other men, that kind of humiliation was regarded by some scholars as a real torture.

Two Iraqi faces that do appear in the photographs are those of dead men. There is the battered face of prisoner No. 153399, and the bloodied body of another prisoner, wrapped in cellophane and packed in ice. There is a photograph of an empty room, splattered with blood.

The abuse of prisoners seemed routine, the solders involved did not feel that they should hide it. On April 9th 2004, at an Article 32 hearing (the military equivalent of a grand jury) in the case against Sergeant Frederick, at Camp Victory, near Baghdad, one of the witnesses, Specialist Matthew Wisdom, told the court what happened when he delivered seven prisoners, to the so-called "hard site" at Abu Ghraib, where the prisoners who were considered the most dangerous were jailed. The men had been accused of starting a riot at another section of the prison. Wisdom said:

"SFC Snider grabbed my prisoner and threw him into a pile.... I do not think it was right to put them in a pile. I saw SSG Frederic, SGT Davis and CPL Graner walking around the pile hitting the prisoners. I remember SSG Frederick hitting one prisoner in the side of his ribcage. The prisoner was no danger to SSG Frederick"

At another session, Wisdom testified:

I saw two naked detainees, one masturbating to another kneeling with its mouth open. I thought I should just get out of there. I didn't think it was right...I saw SSG Frederick walking towards me, and he said, "Look what these animals do when you leave them alone for two seconds." I heard PFC England shout out, "He's getting hard."

Wisdom testified that he told his superiors what had happened, and assumed that "the issue was taken care of." He said, "I just didn't want to be part of anything that looked criminal."

The abuses became public because of the outrage of Specialist Joseph M. Darby, a role emerged during the Article 32 hearing against Chip Frederick. A government witness said "The investigation started after SPC Darby…got a CD from Graner…. He came across pictures of naked detainees

Questioned further, the Army investigator said that Frederick and his colleagues had not been given any "training guidelines" that he was aware of.

Witnesses had testified also that Frederick, on one occasion, "had punched a detainee in the chest so hard that the detainee almost went into cardiac arrest."

At the Article 32 hearing, the Army informed Frederick and his attorneys, Captain Robert Shuck, an Army lawyer, and Gary Myers, a civilian, that two dozen witnesses they had sought, including General Karpinski and all of Frederick's co-defendants, would not appear. Some had been excused after exercising their Fifth Amendment right; others were deemed to be too far away from the courtroom. "The purpose of an Article 32 hearing is for us to engage witnesses and discover facts," Gary Myers told me. "We ended up with a c.i.d. agent and no alleged victims to examine." After the hearing, the presiding investigative officer ruled that there was sufficient evidence to convene a court-martial against Frederick.

Gary Myers, who was one of the military defence attorneys in the My Lai prosecutions of the nineteen-seventies, told Seymour Hersh that his client's defence will be that he was carrying out the orders of his superiors and, in particular, the directions of military intelligence. He said, "Do you really think a group of kids from rural Virginia decided to do this on their own? Decided that the best way to embarrass Arabs and make them talk was to have them walk around nude?"

In letters and e-mails to family members, Frederick repeatedly noted that the military-intelligence teams, which included C.I.A. officers and linguists and interrogation specialists from private defence contractors, were the dominant force inside Abu Ghraib. In a letter written in January, he said: (from the New Yorker)

"I questioned some of the things that I saw, such things as leaving inmates in their cell with no clothes or in female underpants, handcuffing them to the door of their cell—and the answer I got was, "This is how military intelligence (MI) wants it done." MI has also instructed us to place a prisoner in an isolation cell with little or no clothes, no toilet or running water, no ventilation or window, for as much as three days".

The military-intelligence officers have "encouraged and told us, 'Great job,' they were now getting positive results and information," Frederick wrote. "CID has been present when the military working dogs were used to intimidate prisoners at MI's request." At one point, Frederick told his family, he pulled aside his superior officer, Lieutenant Colonel Jerry Phillabaum, and asked about the mistreatment of prisoners. "His reply was 'Don't worry about it.'"

In November, Frederick wrote, an Iraqi prisoner under the control of what was called "O.G.A.," or other government agencies, which is the C.I.A. and its paramilitary employees was brought to his unit for questioning. "They stressed him out so bad that the man passed away. They put his body in a body bag and packed him in ice for approximately twenty-four hours in the shower. The next day the medics came and put his body on a stretcher, placed a fake IV in his arm and took him away." The dead Iraqi was never entered into the prison's inmate-control system, Frederick said "and therefore never had a number."

One sergeant provided graphic descriptions to Human Rights Watch investigators about the abuse carried out by him and others: "The first interrogation that I observed was the first time I saw a PUC pushed to the brink of a stroke or a heart attack. At first I was surprised, like, 'This is what we are allowed to do?'"

The sergeant said if he was told that prisoners had been found with homemade bombs, "we would f*** them up, put them in stress positions and put them in a tent and withhold water...It was like a game.

He explained: "To 'f*** a PUC' means to beat him up. We would give those blows to the head, chest, legs and stomach, pull them down, and kick dirt on them. This happened every day. To 'smoke' someone is to put them in stress positions until they get muscle fatigue and pass out, which happened on daily basis

Iraqis were "smoked" for up to 12 hours. That would entail being made to hold five-gallon water cans in both hands with out-stretched arms, made to do press-ups and star jumps. At no time, during these sessions, would they get water or food apart from dry biscuits. Sleep deprivation was also "a really big thing"

To prepare a prisoner for interrogation, military intelligence officers ordered that the Iraqis be deprived of sleep.

They'd also pour cold water over prisoners and then cover them in sand and mud. On some occasions, prisoners were tortured for revenge. "If we were on patrol and caught a guy that killed our captain or my buddy last week...man, it is human nature," said the sergeant—but on other occasions, he confessed, it was for "sport".

Many prisoners were completely innocent and had no part in the insurgency, but intelligence officers had told soldiers to exhaust the prisoners to make them co-operate. He said he now knew their behaviour was "wrong", but added "this was the norm".

In fall 2004 General Sanchez ordered Ryder to review the prison system in Iraq and recommend ways to improve it. Ryder's report, filed on November 5th, concluded that there were potential human-rights, training, and manpower issues, system-wide that needed immediate attention. It also discussed serious concerns about the tension between the military police and the intelligence teams who wanted to interrogate them. Army regulations limit intelligence activity by the M.P.s to passive collection. But something had gone wrong at Abu Ghraib.

There was evidence dating back to the Afghanistan war, the Ryder report said, that M.P.s had worked with intelligence operatives to "set favourable conditions for subsequent interviews"—another phrase for breaking the will of prisoners." General Karpinski's brigade, Ryder reported, "Has not been directed to change its facility procedures to set the conditions for MI interrogations, nor participate in those interrogations."

Ryder said that the situation had not yet reached a crisis. Though some procedures were flawed, he said, he found "no military police units purposely applying inappropriate confinement practices."

Taguba said. "Unfortunately, many of the systemic problems that surfaced during [Ryder's] assessment are the very same issues that are the subject of this investigation," he wrote. "In fact, many of the abuses suffered by detainees occurred during, or near to, the time of that assessment." He continued, "Contrary to the findings of MG Ryder's report, I find that personnel assigned to the 372nd MP Company, 800th MP Brigade were directed to change facility procedures to 'set the conditions' for MI interrogations." Army intelligence officers, C.I.A. agents, and private contractors "actively requested that MP guards set physical and mental conditions for favourable interrogation of witnesses."

Taguba backed up his conclusions by evidence from sworn statements to the C.I.D. investigators. Specialist Sabrina Harman, testified that it was her job to keep detainees awake, including one hooded prisoner who was placed on a box with wires attached to his fingers, toes, and penis. She stated, "MI wanted to get them to talk. It is Graner and Frederick's job to do things for MI and OGA to get these people to talk."

Common phrases used by MI

Loosen this guy up for us

Make sure he has a bad night

Make sure he gets the treatment

Good job, they're breaking down real fast

They answer every question. They're giving out good information

The soldiers referred to their Iraqi captives as persons under control (PUC)

and used the expressions "f***ing a PUC

"Smoking a PUC" to refer respectively to torture and forced physical exertion.

It was later revealed that at least one of these detainees died in custody of the American forces, several of those deaths were believed to be related to torture or ill-treatment of the prisoners.

The Taguba study noted that more than sixty per cent of the civilian inmates at Abu Ghraib were deemed not to be a threat to society, which should have enabled them to be released. Karpinski's defence, Taguba said, was that her superior officers "routinely" rejected her recommendations regarding the release of such prisoners.

General Taguba spent more than four hours interviewing Karpinski, whom he described as extremely emotional: "What I found particularly disturbing in her testimony was her complete unwillingness to either understand or accept that many of the problems inherent in the 800th MP Brigade were caused or exacerbated by poor leadership and the refusal of her command to both establish and enforce basic standards and principles among its soldiers."

Taguba recommended that Karpinski and seven brigade military-police officers and enlisted men be relieved of command and formally reprimanded. No criminal proceedings were suggested for Karpinski; apparently, the loss of promotion and the indignity of a public rebuke were seen as enough punishment. After the story broke on CBS the Pentagon announced that Major General Geoffrey Miller, the new head of the Iraqi prison system, had arrived in Baghdad and. He had been the commander of the Guantánamo Bay detention centre. General Sanchez also authorized an investigation into possible wrongdoing by military and civilian interrogators.

As the international fury grew, senior officers, and President Bush, insisted that the actions of some solders do not reflect the conduct of the occupation military as a whole. Taguba's report, amounts to collective mistake and the failure of the leadership at the highest levels.

There was concern that most of the investigations were conducted by the American Army itself, which did not have the power to prosecute or even investigate the higher officials of government. The activities of the CIA in Iraq remained largely shrouded by secrecy. No investigation dealt with the USA's alleged involvement in secret transfers between countries and any torture or ill-treatment that may have taken place.

Released detainees have alleged that they had been tortured or ill-treated while in US custody. Evidence also emerged that Federal Bureau of Investigation (FBI) agents and the ICRC, had found that such abuses had been committed against detainees. No further actions were taken.

Regardless of who was responsible Abu Ghraib had seen flagrant violation of Army regulations and the Geneva conventions, and in which management of the prisoners of war was handed over to military-intelligence and civilian security contractors. Interrogating prisoners and getting intelligence, including by intimidation and torture, was the priority.

A letter smuggled out of the prison by a woman called as "Noor", containing allegations of rape, was found to be entirely accurate. Other witnesses interviewed by the Guardian newspaper have said that US guards "repeatedly" raped a 14-year-old Iraqi girl. They also said that guards made several of the women inmates' parade naked in front of male prisoners.

The crimes of Abu Ghraib had tremendous impact on the Iraqi society, who saw the 'liberating Army" tortures and kills innocents, women and teenagers; there were also rumours of rape and sexual violations of many kinds. That had enthused the Iraqi youth in particular in the middle part of Iraq to join the resistance and fight the occupation.

Under the fourth Geneva Convention, an occupying power can jail civilians who pose an "imperative" security threat, but it must establish a regular procedure for insuring that only civilians who remain a genuine security threat be kept imprisoned. Prisoners have the right to appeal any internment decision and have their cases reviewed. Human Rights Watch complained to Secretary of Defence Donald Rumsfeld that civilians in Iraq remained in custody month after month with no charges brought against them. The US investigations had revealed that Rumsfeld had authorized the Central Intelligence Agency (CIA) to keep at least one detainee off the prison register.

Abu Ghraib had become another infamous Guantánamo bay Camp. As the photographs from Abu Ghraib made it clear, these detentions and abuses had enormous impacts on the imprisoned civilian Iraqis, many of whom had nothing to do with the insurgency; and for the United States' reputation in the world.

Since then American soldiers who personally tortured Iraqi prisoners have come forward to give testimony to human rights organisations about crimes they committed. Three soldiers—a captain and two sergeants—from the 82nd Airborne Division stationed near Fallujah in Iraq have told Human Rights Watch how prisoners were tortured both as a form of stress relief and as a way of breaking them for interrogation sessions. These revelations about the torture of Iraqi detainees come at a time when the Bush administration thought it could draw a line under the scandal of Abu Ghraib following imprisonment of Lynndie England for her infamous role in the abuse of prisoners and the photographing of torture. The 82nd Airborne soldiers at FOB Mercury earned the nickname "The Murderous Maniacs" from local Iraqis and took t According to Captain Ian Fishback of the 82nd Airborne Division, army doctrine had been broken by allowing Iraqis who were captured by them to remain in their custody, instead of being sent "behind the lines" to trained military police.

However, Fishback told his company commander about the abuse and was told "remember the honour of the unit is at stake. Fishback then told his battalion commander who advised him to speak to the Judge Advocate General's (JAG) office, which deals with issues of military law. The JAG told Fishback that the Geneva Conventions "are a grey area". When Fishback described some of the abuses he had witnessed the JAG said it was "within" Geneva Conventions.

Fishback spent 17 months trying to raise the matter with his superiors. When he attempted to approach representatives of US Senators John McCain and John Warner about the abuse, he was told that he would not be granted a pass to meet them on his day off. Fishback says that army investigators were currently more interested in finding out the identity of the other soldiers who spoke to Human Rights Watch than dealing with the systemic abuse of Iraqi prisoners.

While the pictures and the video clips obtained by the American army speak for themselves, we will outline some of the atrocities.

Ref

SEYMOUR M. HERSH, American soldiers brutalized Iraqis. How far up does the responsibility go?. The new Yorker30-04-2004

Human Right Watch

Did abuses go beyond Abu Ghraib?" CBS News, May 29, 2004

Kate Zernike, "Only a few spoke up on abuse as many soldiers stayed silent," *New York Times,* May 22, 2004.

Douglas Jehl and Andrea Elliott, "Cuba base sent its interrogators to Iraqi prison, New York Times, May 29, 2004

Douglas Jehl and Neil A Lewis "US disputed protected status of Iraq inmates" *New York Times* May 23 2004. See also, Alberto R. Gonzales, "The Rule of Law and the Rules of War," *New York Times*, May

R. Jeffrey Smith, "Memo gave intelligence bigger role: increased pressure sought on prisoners," *Washington Post*, May 21, 2004

Chris Hansen, "Profile: death in custody; investigation into death of Iraqi detainee Kareem Abdul Jaleel reveals more prison atrocities, NBC News Transcripts, May 23, 2004.

See Letter on HRW's Concerns about the Rights of Iraqi Detainees, February 10, 2004, http://hrw.org/english/docs/2004/02/10/iraq8471.htm.

Sewell Chan and Thomas E. Ricks, "Iraq prison supervisors face army reprimand," *Washington Post*, May 4, 2004.

Arthur Kane and Miles Moffeit, "Carson GI eyed in jail death Iraqi general died in custody," *Denver Post*, May 28, 2004.

Women in Abu-Ghraib

In a letter smuggled from the prison a woman wrote "Please, bomb us with bombs, and even with nuclear weapons, because we are all pregnant by American soldiers," reads one version of the letter. "Every day they walk us naked in front of soldiers and other prisoners. We want you to know that if you have a daughter in here, or a mother, or a sister, that she has been raped and is pregnant by these American soldiers."

The pictures would horrify anyone: hooded US soldiers raping and torturing naked Iraqi women at gunpoint. But for Farah al-Azzawi, these blurry photos burn with agony and shame. It is reported that members of the United States Congress were shown photographs of three American soldiers forcibly taking an Iraqi female detainee to an isolated spot and raping her collectively; Iraqi female detainees were forced at gun point to expose their breasts and other private body parts, made to disrobe in front of American soldiers and then photographed. And also in the Taguba report an American MP (military policeman) was pictured having sex with an Iraqi female detainee.

A particularly moving story is the following that was reported by The Guardian and Christian Science Monitor. Huda Alazawi was one of the few women held in solitary in the notorious Iraqi prison. Following her release, she spoke to Luke Harding 9from The Guardian) about her ordeal

In November 2003, 39-year-old Huda Alazawi, received a demand from an Iraqi, who was recruited as informant for the Americans in Adhamiya, district of Baghdad, which had seen continued hostility towards the occupation. He demanded $10,000. If otherwise, he would write a report to the occupation authorities claiming that she and her family were working for the Iraqi resistance. He wrote a report that prompted US soldiers to perform several raids on the families' house.

On December 23, the Americans arrested her other bother, Ayad, 44, she decided to confront the Americans directly. Alazawi was about to experience the reality of the Bush administration's "war on terror". Then she was arrested.

"They handcuffed me and blindfolded me and put a piece of white cloth over my eyes. They bundled me into a Humvee and took me to a place inside the palace. I was dumped in a room with a single wooden chair. It was extremely cold. After five hours they brought my sister in. I couldn't see anything but I could recognise her from her crying." "The US officer told us: 'If you don't confess we will torture you. So you have to confess.' Her three brothers were also arrested.

Like most Iraqi women, Huda was reluctant to talk about what she saw but says that her brother Mu'taz was brutally sexually assaulted. Then it was her turn to be interrogated. "The informant and an American officer were both in the room. The informant started talking. He said, 'You are the lady who funds your brothers to attack the Americans.' I speak some English so I replied: 'He is a liar.' Then she was hit by the American solder

Alazawi says that American guards then made her stand with her face against the wall for 12 hours. Afterwards they returned her to her cell. "The cell had no ceiling. It was raining. At midnight they threw something at my sister's feet. It was my brother Ayad. He was bleeding from his legs, knees and forehead. I told my sister: 'Find out if he's still breathing.' She said: 'No. Nothing I started crying. The next day they took away his body."

The US military later issued a death certificate, seen by the Guardian, citing the cause of death as "cardiac arrest of unknown aetiology". The American doctor who signed the certificate did not print his name, and his signature is illegible. The body was returned to the family four months later, on April 3, after the Abu Ghraib torture scandal broke. The family took photographs of the body, also seen by the Guardian, which revealed extensive bruising to the chest and arms, and a severe head wound above the left eye.

The US guard broke her shoulder as she left the lavatory, then she was transferred—first to a police academy in Baghdad's interior ministry and then, on January 4 2004, to Abu Ghraib prison. Alazawi, spent the next 156 days in solitary confinement. Along with five other Iraqi women, she was held in Abu Ghraib's infamous "hard site"

She said to Luke Hardy "The guards used wild dogs. I saw one of the guards allow his dog to bite a 14-year-old boy on the leg. The boy's name was Adel. Other guards frequently beat the men. I could see the blood running from their noses. They would also take them for compulsory cold showers even though it was January and February. From the very beginning, it was mental and psychological war." While in the prison, she managed to find a pen, and recorded incidents of abuse.

She evidently came across an old woman prisoner who had collapsed from hunger. She found some food in a packet in a bin and gave it to her. "They caught me and threw me in a one-metre-square punishment cell. They then poured cold water on me for four hours." She wrote the date of that as : February. 24. 2004.

In May, Major General Geoffrey Miller, assigned to Abu Ghraib by Washington in the aftermath of the torture scandal, escorted a large group of journalists around the prison for the first time. The previous night, Alazawi says, US guards evacuated all the juveniles and male detainees from her cellblock, leaving only her and a handful of other women upstairs.

Finally, on July 19, a helicopter took Alazawi to Al Taji, a military base just north of Baghdad. She was released free after 8 months.

"For a woman in an eastern society to spend months in US custody is very difficult," she said to Luke. Several of the other former women detainees in Abu Ghraib are believed to have disappeared; others have husbands who have also disowned them.

All the other women detainees, meanwhile, have refused to talk about their ordeal; she is the first to give testimony. As Iraq lurches from disaster to disaster, from kidnapping to suicide bombing, from insurgency towards civil war, from death to death, what does she think of the Americans now? "I hate them," she says.

Another Tragedy

Ms. Azzawi is part of a secret sisterhood: her mother is one of three women inside Abu Ghraib,. That's why some anonymous ill-wisher slipped a newspaper with the rape photos on the front page under her front door.

The pictures in the paper were fakes, bad copies lifted from a porn website and now circling around the Internet. But in Iraq, where the photos circulate on floppy discs and CDs and splash across newspapers and TV screens, most people believe them.

"I know they're not real, but people won't believe it," says Azzawi, a pretty 20-year-old, holding up the paper with a shaking hand. "Who's going to marry their daughters after they see a thing like that?". Among the 1,800 or so pictures taken by American soldiers at Abu Ghraib, there are others, viewed by Congress but not released to the public, of at least one Iraqi woman forced to bare her breasts. And a US military investigator Antonio Taguba, cited at least one case of a military police guard "having sex with" a female prisoner.

But in Iraq, where rumours alone can destroy a woman's reputation, the consequences of US detention are much more severe for women than for men

Now that there are real pictures of US troops sexually humiliating Iraqi women, reality and rumours have mixed together. Rumours of prison rape have been eddying for months. They started with a letter, allegedly smuggled out of Abu Ghraib by a female prisoner. Passed from one person to another In addition to citing numerous cases of violence at the hands of anti-occupation rebel factions, AI noted that Iraqi women have suffered torture and abuse at the hands of US forces. Huda Hafez Amad, reportedly one of the last women detainees released from Abu Ghraib prison, testified that she was hit in the face by US interrogators who made her stand for twelve hours with her face against a wall.

Luke Harding the Guardian Monday September 20, 2004
Annia Ciezadlo; Correspondent of the Christian Science Monitor May 28, 2004

31

Random actions

Ishaqi province (March 16, 2006)

In the heated battles between the insurgency and the American army, the innocent civilian people again fall victims to the conflict look at this story

Police and witnesses said eleven members of one family were killed in a US raid overnight in Ishaqi province north of Baghdad.

A senior Iraqi police officer said autopsies on the bodies, which included five children, showed each had been shot in the head, again execution style killing; you wonder what they did to deserve this.

The bodies of those children were shown on TV in addition to two men and four women in the morgue. All the children seemed younger than school age. Even there was an infant who had a large gaping wound in his head.

While the American army officials said they were targeting Alaqaeda militants; Ishaqi police said US forces had landed on the roof of one house and shot the 11 members of that family, autopsies shown that all had been shot in the back of the head. Their hands were bound and they were dumped in one room before the house was destroyed. There is no doubt that this was a crime, in fact the police has insisted to lay charges, but who cares.

Those days Saddam trial was aired on television (Saddam and others are facing charges of crimes against humanity for the killing of 148 Shiites after an assassination attempt in 1982 in Dujail. He was saying "I call on the people to start resisting the invaders instead of killing each other". When I heard this I was moved, perhaps it is the first time ever he said something realistic.

In those days Iraq came very close to civil war that was immediately in the aftermath of bombing AL-Imam Alhadi and AL-Askari golden top mosque in Samarra. Although religious leaders from both Sunnis and Shiites have denounced the action, this ignited a series of attacks and many people lost their lives. The Irony of that is we do seem to make excuses for killing each other and we as Iraqi people did not waste any chance to do that.

The ministry of the internal affairs

Ever since Jabr Sollagh was appointed Interior Minister after the January 2005 election brought a religious Shiite coalition to power, he surrounded himself with people who have been persecuted by Saddam, which left them angry and bitter, thirsty for revenge, they launched a secret assassination campaign. Sollagh was member of the Supreme Council for the Islamic Revolution in Iraq (supported by Iran) Sollagh fled to Iran in the 1970s to avoid Saddam's crackdown on the Daawa party members.

Sollagh background and experience with Saddam's regime has left him bitter and distrustful of anyone he suspects has ties to the previous regime. That would most certainly include the former members of Saddam's Special Forces and Republican Guards, the police force under Ayad Allawi was mainly formed from previous members of the republican guard, and that was the case when Sollagh came to the ministry of internal affairs.

To help facilitate his transformation of the police forces, Sollagh enlisted the help of armed wing of the Islamic Revolution, the Badr Organization. Members of the militia have been a growing presence in the National Police, which now consists of nine brigades, with about 17,500 members "Leadership and high rank positions has been turned over to Badr," "And new recruits are mostly Badr.".

When J Sollagh was first appointed Interior Minister, where Sunni men were killed execution-style by Interior Ministry police or Shiite militias. In each case, J Sollagh has said he ordered an investigation, and in each case the investigation had yet to report any findings.

In an interview with time magazine (4th, April, 2006) Jerry Burke, a former civilian senior police advisor to the Interior Ministry of the United States Said

"J Soullagh was at least indirectly responsible for the deaths of hundreds of military-age Sunni men whose bodies have turned up at the sewage plant in southeast Baghdad since late December. Men in police uniforms and vehicles routinely travel through the city in daylight hours with bodies in the back of trucks for disposal at the sewage plant, he said. Prisoners often disappear, because they're picked up at night and no one has an accurate account of who is arrested and where they are taken. "The Special Police Commandos," he said, "are most definitely out of control."

Perhaps one of the highlights of the era of the American occupation is the ministry of internal affairs and its infamous minister (Jabr Soullagh). They have the National Guard force, which is a police force that was built after the fall of Saddam. They are trained locally by the Americans to control the local security.

It is ruled mainly by people who were refugees in many countries mainly Iran, mostly they belong to the Islamic Daawa party; the force is a significant authority these days, they patrol the streets usually with the American army, but they have the initiative to conduct raids on suspected terrorists round them up and detain them.

Horror stories started coming up soon after the formation of that guard. They evidently have secret jails, some of them were eventually discovered like the one in AL-Jadiriah section in Baghdad, where people were held, tortured and abused. Unverified stories about using drill to drill the bones and skulls of the detainees in order to squeeze a confession out of them

Going back to the roots of the civil society in Iraq there had been some form of ethnic based hatred between different sectors of the society, it is true that we do not admit it in public, but it is there and only surface very quick at times of difficulties, the strange mix of the society did not help at all.

Added to that the rule of Saddam had fuelled the sectarian discrimination by his irrational policies During that era we all witnessed that everything is done by violence, the only way we as a society dealt with differences and conflicts is by force.

Soullagh and his internal ministry was a natural product of the preceding era. Saddam and his thug ruled for 35 years, changed the standards of the society, built that hatred between the Sunnis and the Shiites. The conduct of the internal ministry was nothing but shameful, whatever we had from abuse for human rights in Saddam time has again repeated itself and even worse, I wonder how unlucky could we be?

The interior ministry had what seems to be an offshoot branch of a well trained militia specialised in people abduction, torture and execution for variety of reasons. We all agree that Saddam was a coward who hid himself behind all the atrocities he did, but you got to respect him (in a hind sight) at least he admitted that. The enemy now is actually not known. The motivations are not always clear.

When people walk in Baghdad streets the risks are many and it is a lucky day if you escape unhurt. The risk could be a roadside bomb, a suicide attempt by some brain washed teenager, an attack on or by American envoy, the army of the internal ministry, the paramilitary militia, or simply you get caught in the middle of the fire.

Baghdad is not the House of Peace (as it is used to be called), it is rather the house of massacres.

Many of the 110,000 policemen under the ministry's control are suspected of being members of the Badr Brigade. The counter-insurgency units such as the Wolf Brigade, the Scorpions and the Tigers, also the commandos and even the highway patrol police have been accused of acting as death squads.

32

Post war clerics and politics

Moqtada AL-sadr

A very controversial figure in Najaf; son of Muhammad Sadiq AL-Sadr (known Shiites religious authority assassinated in 1999), reportedly by agents of the Iraqi intelligence Moqtada Sadr was virtually unknown outside Iraq before the American invasion in March 2003. Moqtada is in his early thirties when he appeared on the radar of the political scene in Iraq, no one heard of him before. He is radical with extreme and unstable views, certainly very confusing to analyse. At the first instance he called for a national rebellion against Anglo-American occupation and sent out his (AL-Mahdi) militiamen to confront the invaders and they clashed several times with the occupying armies as well as the Iraqi police. At others he has seemed more compromising, seeking for a political role within the new Iraq.

The Sadr name clearly has powerful influence in the society; of Baghdad. Saddam City was renamed AL-Sadr City after the fall of the Baathist government. In Baghdad.

Moqtada AL—Sadr has built on his father's reputation and created AL-mahdi militia that has overshadowed most of Shiite authorities, who have remained largely silent and supported the occupation on the premises they get to rule the country.

In June 2003 he established the Mahdi Army, in defiance of the American forces, pledging to protect the Shiites religious authorities in the holy city of Najaf. He also set up a weekly newspaper, (Al-Hawzah). The US-led authorities imposed a ban on the paper in March 2004, accusing it of inciting anti-US violence.

He and his followers seem to believe that he is a religious leader, however that does not sit well with the general populace feeling about Ayatollah who is usually old and experienced.

Moqtada al-Sadr doctrines are mixture of, and oscillate between Iraqi nationalism and Shia radicalism. He surrounded himself by many of Iraq's poor Shiites Muslims. He certainly actively sought to stand out and gave many Fatwa that contradict the will of the highest Shiite Authority (ayatollah Al-Sistani) probably felt that will make him more appealing to the majority of the Shiites Iraqi population.

This man may have been actually accomplice to a murder of a prominent religious Imam (Abdul Majid al-Khoei), who was attacked soon after the American invasion, Abdul Majid al-Khoei was in Britain and Tony Blair had views of him as possible future leader. He was moderate well acculturated man, and probably had no radical views. He was attacked and killed by stabbing in Najaf. A relative of AL-Sader was charged with his murder.

The unexplained problem is that Al-Sader was also charged and there was an arrest warrant on him for that particular case; however neither the occupation nor the Iraqi authorities have followed suit. He remained free sticking his head every now and then to make some noise. Probably the American wanted to calm the waters by not prosecuting him, else they will face civil riot, which might make unstable situation even more volatile.

He is also known for his fiery rhetoric speeches against the presence of foreign troops in Iraq. Moqtada AL-Sader has led uprisings against US forces centred on Najaf.

Using the sentiments of the common people Moqtada demanded that the occupying army leave the Najaf city, he threatened with suicide attacks against American forces if they try to displace him out of Najaf

On 05 August 2004 Moqtada al-Sadr called on his militia to rise up and fight the American occupying troops. The message comes as clashes broke out in at least three cities between his supporters and US and Iraqi security forces.

By August 2004 the US military that 300 men from the Mahdi army were killed in the city of Najaf in two days of fighting. Heavy fighting has also erupted in the streets of Sadr City in Baghdad, at least 19 people have been reportedly killed over the same period. Sadr's spokesmen sent mixed messages, one saying al-Sadr wanted to truce with the Americans, and another saying he had declared America the enemy and urged Iraqi people to resist the occupation..

Fighting began in April 2004 that battle was nothing but a disaster for the people of Najaf, large number of his militiamen was killed and the city citizens were forced to leave because of the ongoing conflict and lack of life necessities. Fragile truce was agreed upon after the mediation of Grand Ayatollah Ali Sistani.

Fresh clashes erupted in the holy city of Najaf in early August 2004, which again required the ayatollah's intervention.

His supporters (AL-Mahdi militia) have also clashed with the mainstream Shiites supporters of Ayatollah Sistani, who has become very influential in the run-up to the handover of power to Iraqis on 30 June 2005.

Moqtada Sadr's appeal to the poor accounts for much of his popularity among the Shiites, the Sunnis also saw him as a useful power to oppose the majority political leaders who are endorsed by Sistani. A lot of Iraqis also see him as symbol of resistance to the American occupation.

Previously, Moqtada al-Sadr has rejected invitations to participate in a national conference to facilitate the formation of a national government, and had not indicated any willingness to take part in the elections scheduled for January (2005). Al-Sadr vowed on 9 August(2005) to fight until the "last drop of blood" is spilled. Latter in August 2005, Muqtada al-Sadr called for a nationwide cease-fire and announced that he would join the political process in the following days. The announcement followed discussions between al-Sadr and the Iraqi government as well as coalition officials.

His alliance with the Sunnis was clear as he supported the rebels in their fight in Fallujah, he supported with money, food and arms; however due to his unstable stance they found him unreliable and dangerous. Their fears were further fuelled in the bloody two days after the attack that followed the bombing of Imams in Samara, when Iraq became a slaughterhouse, Shiites and Sunnis are killing each other. Militiamen from Moqtada al-Sadr's Mahdi Army vandalised Sunni mosques and swarmed over Sunni neighbourhoods.

There is clear evidence that the Mahdi militiamen were involved in the abduction and torture and summary executions of their enemies mostly from the Sunni section of Baghdad community

Abdul Majid al-Khoei

Abdul-Majid was born in Najaf. During the Shiites uprising of 1991 he acted as a moderator attempting to minimize the crisis and the consequences of revenge killings. When the uprising was crushed he was forced to leave Iraq.

In London he founded the al-Khoei Foundation a charitable foundation set up by his father, became the head of the foundation in 1994. He was also an outspoken critic of Saddam Hussein's rule: "The regime's criminal acts, beginning in 1968, have been never-ending. Executions, the closing of schools, mosques and shrines sacred to Shiites worshipers; the burning of old religious scriptures; looting the sacred sites of gifts left by presidents and kings."

He returned to Iraq in April 2003 after the fall of Baghdad despite being warned of the dangers. Though assigned protection, the protective unit could not follow him into the shrine of Imam Ali in Najaf on April 12, 2003. Here he was attacked and hacked to death.

Moqtada al-Sadr was suspected by U.S. and Iraqi authorities of ordering the assassination. According to witnesses, at the mosque they were confronted by an angry mob, some of whom are reported to have shouted "Raifee is back" and others "Long lives al-Sadr". The mob killed Raifee with knives; al-Khoei was chased down and killed in an alley near the nearby headquarters of al-Sadr.

Al-Sadr claims the murderers were not his followers and that he sent men to protect al-Khoei, he seemed unconcerned over the death. Additionally witnesses say that members of the mob claimed to be there on al-Sadr's orders, and that he had instructed them not to kill al-Khoei inside the mosque. Al-Khoei's followers publicly blamed Baath party members who also hated al-Khoei. On April 5, 2004, a warrant was issued for Sadr's arrest in connection with this killing.

Sistani

Ali al-Sistani was born in Mashhad, Iran to a family of religious scholars. His grandfather, for whom he was named, was a famous scholar who had studied at Najaf. Sistani's family comes from the area of Iran known as Sistan. Sistani began his Islamic education as a child in Mashhad and then moved to Qom in central Iran. After spending a few years inn Qom, he went to Iraq to study in Najaf under Grand Ayatollah Abul-Qassim Khoei.

There Sistani settled down, he raised a family and became essentially a member of Najaf community. He was certified as a mujtahid by Khoei in the 1960s. Among other things, Sistani follows Khoei's belief of separating the religion from the state. Subsequently he kept out of great political involvement. That line of theoughts probably saved him from being persecuted by the ruling Baath Party. However, he was imprisoned after the Rebellion of the south of Iraq that followed the war of Kwait invasion and the subsequent Gulf War. He was the target of a number of assassination attempts during the 1990s.

Khoei died in 1992, but not before naming Sistani as his replacement. Ayatollah Sistani cemented his relationship as successor to Khoei by leading the funeral prayers of his teacher. Khoei's death brought Sistani as the most respected of the Shiite Ayatollahs in Iraq. His position was contested by other clerics, including Mohammad Sadeq al-Sadr, but his role as successor to the legacy of Abdul-Qassem Khoei gave him an edge. His authoritywas further established after the assassination of Sadr by Saddam Hussein.

Sistani oversees sums of millions of dollars from Zakat, which he distributes in many ways, including payment for the religious education across the Muslim world, helping the poor and the needy..

While Sistani had survived the persecution that killed many other Shiites clerics, his mosque was shut down in 1994, and did not reopen until after the American invasion. Since around that time, he has usually stayed at his house in Najaf, probably to avoid persecution. Despite his seclusion, Sistani exerts control over the Shiites population of Iraq, and is seen as the leader of the majority. It is because of this influence that he continues to play an important role in the current politics of Iraq.

In early August 2004, Ayatollah Sistani, had suffered serious heart problems. He had been transported to London for medical treatment. On August 25, Ayatollah Sistani returned from London and facilitated an agreement that ended the standoff in Najaf between the American occupying army and Muqtada AL-Sadr's Mahdi militia.

Role after the invasion

Since the American invasion of Iraq in 2003, Sistani has played a heavy role in the political lirfe in Iraq. Western media universally call him the most politically influential figure in post-invasion Iraq. On the Eve of the 2003 invasion, His fatwa as the Shia Supreme leader to Iraqis not to resist the occupation forces resulted in swift victory for the allied forces. This decision, although is very pragmatic given the overwhilming american power, was not congrous with the orthodex doctrine of Islam, which is clearly against foreign occupation.

Muqtada al-Sadr, who is a young clric and the head of an independent militia known as the Mahdi army, has risen to prominence in the course of 2004 and is often referred to as a potential rival, but the two overcame considerable tensions to agree on a common representatives of Shiite candidates in the elections of Jan. 2005. Observers note that their social base is quite different, with Sistani's support strong among the majority of Iraqi Shiite, and Muqtada was driving his support from the urban poor shiite society, who provide most of the members of the Mehdi army.

Immediately after the American invasion, Sistani issued fatwa calling on Shiite religious leadersnot to get involved in politics. However, as the summer of 2003 approached, Sistani became more involved, though always through representatives, never directly. his increased political activities since 2003 was usually through representatives, has been interpreted as a response the dire and deteriorating conditions in Iraq.

He called for the formation of a constitutional convention, and later demanded a direct vote for the purpose of forming a transitional government, seeing this as a sure path to Shiite dominance over Iraq's government, since most institutions say that Shiites make up 60% of Iraq's population. Sistani had criticized American occupation for appointing an interim Iraqi government as not being democratic enough.

Sistani's rulings and Fatwas have provided many Iraqi Shiite backing for participating in the January 2005 elections—he urged, in a statement on October 1, 2004, that the people should realize that this was an "important matter" and he hoped that the elections would be "free and fair…with the cance of participation of all Iraqis". Sistani's message is that Iraqis have a religious obligation to vote.

He called upon the Shites not to respond to the violent attcks of suicidal bombing Which became commonplace in the middle part of Iraq, particularly the area south of Baghdad known as the "triangle of death". This insistence on non-violence earned him a nomination for the 2005 Nobel Peace Prize.

One of the most important rivals for the Hawza (the highest religious authority of the shiite in Iraq) was Mohammed Baqir al-Sadr, who was assassinated in 1999 along with two of his sons (Saddam's secrete Mukhabarat are suspects of his murder). Sadr preferred the more vilent, Khomeini-like tradition, urging secret resistance against Saddam's rule. Sadr and other critics portrayed Sistani as a coward and referred to him as the "silent authority,". Sadr's son Muqtada has positioned himself as a rival to Sistani.

Al-Sustain is a reasonable religious figure who is capable of weighing the difficulties before him, which does guarantee that Iraq will not be led toward some adventures with unknown consequences. This does not imply surrender, but the patience and wisdom necessary to achieve independence and sovereignty.

He favors an Islamic state, but not a theocracy as in neighboring Iran. Sistani has said that no law in Iraq should conflict with Islamic principles, and he wants Islam to be recognized in law as the religion of the majority of Iraqis. Sistani supports an Islamic state that has elections, freedom of religion, and other civil liberties. The essence of Al-Sistani's position is that the Iraqis do not need to resort to violence to acquire their rights as long as they have peaceful means available to them. But should these means no longer be available, then other means, including armed resistance should be used.

The religious figure, after consulting and meeting with the Governing Council, has insisted on holding elections. Al-Sistani has also urged a bigger role for the United Nations. Ambassador Paul Bremer] received the news with dismay. [U.N. Secretary General Kofi] Annan, on the other hand, welcomed the initiative and invited the Governing Council for a meeting in New York in the presence of Bremer.

clash with the United States

After their experience with Khomeini, whose popularity they thought was just a passing phase in the Iranian revolution, the Americans recognized Al-Sistani's strong position in Iraq. Initially it was thought that Al-Sistani lacked a clear political vision for Iraq, which was in fact a position of influence over a large sector of the Iraqi society. The American policy makers were very cautious dealing with Al-Sistani and respected his opinions.

In June 2003, he issued a *Fatwa*, stating that the framers of Iraq's constitution had to be elected, not appointed, by U.S. officials and members of the Iraqi Governing Council.

In November 2003, he issued a statement saying that elections—not a system of regional caucuses suggested by the U.S.-led coalition authorities—would be the proper way to select a transitional government. He also demanded U.N. involvement in supervising the election process. In another difference with U.S. plans, Sistani called for a transitional assembly to ratify an interim constitution drafted by the Iraqi Governing Council and to define the terms under which U.S. and allied troops would remain in Iraq after sovereignty was handed over June 28. All of Sistani's views have been accommodated.

The Iranian revolution had opened a new doctrine about the leartion between relegion and the form of the state. Ayatollah Khomeini was a proponent of an Islamic political theory that emerged in the mid-20th century called (w*elayat Al-faqeeh)*, which means that the government is headed by the most senior religious authority. Sistani has long favoured and practiced the quietist, or being moderate, which means the religious authority is seprate from the state, this incliniation and the fact that he holds so much power made him very respectable to the American official.

His view on elections as being the most legitimate expression of the will of the people. If chosen through elections, "the parliament would spring from the will of the Iraqis and would represent them in a just manner and would prevent any diminution of Islamic law," he wrote in his November 2003 Fatwa statement. This approch almost gurantees that the government will run by shiites.

Sistani had rejected the Iraqi Governing Council's (IGC) proposal to allow for the transfer of power to an interim government, which would not be elected by Iraqis but appointed by a transitional council comprised of IGC-appointed representatives. Followers of al-Sistani had organised very large demonstrations, calling on the Americans to allow for open elections.

(SCIRI

The Supreme Council for the Islamic Revolution in Iraq (SCIRI) was established in 1982 in Iran by the late Mohammed Baqir Ai-Hakim (who was assassinated in Najaf 2003). Its main aim is to apply the concept of the "Islamic Revolution" from Iran. Their doctrine is Shiite Islamic scholar should be the head of the state (a theocracy led by Shiites Ayatollah). Abdul Aziz Al-Hakim (brother of Baqir) was deputy leader of SCIRI, was a part of the nine-member rotating presidency in the interim leadership. Their popular background is the Shiites inn middle and south Iraq.

However, many Shiites Muslims are terrified of their radical backward views and of the consequences of having them in power. Al-Hakim, Allegedly was responsible for torturing and executing Iraqi POWs in Iran through the Iran-Iraq war and afterward. It has been reported that some prisoners of war were given the choice of working for AL-Hakim or being accused as Baathists and were tortured for refusing to join SCIRI.

Ever since entering Iraq, Al-Hakim had the upper hand in Iraqi politics and the CPA in Baghdad with his major Shiites followers in Iraq'. He entered Iraq with their Badr's Army'. This 'army' is composed of thousands of Iraqi extremists led by Iranians and trained in Iran. During the American invasion they were stationed on the Iraqi-Iranian border, waiting for the end of combat to go inside. In Baghdad, and the south, they have been a source of terror and anxiety to Sunnis and Shiites alike. They were responsible for a large portion of the looting and the burning. They were allegedly involved and probably responsible for hundreds of religious and political abductions and assassinations.

29 August 2003 And Mohammed Baqir Al-Hakim of the Supreme Council of the Islamic Revolution in Iraq (SCIRI founder and leader) was assassinated in the holy city of Najaf. It was not known who was behind his assassination, but many believe it is one of the other Shiites fundamental religious factions. There has been some tension between Al-Sadir's followers and Al-Hakim's followers.

Iraqi Shiites in the south lost hundreds of thousands of lives to the war against Iran—fighting the very regime that is backing SCIRI now—the Islamic Revolution in Teheran. Al-Hakim does have a strong backing from many Shiites fundamentalists who are mostly seen as loyal to Iran, but he also has people who hate him and hate his Badr brigade..

Chalabi

Ahmed Chalabi, the head of the Iraqi National Congress, (INC) was born in 1945 to a Shiite family, known for its banking business and fraud. Some members of his family held governmental positions in Iraq after World War I. He was only 11 years old when he left Iraq in 1956 and spent most of his life in the US or Britain. After studying mathematics at the University of Chicago and the Massachusetts Institute of Technology, he went to Lebanon. There he worked in the American University until the 1975. Chalabi then moved to Amman, and had established unique relations with Prince Al-Hassan. His political career is tainted by his adventures that started with robbing a bank, he does not feel awkward robbing entire country.

Chalabi's relations with politics and economy enabled him to found the private Bank of Batra'a in 1977, which became the second largest private bank in Jordan. It collapsed in 1989 in one of the most infamous scandals of corruption, which cost Jordan $300 million US dollars. He was accused of theft and ran away to Syria, then to Britain where he founded the Iraqi National Congress.

He moved to the politics, claiming the role of Iraqi dissident who is opposing the regime of Saddam Hussein, while never been under that rule. The Jordanian Justice System charged Chalabi with fraud and embezzlement and he was sentenced in absentia to 22 years in prison with hard labour. Since then, Chalabi has been one of the most wanted by the Jordanian Justice Authority. Although he tried to defend himself and repeatedly claimed innocence, he insisted that the plot was a conspiracy fabricated by Saddam's regime.

The American State had revelled that the amount of money provided to finance the Iraqi National Congress, several million dollars, was mostly reported under the item Office Decorations and Gymnasium Expenses!!.

Although Chalabi immigrated to the US to study mathematics and practiced for a while in the academic sector, he became a politician. His network of contacts mainly consisted of politicians, in particular those who were known for their extremist attitudes towards the Arab countries, including his alleged mysterious relations to Israel.

He established great relations with the hawks in Washington, the Pentagon and the CIA such as Richard Pearl, former assistant to Secretary of Defence Donald Rumsfeld and former CIA director James Woolsey, in addition to relations with congressmen from both sides of the aisle.

He used all these relations to found the Iraqi National Congress in 1992 with strong support from the US. In 1995, he managed to convince the Clinton Administration of the possibility of ousting Saddam Hussein via the Kurdish opposition. He accordingly returned to Iraq to lead the Kurds' rebellion in the Kurdish Northern, which failed miserably.

Latter he managed to win the sympathy of those who upheld war on Iraq and gathered support inside Congress to issue the Iraqi Liberation Act in 1998. The Act approved of a plan to provide $100 million to the Iraqi Opposition, on top of which was the Iraqi National Congress.

In 2002 the American Administration was assured that a military offensive would take place against Iraq. Chalabi's name reappeared as the main opposition leader nominated replace Saddam's regime.

The biggest issue of criticism drawn on Chalabi was that he always expresses his desire to establish friendly relationships with Israel. He openly discussed his relations with the Jewish Institute in Washington, which influences issues of American national security. He also has tried to exploit the Shiite issue, since they are the majority, given that fact that the Americans wanted majority rule. He established relations with the religious leaders of the Shiites living in exile in London, on the other side he was talking to the liberals. By the time he made membership of the Iraqi National Congress available to the Kurds, he was establishing strong relations with the Turkmen's (usually enemies of the Kurds). Chalabi was the first Iraqi opposition person acknowledged by Ankara where he met Muhammad Ali Shahin, Vice Prime Minister, before the American invasion of the country.

He repeatedly said that he visualizes a "new federation, diversity, a parliamentary skeleton, and a new pattern similar to the one in the US and Germany". After the invasion he was disappointed, the friends of yesterday had not fulfilled their promises, they have denied him a request to establish an interim government and threatened to stop their financial aid if Chalabi declared the formation of such a government.

Some American officials eventually saw Chalabi as an impostor, as he had led the American Administration to believe that an Iraqi military coup would take place on the Iraqi borders as soon as the US began its war on Iraq; and perhaps had led them to believe that Saddam had weapons of mass destruction. Of course there was fierce resistance tot the US aggression in the south. Other officials see that the reason behind the American rejection of Chalabi lies in his being despised by the other opposition groups and political entities inside Iraq.

After the invasion Ahmed Chalabi, became used to manoeuvring, he responded fiercely to the American stance towards him, accusing the US in a CNN interview of hesitating to provide aid and security to his country.

Soon afterwards, Chalabi changed his tone and announced that he would not assume a fundamental role in any future government in Iraq. He announced, "I don't seek to become president of Iraq; I don't look for official positions, and my mission comes to an end when Iraq is freed from Saddam Hussein's regime."

Soon after that, he was on board an American aircraft heading for Al-Nasyria, south of Iraq, to participate in the conference held to discuss the political future of the country. The demonstrations that broke out against the conference and against any US-sponsored government discouraged him from attending.

People in Baghdad had witnessed his followers looting the public offices and ministries, in particular those with relation to the previous intelligence, and started selling those documents with relation to people who disappeared during Saddam time. Desperate families who wanted to find what happened to their loved ones bought those documents. His followers had confiscated public buildings and made it their headquarters in Baghdad.

An ex-bodyguard complained that when the Chalabi group (INC) first came into Baghdad, they recruiting people, they seemed reasonable. Suddenly, they had overtaken one of the top recreational and cultural Baghdad clubs and turned the INC into a militia and that particular club building as its headquarters. They were hijacking cars in Baghdad during April, May and June 2003, claiming that the cars they were confiscating at gunpoint were 'looted'. The cars were kept in the 'headquarters' and smuggled out of Iraq and to the north of Iraq Kurdish territory. The nicer ones were split amongst the 'members' of the INC. Someone who wasn't getting a share in the booty complained to the CPA and Al-Chalabi was warned not to do that again.

Dreaming of power, which has almost turned into a mirage, Ahmed Chalabi still manoeuvres, unmindful of the fact that he has already become unwanted by everybody, including his American old friends.

33

Women Life under the Occupation

Female detainees were subjected to sexual abuse at Abu Ghraib, and a male Military Police guard raped at least one, according to a report issued in 2004 by Major General Antonio Taguba. US-led forces have also illegally detained Iraqi women and held them as "bargaining chips" in efforts to convince male relatives to turn themselves in or admit involvement in the resistance activities.

To add further to the complexity; Iraqi women who hold important positions, women activists and those who do not abide by strict Islamic dress codes, have become the targets of violence from Islamic extremists.

Acts of violence and intimidation have caused many Iraqi women to withdraw from public life, according to report by Amnesty International (AI). Titled "*Iraq: Decades of Suffering, Now Women Deserve Better,*" the AI report concluded that, on the whole, conditions for women were no better under Iraq's US occupation than they were under Saddam.

Iraq under the invasion has been a mess with loss of security and freedom, on the other hand secular Iraqis fear the second product of the occupation (extremism), fundamentalist militants and the prospect of fundamentalist religious rule.

The year 2005 had seen the murders of several Iraqi women who had been active in human rights, government service and business, combined with the ongoing economic crisis under the occupation and rising suggest that conditions for women in Iraq continue will continue to deteriorate.
Top of Form

Bottom of Form

On a highway near Baghdad recently, the body of pharmacist and women's rights activist Zeena Al-Qushtaini turned up ten days after she was abducted by unknown assailants who had taken her at gunpoint from her pharmacy. She was killed in execution style. Reuters reported that pinned to her clothes was a message that says, "She was a collaborator against Islam,".. The United Nations humanitarian news service, reports that decapitated female corpses has turned up recently, many accompanied by notes similar to the one attached to Al-Qushtaini. Other stories of extreme violence against women are becoming very common. In Mosul, Islamic militants have killed twenty women, most of them professionals and students.

In Basra dozens of armed men attacked college students enjoying a spring picnic. The students' crimes was socializing and playing secular music. Students who escaped the scene say the attackers were members of Shiite cleric Muqtada Al-Sadr's Mehdi militia. Sheik Ahmed Al-Basri, an Al-Sadr loyalist, reportedly said after the incident "We beat them because we are authorized by [God] to do so, and that is our duty". Also targeted were women working for humanitarian agencies. Women have been targeted simply because-Taliban style fundamentalists thought they are talking too much in public.

Women in Baghdad feel under siege in their own suburbs, which have been overrun by gangs and insurgents. There are even warnings in some parts of Iraq warning women not to go out in public without covering their head and face. Those who defy the warning will be punished by death. As a result, many women who never wore traditional clothing are putting on the *hijab* and the *Abaya* before leaving their homes.

Some secular women say they will continue to wear Western-style clothing in defiance of the fundamentalists, while others choose to play it safe. Women blame the "American liberation"; during Saddam time there was no place for the fundamentalists.

Beyond immediate violence, many Iraqi women fear that the rise of Islamic fundamentalism will result in the imposition of law, or *Sharia*, which could take the place of Iraq's long-standing Personal Status Law, a secular civil code that was based on the French law and instituted in 1958 and maintained through the Saddam years. The Personal Status Law in Iraq is considered very progressive compared with the social decrees of other Middle Eastern countries.

Females can no longer leave homes not accompanied by a male relative. The society had gone back hundreds of years. A woman who ventures outside home alone risks anything from harassment to abduction. Women have to plan carefully in this state of total lawlessness. The situation became incredibly difficult to working females and those who go to university. Before the war, around 50% of the college students were females, and over 50% of the working force was composed of women. But not anymore we are seeing an increase of fundamentalism in Iraq which is terrifying.

Before the war about 55% of females in Baghdad wore a hijab (headscarf that covers the hair and neck of women). Hijabs do not signify fundamentalism, it is rather part of the culture. The Burqa (which covers the entire female body) is not part of the Iraqi culture, however with rising with the rising fundamentalism

Iraqi women who used to wear western style clothes pf Jeans and short sleeves are not able to do that anymore, a long skirt and loose shirt with long sleeves became necessary to avoid harassment. Women wearing jeans or other types of pants risks being attacked, abducted fundamentalists, many instances of this kind had been reported to occur around the country and particularly in Baghdad.

Many women lost their jobs for this reason. Girls are being forced to quit schools. Because the Supreme Council of the Islamic Revolution in Iraq and other radical groups are patrolling streets and overseeing schools and coercing girls to abide by strict dress codes

Men in black turbans and dressed in all black, head to foot, observe schools, scanning the girls, sometimes jeering at the ones not wearing a hijab or whose skirts aren't long enough. In some areas, girls risk being attacked with acid if their clothes aren't 'proper'.

A few Mullahs declared 'fatwa', in June 2003 that declared all females should wear the hijab and if they didn't, they could be subject to 'punishment'. Another issued a decree that no single girl over the age of 14 could remain unmarried—even if it meant that some members of the Hawza would have to have two, three or four wives.

This decree included females of other religions. In the south, female UN and Red Cross aides received death threats if they didn't wear the hijab

Iraqi women rights

Women in Iraq were a lot better off than females in other parts of the Arab world (and even some parts of the Western world). They made up over 50% of the working force as doctors, lawyers, nurses, teachers etc they had reasonable freedom. They dressed in the manner they wanted (within the boundaries and restrictions of a conservative society).

It has been estimated in report of Middle East newspaper in Jordan that 2.3 million Iraqi women have been widowed as a result of the wars and the recent violence. Since the fall of Saddam, Iraqi women had complained, their freedoms had gradually been eroded, not by official dictatorship but by religious radicals who had invaded hospitals, universities and schools, insisting that women wore headscarves and behaved as men think was respectable behaviour.

Before the elections of 2005 educated women and men alike were fearful that the rise of fundamentalism of both Shiites and Sunnis was going to robe women their freedom, hence many middle-class and professional people had voted for the secular group headed by Ayad Allawi mainly because of the fear of what would happen if the 'religious' Shiite list swept the majority.

However Allawi and the secular views he represented have lost the elections t to a new sense of religiosity and resurgence of tribal authority that is on the march across most of the Arabic part of Iraq.

The principal of equality that existed in what was once one of the most secular countries in the Middle East's, which protected women's rights even in the midst of Saddam's atrocities, is now under threat even under the new constitution.

The major Shiites religious parties want to replace the civil law that now governs marriage, divorce, child custody and inheritance with Sharia law. A draft of the constitution published in the newspaper run by the Supreme Council for Islamic Revolution in Iraq frames sexual equality specifically in terms of 'the provisions of Islamic Sharia' rather than Iraq's civil legal code. Even if, as has been suggested, the new constitution results in a parallel system where women can choose Sharia or the civil code, women's rights groups are worried they may be forced by male relatives to choose a system that is not in their interests.

In a country where the most basic human rights—to life, freedom from intimidation, freedom from torture, a fair judicial process, and freedom of confession—are routinely abused, the issue of women's rights is low priority.

Female circumcision apparently had resurfaced in north Iraq. Hasira in Kirkuk (northeast Iraq) and its people have become noted for presenting the first statistical evidence in Iraq of the existence of female circumcision, or female genital mutilation (FGM), as critics call it. Thomas von der Osten-Sacken, director of a German nongovernmental organization called WADI "We knew Hasira and nearby villages was one of the areas most affected by the practice,"

Of 1,554 women and girls over 10 years old interviewed by WADI's local medical team, 907, or more than 60 percent, said they had had the operation. But while this practice was suspected in the region, there was never solid proof that the procedure was so prevalent.

A farmer's wife from the nearby village of Milkhasim, she says she learned the techniques from her neighbour, and took over when she stopped performing the operation. "June is the best time of the year," she says, "and the best age for patients is between 3 and 8."

Islamic scholars have variable views on female circumcision. According to the Shafii School (Mainstream Sunnis), circumcision is obligatory for both men and women. The Hanbali (another Sunni School) say it is obligatory only for men." In recent times Shafii Scholars had presented A Fatwa against female circumcision. In Hasira village information is extremely slow to filter through the population. Women are still thought to be promiscuous if they were not circumcised.

Minorities

Christians have become the victims of extremism also. Some of them are being threatened, others are being attacked. Liquor stores are being attacked and bombed. The owner usually gets a 'threat' in the form of a fatwa claiming that if they didn't shut down the store permanently, there would be consequences, which is usually either a fire, or a bomb. Similar threats have been made to hairdressers in some areas in Baghdad.

Security

For a while after the fall of Baghdad, men in residential neighbourhood began arranging 'lookouts' to protect there area from looting and to keep people safe. They would gather in groups, in a street, armed with AK 47s, and watch out for the entire neighbourhood. They would challenge strangers and ask who they were and what they are there for. Hundreds of looters were caught that way and for a short while people felt safe for a brief period. Then the American armoured vehicles started patrolling residential areas, ordering the men off the streets—telling them that if they were seen carrying a weapon, they would be treated as criminals.

The new Iraq era had seen a surge of gangs of robbers and killers for all kinds of reasons. Organised crimes became a commonplace in a city that had no such experience before. Most of the gangs, particularly those in Baghdad, originate from slums on the outskirts of the city; some of them are notorious for poverty and unemployment and low morals. The previous Saddam city is one such example, it is terrifying. Lost cars or even people, you will most likely find them there. Every street is under control by a certain gang, weapons are sold in the streets. Americans don't bother raiding the houses in areas like that. American raids are exclusively for decent people who can't shoot back or attack under the excuse for being part of the resistance. The following incid3etn happened June 2006-06-06

Salhiya area in Baghdad has been particularly busy since the war because people who want to leave to Jordan and Syria all make their reservations from travel agencies in that area. According to eyewitnesses, around 15 police cars pulled up and men dressed in uniforms began pulling civilians off the streets and from cars, throwing bags over their heads and herding them into the cars. Anyone who tried to object was beaten. The total number of people taken away is estimated to be around 50.

This has been happening all over Iraq—mysterious men who work for Ministry of Interior rounding up civilians and taking them away. The disturbing thing is that the Iraqi Ministry of Interior has denied that it had anything to do with this; probably to avoid human rights organizations criticism about mass detentions, torture and assassinations. It is likely that these people will probably be found dead in a matter of few days.

Unemployment

Over 65% of the Iraqi working force is unemployed. It started with Bremer's horrible decisions, to dissolve the Iraqi army, which left 400,000 armed men with families to feed.

Young men unemployed roam the streets looking for work, looking for an answer. They are perplexed, angry and uncertain about tomorrow. The CPA had also dissolved the Ministry of Information and the Ministry of Defences and other institutions. These institutions were full of regular people with usual jobs, engineers, accountants, technicians etc.. These people are now jobless. Companies have been asked to 'cut down' their staff to reduce expenses on the other hand it left more jobless people. Other companies, firms, bureaus, factories and shops shut down as a result of the looting and damage done in the post-war chaos. The salary of employed people is average $50, which is not enough to support one person, let alone a family.

For weeks, after the occupation, men would line up daily by the thousands outside of the governmental offices applying for jobs and begging for work, but there is no work. Men were not willing to apply to the Iraqi police force because they weren't given weapons, and the resistance and the extremists are targeting the police. The Iraqi police were expected to roam and guard the hellish cities without weapons...to stop looters and abductors and to deal with the increasing resistance.

Ref

Chris Shumway the new standard Mar. 30, 2005

http://www.brusselstribunal.org/)

34

Turmoil

The national police as the new age tormentor of the Iraqi people

On Monday, third, April 2006;34 corpses were found.15 more men were found on next day, those were all men between 20 and 40 years of age; they were discovered dead in the back of a white truck in the Al-Khadra district of (mainly Sunni neighbourhood in the western part of Baghdad). Those men have hanged. Those were all Sunnis abducted earlier by armed men wearing the Iraqi police uniform.

The next day 40 more bodies were found scattered in different parts of the capital city, most of them had signs of torture before they were killed (bullet in the head execution-style).

There was another horrific scene; there was a mass grave in the Shiites neighbourhood of AL—Kamaliyah in eastern part of Baghdad containing the bodies of 29 men killed wearing only underwear, their hands were cuffed and their mouths sealed with tapes. This all bears the signature of the deadly squads of the militia that was targeting young people who have voiced their opposition to the occupation and the sectarian authority.

This is only one example to an organised crime in a lawless country, a crime that happens every single day since march 2003, the horrific scene repeats itself on daily basis, right in front of they eyes of the civilised community in the 21st century. And nothing is done about it.

Still at this stage the occupation authorities is dismissing that as no civil war, well if it is not civil war then what do you call it?. These crimes are overlooked by the police force (which is dominated by Shiites figures) and the elected government.

The interior minister has been accused of authorising the death squads that carry out the organised assassination. There is damning evidence that, the high ranking police leader sanctioned by the minister in internal affairs (Jabr Soullagh) have their hands dirty in this civil conflict. Most of the high ranks are dominated by leaders of the para-military militia, most of those were refugees in Iran, they have old scores and it is just the suitable time to settle those scores.

The reputation of the national; police is so bad, after the Feb. 22 bombing of the Mosques in Samarra, Sunnis said the perpetrators were Interior Ministry troops who were looking for a pretext to start a civil war

Instead of protecting citizens from each other, National Police units stood by as Shiite rioters—and rival militiamen from Moqtada al-Sadr's Mahdi Army—stormed Sunni mosques and swarmed over Sunni neighbourhoods,

Assassinations

A terrible tragedy that the Iraqi community had to go through is the assassinations of prominent figures, notably those who are Doctors and University Professors. The scientific community has certainly suffered form poverty and demoralisation in Saddam era, a lot of those have left the country for better life abroad. Others had to drive taxies to live. The fall of Saddam was followed by a remarkable, Iraq got used to the political persecution and assassinations, and however, targeting the scientific community is something new in the nation's history.

The wave of assassinations started with the previous Dean of the Medical School at Baghdad University (Mohammed A. Al-Rawi), admittedly he was Baathist, but what happened in the days to follow has shown a remorseless slaying of doctors and prominent figures. It all was mysterious with no responsibility laid on any party; it is still baffling as to who is responsible.

One of the scenes was the killing of Abdul Razaq al-Na'as, sitting in his car covered by his own blood dead by the assassin bullets.

On January 28 al-Na'as got to his car and drove from his office at Baghdad University, he was blocked by two cars and gunmen opened fire, shot and killed him immediately.. In a letter to a friend evidently, Abdul Razaq al-Na'as, was grieving for friends and colleagues who were assassinated, wrote to one of his friends in Europe and said "I wonder who is next!" it was him!

Al-Na'as is not the first academic to be killed. Hundreds of academics and scientists have met this fate since the American invasion, March 2003. Baghdad universities alone have lost over 80 members of staff. According to the ministry of education during the year 2005, 296 members of university academic staff were assassinated and 133 wounded.

None of those crimes has been investigated by the occupation forces or the elected governments. They leave that to international humanitarian groups and anti-war organisations.

One of those organisations is the Brussels Tribunal that has compiled a list of the crimes and the victims to persuade the UN special sector on summary executions to investigate those assassinations. The information available so far on those killed seems to be from all ethnic groups with no discrimination. Who is the perpetrators and who is behind all this. I am sad to say regardless of who is responsible this had grave consequences of the society that is already grieving the loss of family members and friends. They mostly were killed cold-blooded assassination. No one has claimed responsibility.

The following is appeal from the Brussels Tribunal

Those assassinated paid heavily for voicing their concern and opposition to the American occupation, all I can say *"goodbye Tyranny and welcome Freedom"*. If we ever knew that was the price we have to pay for the freedom, I suspect we would have not complained so much about Saddam

The Iraqi academics, who risk their lives in the process seems to push for investigation and prosecution of the perpetrators. This fell on deaf ears from the *"democratically elected national administration"*

My concern is that this does appear to be a planned eradication of the intellectuals in the country; I am afraid the only party that has interest in that is the occupying force. Just consider the following about al-Na'as

Dr al-Na'as had often appeared on Al-Jazeerah TV and attacked the continued presence of occupation forces in Iraq, and criticised the interim governments. He often lashed at the militias that are offshoot from certain sectarian groups.

Alna'as assassination has sparked wide spread criticism to the government and a group of journalists have gone on strike demanding the government investigations. We know that again fell on deaf ears. Often the authorities have blamed that on unknown groups of killers of unknown motives, it is a dirty war, the difference between this era and Saddam era is now we don't know who the enemy is, and the victim of this is a single word "IRAQ". Al the circumferential evidence is damning to the authority, true there is no evidence of direct link; but there were no investigations, so you be the judge.

The law of occupation states that: "All foreign soldiers, diplomats or other workers implicated in the killing or torture of Iraqi civilians are immune from arrest or trial in Iraq." Were is the justices in that, is this the new Iraq that we were promised, free of the torture chambers?

Both the British and U S governments turn a blind eye to the systematic violations of human rights and murders committed by their troops in Iraq.

The year 2005 has seen the July London bombings. The British people blamed their leader as it is clearly a revenge for the British involvement In Iraq. This is going to be lesson to the British people who will reflect on that for generations to come.

Ref

http://www.brusselstribunal.org/)

35

The Militia

The development of armed militia was a direct result of a combination of societal oppression, poverty, ignorance and lack of promising life prospects. Militias have replaced the disbanded Iraqi army, applying their own rule of law. Some units operate under some cover of "legality", the "wolf brigade", was founded by a previous army general, it was attached to the interior ministry, it was infamous for its terror raids on mosques and homes and the abduction and torture of civilians.

December 2003, David Gompert, the former National Security Advisor for the Coalition Provisional Authority, realized the dangers sectarian militias posed to Iraq's stability in the days of the Coalition Provisional Authority. Paul Bremer issued Order 91, which was intended to integrate nine militias ; about 100,000 men into the Iraqi security forces. But the Kurdish *pesh merga* and the Badr Organization, still exist today because the order was never completely carried out. Despite repeated U.S. requests for them to disband, Iraq's various ethnic and sectarian militias continued to exist, and more disturbing is the fact that some of those militia, are on a path to being recognized as part of the security system.

Some othose militia were supported by the governemnt and the occupation perhaps to fill in the security gaps left by the local police and army. Their use is part of the strategy by the Iraqi government to "get tough" on insurgents, are willing to use brutal methods and have emerged because of Iraq's security vacancy.

They are generally drawn from sectarian or ethnic sections in Iraq, whether Sunni, Shiite, or Kurd. In Iraq increased sectarian tension can result when members of one ethnic group are charged with policing and arresting people from another group.

Iraqi President Jalal Talabani praised an Iran-trained Shiite militia known as the Badr Organization and the Kurdish *peshmerga* security force for their role in the post-war Iraq. The continued operation of these militias had led to increasing sectarian violence and the security responsibilities in Iraq became diffuse and was not the resposibility of a well organised national system, but by a diverse group of militias that had deepened the nation's sectarian divisions.

Added to the complexity is the fact that there are a growing number of small, paramilitary brigades being formed by local tribes, religious leaders, and various political parties. Some battle Iraq's resistance to the occupation alongside official Interior and Defense ministry troops; others operate without official role. The larger, more established militias, such as the Badr Organization and *peshmerga*, are tied to Iraq's leading political parties, organized along sectarian lines, and enforce order in their respective regions.

The Kurdish liberation army (pesh merga) whose name translates to "those who face death." their roots stretch back to the 1920s, fought against Saddam during the Iran-Iraq war and provided military backup during the U.S.-led invasion in 2003. The *peshmerga* is now believed to comprise some 100,000 troops, and serves as the security force for the Kurdistan Regional Government in northern Iraq. Iraq's Kurds have repeatedly insisted that the *peshmerga* remain intact as a Kurdish force as a condition of their remaining loyal to Baghdad instead of seeking an independent state.

Badr Organization is the Iranian-trained wing of the Supreme Council for the Islamic Revolution in Iraq (SCIRI), Badr was formed and trained in Iran in cooperation with the Iranian government, and its members staged raids into Iraq during the war between the neighbouring countries in the 1980s. During the U.S.-led occupation government's crackd own on militia groups in 2003, the 10,000-strong militia changed its name from the Badr Brigade to the Badr Organization of Reconstruction and Development and pledged to disarm. The group, however, remained armed. One of Badr's recent offshoots is a feared, elite commando unit linked to the Iraqi Interior Ministry called the Wolf Brigade. Which have been accused the of revenge killings against Sunni religious leaders and unlawful kidnappings.

The Mahdi Army is loyal to the young cleric, Muqtada al-Sadr, this group of thousands of armed loyalists fought U.S. forces for much of 2004 before agreeing to an October 2004 ceasefire. The militia controls much of Sadr City, a Baghdad slum of some 2.5 million Shiites, Muqtada al-Sadr has refused to participate directly in the Iraqi government, though some of his followers were elected to seats on the Iraqi National Assembly.

Defenders of Khadamiya is a group comprised of roughly 120 loyalists to Hussein al-Sadr, a distant relative of Muqtada al-Sadr and a Shiite cleric who ran on former Prime Minister Ayad Allawi's ticket in the January 30 elections. The brigade was formed to guard a shrine in northern Baghdad popular among Shi-ites, and is one of a number of similar local forces that have emerged.

The most feared and effective commando unit in Iraq was the wolf brigade. Formed October 2004 by a former three-star general and SCIRI member who goes by the name of Abu Walid, the Wolf Brigade is roughly 2,000 fighters, mostly young unemployable Shiites from Sadr City. Members of the group reportedly earn as much as 700,000 Iraqi dinars, or $400, per month, a large amount of money in the current situation in Iraq. They dress in olive uniform and red beret.

December 2004, the Wolf Brigade backed up by the Iraqi army and U.S. mil-itary achieved its infamous reputation after launching a series of attacks against claimed resistance in Mosul. They Coereced susoects by torture to confess crimes on Iraqi TV channels. The Wolf Brigade was accused of targeting Palestinian ref-ugees in Iraq, and killing six Sunni clerics. The brigade denied those charges, which have deepeved the sectarian division. Human-rights groups accused cre-ators of the counterterrorism Iraqi television show of violating the Geneva Con-ventions by publicly humiliating detainees. Among Shiites, however, there are patriotic songs devoted to the group..

There was one counterinsurgency unit headed by a former officer of Saddam Army. "The Special Police Commandos", like the Wolf Brigade, has a reputation for brutality, it is also considered one of Iraq's most effective and well trained counterinsurgency units. It was formed September 2004 by General Adnan Thabit, a 63-year-old Sunni and former intelligence officer in the Iraqi Air Force who was thrown in prison for plotting a coup against Saddam Hussein in 1996. Armed by the Iraqi government, it has heavy ammunition, rocket-propelled gre-nades, and AK-47 assault rifles. It is comprised of 5,000 members who are selected by Thabit and are former members of Saddam's Republican Guard. In a May *New York Times Magazine* article on the Special Police Commandos, Peter Maass wrote, "The integration of the commandos into the security forces staunches one flow of experienced fighters into the insurgency."

Although initially the occupation force refused to sanction the militia, on June 8 2005, Sean McCormack, a State Department spokesman, told reporters that the Iraqi government's growing use of militias "is an Iraqi issue that they will decide and that they will deal with". Then the U.S. military fought alongside the Wolf Brigade and other militia units in "counterinsurgency" operations in Mosul and Samarra. "These commando units may be a marriage of convenience and ultimately may be absorbed into the army or disbanded" according to some US officials.

Oil Militia

Iraq has lost more than $10 billion in oil revenues in the first three years of the invasion. Corruption and sabotage are largely to blame. U.S. and Iraqi officials are blaming the insurgence. But many say the Oil Ministry's own militia, contracted to protect the oil industry infrastructure, seems to be the centre of the problem. Sixteen battalions of Iraqi troops are tasked with protecting the oil infrastructure.

Iran and the Militia

U.S. and Iraqi officials say the Iranian-backed Badr Organization has taken over many of the Iraqi Interior Ministry's intelligence activities and infiltrated its top command ranks.

Rumsfeld told members of the defence subcommittee of the Senate Appropriations Committee on May 17.2006 that U.S. forces continue to find Iranian-manufactured weapons in Iraq,. "The problem we've got is unless you catch somebody from Iran, from the government of Iran, physically bringing a weapon into Iraq, and you can tie a string between the two, you can't assert that it necessarily was government-sponsored," he said.

Current and former Ministry of Interior employees told Knight Ridder about that "it enabled the militia to use Interior Ministry vehicles and equipment; to carry out revenge attacks against the Sunni Muslims"

Tom Lasseter wrote in Knight Ridder "The officials, some of whom agreed to speak only on the condition of anonymity for fear of violent reprisals, said the Interior Ministry had become what amounted to an Iranian fifth column inside the U.S.-backed Iraqi government, running death squads and operating a network of secret prisons".

The American stance is summarised by one official, Gen. George W. Casey, the top U.S. general in Iraq "They're putting millions of dollars into the south to influence the elections; it's funded primarily through their charity organizations and also Badr and some of these political parties,". "A lot of their guys (Badr) are going into the police and military."

Those militia activities had enraged Sunnis and pushed many to join the resistance. And by supporting Badr and other Shiite groups, Iran—a member of President Bush's "axis of evil" had gained unprecedented access to meddle in the internal affairs of Iraq in the presence of the American occupation.

Current and former ministry officials said the American military hadn't interfered with Badr's infiltration of the ministry, either because U.S. officials weren't fully aware of what was happening or because they didn't want to risk arresting militia leaders who had powerful political positions and tens of thousands of followers.

Interior Ministry and Badr officials have denied any involvement in the prisons or death squads, but Gen. Muntadhar Muhi al-Samaraee, a former head of special forces at the Interior Ministry, told Tom Lasseter (of the Knight Ridder) that the prisons were run by Badr operatives.

According to Donald Rumsfeld Iran has deployed elite forces to confront the U.S. military in Iraq in what has been termed a major escalation in the Iran nuclear issue.

Defence Secretary Donald Rumsfeld said "They are currently putting people into Iraq to do things that are harmful to the future of Iraq," American officials said Iran has deployed members of the Islamic Revolutionary Guard Corps in Iraq in early 2006. They said the IRGC operatives helped foment unrest and bolster Shiite militias in Iraq amid sectarian violence triggered by the bombing of the Golden Dome mosque in Samara on Feb. 22.

Rumsfeld said Iran was deploying members of the Quds Brigade of the IRGC. The Quds Brigade has been regarded is specialized in insurgencies abroad. The brigade has been identified as the trainer and controller of Hizbullah in Lebanon. In February, John Negroponte (intelligence director) reported Iranian attempts to strike U.S. forces in Iraq. "The Revolutionary Guard doesn't go milling around willy-nilly, one would think," Rumsfeld said. "Is it possible some more Iraqi civilians will be killed? Sure."

Peter Pace, chairman of the Joint Chiefs of Staff, said the reports of the Quds Brigade infiltration in Iraq had marked the most recent developments that aroused from Iran. Pace added" We're working with the Iraqi government to enhance the capacity, the total numbers dedicated to border control, and also their capacity,"

Ref

TOM LASSETER Mon. 12 Dec 2005, Knight Ridder Newspapers

SPECIAL TO WORLD TRIBUNE.COM; Friday, March 10, 2006

Peter Mass, The New York Times Magazine May 01,2005

Lionel Beehner, staff writer, cfr.org

Ministry of Interior affairs

Sunni groups, including the Iraqi Islamic Party and the Muslim Scholars Association, have documented hundreds of instances in 2005 in which men wearing police uniforms raided Sunni neighbourhoods at night and abducted men who later were found dead.

On one instance a raid on a detention centre belongs to the Interior Ministry building found 13 men who had been tortured and needed medical treatment.

In November 2005; the secret was revealed as 169 men, most of them Sunnis, were found in an Interior Ministry bunker in Baghdad's Jadriyah neighbourhood. Many of them had been beaten with leather belts and steel rods and made to sit in their own excrement, according to a U.S. military statement and an Iraqi who was held at the centre. The evidence was damning when a police officers with knowledge of the jail said Badr ran it.

A Human Rights Ministry official has declared that there are other secret jail centres that the Human rights did not know anything about its conditions.

A senior U.S. military official speaking on the condition of anonymity to Knight Ridder acknowledged that the torture at the Jadriyah site was carried out by Interior Ministry intelligence group.

After Iraq's national elections January 2005, the Supreme Council for Islamic Revolution in Iraq and its Badr militia, took power and installed a man with strong ties to Badr, Bayan Jabr, as the head of the Interior Ministry. The ministry's ranks, particularly intelligence units were delegated to Badr militia members. The American officer said it would be up to the Iraqi government to deal with the Badr organization and other militias. People who signed up for the security forces had remained loyal to a militia leader more than their loyalty to the commanders of police.

There have been allegations that the militia that's loyal to radical cleric Muqtada al-Sadr, who also has Iranian support, is responsible for part of the killings.

Tom Lasseter said a document obtained by Knight Ridder appeared to reveal the existence of an Interior Ministry death squad.

"A memo written by an Iraqi general in the ministry operations room and addressed to the minister's office says on its subject line: "Names of detainees." It lists 14 men who were taken from Iskan, a Sunni neighbourhood in western Baghdad, during the early morning hours of Aug. 18.2005 It also marks the time of their detention: 5:15 a.m. The bodies of the same 14 men were found in the town of Badrah near the Iranian border in early October. Hussein Sayhoud, a doctor at Baghdad's main morgue who examined the bodies and signed one of the death certificates, said that most of the men had been killed by single gun-shots to their heads". The bodies were decomposed and signs of torture could not be confirmed or excluded.

The general who signed the Interior Ministry memo, Brig. Gen. Abdul Kareem Khalaf, confirmed its authenticity. Pressed for more details, Khalaf said: "The minister is very upset. He wants to know how such a document slipped out of the ministry."

There've been reports of several instances in DiSalvo's area of Sunni men being rounded up by vehicles with Interior Ministry markings, then found murdered.

Ref

Tom lasseter Mon. 12 Dec 2005, Knight Ridder Newspapers

TOM LASSETER Mon. 12 Dec 2005, Knight Ridder Newspapers

SPECIAL TO WORLD TRIBUNE.COM; Friday, March 10, 2006

Peter Mass, The New York Times Magazine May 01,2005

Lionel Beehner, staff writer, cfr.org

36

Snapshot of Iraq daily life under the occupation

(voice from the wilderness)

Lack of basic services is prompting growing protest against Iraqi officials and the occupation. Three years since the fall of Baghdad, has been the worst with regard to basic services. Interruptions to electricity and water supplies—caused by both lack of maintenance and sabotage—are depriving Iraq and fuelling up the frustrations of the millions.

The south has been relatively stable with no tangible evidence of violence; yet towns of south Iraq is lacking basic services, protests in Samawa in summer 2005 over joblessness and limited electricity and water supplies turned into violence outside the governor's. The riot ended when police opened fire at the protesters killing one.

In Baghdad, the militant cleric Moqtada al-Sadr has called for Friday protests against the lack of power and water.

Iraq's electricity problems—are a combination of a run-down system, wartime damage, and lack of maintenance due to violence. This power shortage in turn leads to pump shutdowns, which deprive many neighbourhoods of water supply, and frequently leave pools of sewage in the streets.

Electricity

The US occupation had declared that is in the process of spending about $19 billion on long-term water and electricity projects, but about a quarter of this money has been diverted to security because of the resistance according to the US. Maintenance has not been effective whatever the reason was.

Iraqi officials said that the country would need an estimated $20 billion over the next five years to restore full electric power capacity and keeps power flowing to the entire country. Iraqi Electricity Minister of power seemed confident that

Iraq would be able to restore full power within two years and that daily demand—estimated by the US General Accounting Office to reach 8,500 megawatts this summer will go up to18,000 megawatts by 2010.

But Baghdad people want reliable electricity and more water supplies right now. Baghdad summer heat is turning homes into an "oven" by summertime in Baghdad the temperature ranges between 45 and 48 degrees. Iraqi politicians and the occupation authorities had made many promises to rehabilitate the power and water supply and they have not fulfilled their promises and lost any credibility. Some neighbourhoods had local supply by privately owned generators, however many of them had to sell theirs because of the death threats they received from local insurgency fighters.

For example some people are fortunate to get few hours' electricity a day in; most people at night to the rooftop of their house for cooler nights; those who live in apartments, however don't have that option. A cool shower is not an option, since the water is turned off for days at a time.

But at least someone is profiting from Baghdad's decaying infrastructure. Haider al-Turki (an auto mechanic) spoke to Dan Murphy of Christian Science Monitor he said. "*I'm making a lot of money thanks to cheap Chinese generators and the terrorists,*" he added, "*I'm the only person I know who's benefiting from this situation.*" And also he felt sorry for others "*Most Iraqis can't afford a generator, and they're just trying to live through this.*"

Small businesses have suffered a lot from power cuts, some had to shut down totally because of that. Corruption is an added burden on small businesses and the public. Electricity workers had reportedly cut the power supply and demanded bribes whenever they wanted.

Internal displacement

MORE than 100,000 people have fled their homes in Iraq since late February because of the insurgency and rising sectarian bloodshed, up from 65,000 just over two weeks ago, Iraqi officials said. The Iraqi government reported almost 7680 families moved to the Shiite provinces in southern Iraq and about 3200 to mainly Sunni provinces such as western Anbar and central Salahiddin.

These are only those who have registered with the Migration Ministry for financial support between the bombing of a Shiite Muslim shrine on February 22 2006 in the city of Samarra, and April 2006. In mid-April, the ministry said 65,000 people had left their homes since the February 22 shrine bombing

About 15,000 families, roughly split among majority Shiite Muslims and Sunni Arabs in the same proportions as the general mix of Iraq's 26 million people, have left their towns, according to the ministry's report. Not all refugees register with the ministry. Many of the better off move in with relatives or rent homes in new areas

Some wealthy families, held back from telling authorities they had left their homes for new ones because they don't need any help from the government.

Targeted Killings Surge in Baghdad

Nearly 4,000 civilian deaths, many of them Sunni Arabs slain execution-style, were recorded in the first three months of 2005. In Baghdad more civilians were killed in Baghdad during that period of the year than at any time since the toppling of Saddam Hussein's regime, many of them found shot in the head execution-style, with hands tied behind them and signs of torture. Others were strangled, electrocuted, stabbed, garrotted or hanged. Many bore signs of torture such as bruises, drill holes, burn marks, gouged eyes and severed limbs.

Every single day, about 40 bodies arrive at the central morgue in Baghdad, according to some Iraqi officials. The numbers demonstrate a shift in the nature of the violence, which increasingly has targeted both sides of the country's Sunni and Shiite. However the crime is now more organised and the killings are systematic and personal. Masked gunmen storm houses, and the victims (the majority of them Sunnis) are never again seen alive. Such killings now claim nine times more lives than suicidal car bombings (figures provided by a high-ranking U.S. military official, who released them only on the condition of anonymity, to Christian Science monitor)

Statistics obtained at the Baghdad morgue showed a steady increase in the number of shooting deaths and other types of targeted killings, with a stunning surge in March 2006, after the Feb. 22 bombing of the Golden Al-Askary Mosque in Samarra.

At the central morgue, the freezers are filled with bodies, and forensic workers are overwhelmed. Louise Roug visited the central morgue and reported "*On a recent day, coffins were stacked against the wall outside the morgue, waiting to be filled. Every half hour or so, police officers arrived, unloading bodies from their pickup trucks. Each time, crowds of people rushed forward to see whether their missing relatives were among them*".

The statistics 3,472 violent deaths in Baghdad from January through March 2006 do not present the full picture of the violence in Baghdad. That number does not include those killed in bombings or during gunfights between insurgents and security forces because they are not brought in for autopsy at the central morgue. According to reports by hospital and police officials at least 351 civilians were killed in bombings across the capital during the first three months of 2006. These figures do not include those killed by the occupation army or the police killed by bombing or fighting with the resistance, neither it includes those killed outside Baghdad.

The figures obtained from numerous other sources, however, show the sectarian nature of a conflict that is increasingly targeting civilians.

In the cemeteries serving Baghdad (6 million people), demand for tombs is so high that people are buried between old graves or at the edges of the burial grounds.

Sunni leaders allege that police officers and special commandos, most of whom are Shiites, run death squads that target Sunnis in a big campaign of sectarian cleansing.

The culprit remains largely unknown; Shiite politicians declared that criminals steal or buy official uniforms to disguise as security force and terrorize Baghdad. U.S. military officials lay the blame on Abu Musab Zarqawi, saying he is trying to provoke a civil war.

According to the numbers provided by the U.S. military official, the number of civilian deaths has increased steadily since 2003 and the incidence of execution-style killing started to rise in spring 2005, the violence increased by 86% in the few weeks after the Golden Mosque bombing, Targeted killings now account for most of the violence.

The central morgue director told Louise Roug "On a daily basis, he said, the morgue receives about 40 bodies and this number is constant, if not increasing." Gunmen operate throughout Baghdad, killing during daytime and moving with impunity during curfew. There has been so far no investigation in to these killings, neither by the Iraqi officials nor by the occupation.

The following is excerpt from Louise Roug of La Times, the story is a remarkable event that is now a commonplace in Baghdad "On the day of the Samarra bombing, the Ubaidis, a Sunni family of teachers and students enjoying the lull of a midterm break, had just finished lunch when someone knocked on the door of their home in Shaab, a mixed Shiite-Sunni middle-class neighbourhood in Baghdad. Six men wearing masks and dressed in black demanded to see Ziad and his father Tariq. The men forced the two into the trunks of waiting cars as Ziad's mother, Muazzaz, watched from an upstairs window. Four days later, their bodies were found in a Baghdad suburb. At the central morgue, workers duly noted the deaths. Muazzaz's eldest son and her husband of 22 years became two more entries, numbers 30948 and 30952, respectively, in the morgue's Byzantine record-keeping system. "My husband and son were killed for sectarian reasons," said Muazzaz, a teacher who had lived in the neighbourhood for 19 years. "In a while, this area will be 100% Shiite.... It's definitely sectarian cleansing."

The Sunni revenge is happening as well, by suicide bombs and otherwise. Shortly after the Samarra bombing three suicide bombers walked into the Bratha Mosque—(an extremely important Shiite shrines in the Baghdad) and detonated themselves, killing 78 people and wounding150 during prayers.

Another story:

Halale Ubaidi, a Shiite who married a Sunni. Her 29-year-old son, Haitham, raised Sunni, was kidnapped along with his younger brother, Othman. "My two sons were taken in front of my eyes, and one of them is dead," said Ubaidi, who is not related to the other Ubaidi family. One night, attackers charged into the cramped apartment where the family squatted among Shiite neighbours. "You, the Sunnis," said the gunmen, taking Haitham and Othman, said their sister, Maryam. The attackers took the brothers to a house where, during their torture and captivity, they could hear the sounds of children and a woman cooking in the room next door, Othman told her. Haitham was beaten and tortured to death in that house, said Othman, who managed to escape while he was being taken to a deserted area where, his captors had told him, he, too, would be killed. Haitham's mutilated body was found five days later in a dump near the vast Shiite neighbourhood of Sadr City.

Halale Ubaidi said she had spent her adult life living and praying alongside Sunnis. "I didn't care," she said, still stunned by her son's death.

Haitham's captors had gouged one of his eyes, cut his face with a razor, smashed his skull, broken his jaw, slit his back and cut off his penis, his sister and mother said. A copy of Haitham's death certificate says he was shot 14 times.

"We are living in a state of panic and fear," his sister said. "Maybe they'll come again…. Nobody knows when his turn will come to be captured and killed by these gunmen

Ref

Louise Roug; Times Staff Writer *from the Los Angeles Times* May 7, 2006

11 Aug 2005 Christian Science Monitor by Dan Murphy | Staff writer of The Christian Science Monitor

Education

10 Aug 2005

A deteriorating security situation in Iraq has caused parents to fear for students going to school, and also increased teachers' concern for their own safety. The capital, Baghdad, has been one of the most affected areas in Iraq and, the quality of education is remarkably reduced. Iraqis suffered the ill effects of an education system under severe pressure of the security concerns with declining standards.

Education Ministry official told Alert Net that the reason for such decline in education was that most teachers were afraid to stay for long time in schools, and try to finish their job as early as possible to get off the streets to the relative safety of their homes.

The families of many students who are concerned about the quality of education have now started to search for alternative ways to have their children educated abroad in Jordan or Syria, for instance, despite the expense involved.

Iraq seed Industry

The war had destroyed Iraq's seed industry, putting the country's food supply at ruins, the United Nations food agency had appealed for aid to rebuild farming and agricultural resources. The Food and Agriculture Organisation said it needed $5.4 million to help the agriculture ministry rebuild a seed industry. FAO declared in a statement "Iraq had a relatively stable and functioning public-sector-controlled seed industry before the war in 2003. After the war, research and seed production facilities have greatly deteriorated,".

Iraq under the occupation covers only 4 percent of its demand for seeds from its own resources. FAO Iraq project manager "Iraq has currently no system in place that provides certified high-quality seeds of improved varieties. As a result, crop productivity remains very low because farmers are using their own, mostly low-quality, seed," "If no immediate action is taken, serious seed shortages can be expected in the near future, threatening the country's food security."

ECONOMIC PUSH TO PROSTITUTION

This increase is attributed to economic pressure faced by families across the country and the presence of new prostitution rings that have sprung up since the invasion. With society in turmoil, child protection has not been uppermost in the priorities of the transitional government. Rising unemployment had led to the desperate search for money to survive, despite the physical, psychological and health dangers involved in commercial sex work. According to a survey by the Iraqi Ministry of Planning and Development Cooperation released in April, 48 percent of youths in the country are unemployed, most of them discouraged by poor salaries in those jobs that are available.

"We are a poor family and my husband cannot work because he has serious epilepsy," Um Zac, a mother of two child sex workers, said. "Three months ago, Abu Weled came to our house offering us money if we let our two teenage [aged 13 and 14] boys work with them.

"Thanks to him, today we have a good income. People may find it surprising, but at least we can eat now and I'm proud of them."

Unofficial information suggests there could be as many as 4,000 male commercial sex workers. There are no statistics on the number of boys caught up in the business countrywide, but officials fear that it could be in the hundreds.

Based on information supplied by the Ministry of Labour, two small local NGOs are trying to help the child sex workers. On of them, Iraqi Peace and Better Future (IPBF), has collected the names of more than 50 teenage boys who say they cannot leave the trade because of threats. Meanwhile many boys in Baghdad are living in fear, urging that someone, somewhere come up with a solution to their plight.

Y H is 15 year-old boy said to alert net "I hope that one day I will live without the fear that I may find my father with a gun or a knife ready to kill me because he has discovered what I do for a living,"

Ref

Baghdad correspondent, Herald Sun, 8.May 2006

Peter Beaumont, The Observer14 Aug 2005; foreign affairs editor

Nicholas Birch, Contributor to the Christian Science Monitor; 10 Aug 2005 Christian Science Monitor

ROME, Aug 8 (Reuters)

BAGHDAD, Aug 2005, Alert net.org

Fleeing the violence

In the previous three years, the killings have been random. Violence came mostly in the form of bombs wielded by the Sunni Arab-led insurgency that primarily targeted the coalition forces and the Shiite: balls of fire and shrapnel tearing through the bodies of those riding the wrong bus, shopping at the wrong market or standing in the wrong line. In 2005 the process has changed more into organised crimes.

Large numbers of Iraqis are leaving, as if there is no tomorrow—huge numbers waiting in long, endless lines at check points on the borders with Jordan and Syria. It could take you 48 hours at the Iraqi-Jordanian border to have an exit visa; huge numbers and slow work. Since the 2003 war and the beginning of the occupation, the security situation, among other things, deteriorated so badly that is forcing people to leave..

The Occupation had utilised the principle of divide and conquer to control the country, the favouring of the Kurds and the Shiites over the Sunnis had deepened the ethnic divide and created internal clashes between different sects of the society perhaps to distract the attention and directed away from the occupation. The people of Iraq became so divided to an extent it is openly discussed whether they were Shiites or Sunnis. The media had helped to shape up the world idea about the country by a phrase that almost universal to any western report it "the Shiites majority who were largely oppressed under the rule of the Sunni minority".

Sectarian violence has targeted the Sunnis in particular, prominent doctors university professors, scholars and previous military leaders from the Sunni section are systematically eliminated by abductions, and assassinations. This had led to many of them to leave the country, basically being Sunni made many people falsely accused and labelled as terrorists. Practically any male between 18 and 40 can be arrested and executed; and some of these bodies are found latter tortured to death or executed. The situation amounts to a secret state sponsored terror, under the nose of the occupation.

Huge numbers of people are unemployed, if you are looking for a job in the public sector, you will need a letter of good standing from the Daawa Party, SCIRI, or Sadr offices, qualifications and resumes don't matter that much. Those problems had forced the educated elite of the country, Sunnis, Christians and Shiites to leave the country in large numbers.

Iraq is not for sell

Abdul Aziz Al-Hakim's call to establish a federal Shiite state in southern Iraq Al-Hakim made his call in front of a large crowd of Shiite mourners, who gathered in Najaf on August 11, 2005 to commemorate the second anniversary of his brother's (Baqir Al-Hakim) death. Al-Hakim suggested to group nine southern Iraqi governorates in order to establish a Shiite entity, which would eventually break up from the mother homeland of Iraq. The call stirred anger and disgust among Iraq's Shiite and Sunnis and other sects. Despite the huge cash and propaganda utilized to back the call, it did not receive the desired support; protesters marched all over Iraq holding banners that read, "Sunnis and Shiites, we will not sell this country."

The death of hundreds of Iraqi Shiites on August 31, 2005 in a Baghdad stampede across a bridge that join Kadymia to Aadamyia was a disaster. The scene on that day was a demonstration of the failure of the US occupation's plans to divide the country, and showed there is still some hope that the society that had show solidarity along the centuries is still unified.

The US-led occupation and the collaborators who came not only seeking power but aiming to split the country and erase it identity; have made every effort to deepen the sectarianism. Starting from the cabinet to the lowest governmental posts Reports from Baghdad had revealed the real Iraqi spirit of unity and cooperation, the bridge disaster prompted Iraqis from different sects of the community to offer help in every possible way and demonstrated a deeply rooted Iraqi solidarity.

The stampede took place in Kadhimiya, a Shiite-dominated Baghdad district; Adhamiya, a neighbouring Sunni-dominated district. Sunni and Shiite mosques in different Iraqi cities were urging people through loudspeakers to help. Iraqis from all sects and religious affiliation donated blood to the victims. A Sunni teenager from Adhamiya gave a striking example of Iraqis' unity. Uthman Al-Ubeidi died while saving his fellow Iraqis from drowning into the Tigris River. Uthman saved seven people and died of exhaustion while he was trying hard to save the eighth one.

As the Sunni Arabs were fighting the constitution battle to abort the potential division of Iraq into separate states, Shiite Arabs in the south were opposing Al-Hakim's plans. Shiite tribal leaders voiced their rejection of Al-Hakim's proposal; as a result, Al-Hakim's parliamentary bloc dropped their demand of a Shiite self-rule region.

The message has been clear to those who aim to hit the country in the heart of its identity. The people of Iraq want to remain united and the odds are they will.

Ref

Ahmed Ahmed. *Freelance Writer* Sep 07, 2005

Khalid Jarrar Freelance Writer—Jordan Mar. 05, 2006

37

Revisiting Halabja Issue

Saddam had long being accused of using chemical weapons against the Iraqi people and the most commonly occasion referred to is the gassing of Iraqi Kurds at the town of Halabja in March 1988, closer to the end of the Iran-Iraq war. President Bush had cited Iraq's "gassing its own people" specifically at Halabja, as one acceptable reason to topple Saddam Hussein regime. "The dictator who is assembling the world's most dangerous weapons have already used them on whole villages, leaving thousands of his own citizens dead, blind or disfigured." President Bush, lacking smoking-gun evidence of the WMDs programs in Iraq, used his State of the Union address to emphasize the moral case for an invasion

Kurds were bombarded with poison gas in March 1988 at Halabja. No official source could say with any degree of certainty that Iraqi chemical weapons killed the Kurds. There is other twist to the story.

Stephen C. Pelletiere said he is in a position to know because, "as the Central Intelligence Agency's senior political analyst on Iraq during the Iran-Iraq war, and as a professor at the Army War College from 1988 to 2000" he said "I was privy to much of the classified material that flowed through Washington having to do with the Persian Gulf. In addition, I headed a 1991 Army investigation into how the Iraqis would fight a war against the United States; the classified version of the report went into great detail on the Halabja affair".

The gassing at Halabja happened in a battle between Iraqis and Iranians on the northeast borders of Iraq. Iraq used chemical weapons to try to kill Iranians who had seized the town, which is on the borders between Iran and Iraq.

Stephen C. Pelletiere said "The Kurdish civilians who died had the misfortune to be caught up in that exchange. But they were not Iraq's main target". Immediately after that battle "the United States Defense Intelligence Agency investigated the matter and produced a classified report", he added "which circulated within the intelligence community on a need-to-know basis. That study asserted that it was Iranian gas that killed the Kurds, not Iraqi gas.

Probably both sides had used chemical weapons, however the dead Kurds' bodies examination indicated they had been killed with the blood agent (cyanide-based gas), which Iran was known to use. The Iraqis, who are thought to have used mustard gas in that battle and other battles, are not known to have possessed blood agents at the time.

According to Stephen C. Pelletiere "I am not trying to rehabilitate the character of Saddam Hussein. He has much to answer for in the area of human rights abuses. But accusing him of gassing his own people at Halabja as an act of genocide is not correct"

Before the Persian Gulf War, Iraq had built an extensive system of dams and irrigation projects, the largest being the Darbandikhan dam in the Kurdish area. Pelletiere thinks it was this dam the Iranians were aiming to take control of when they seized Halabja…

By invading Iraq "America could alter the destiny of the Middle East in a way that probably could not be challenged for decades—not solely by controlling Iraq's oil, but by controlling its water' Pelletiere said.

State Department gave a "green light" to Saddam Hussein to go into Kuwait in August 1990. The first gulf war could have been averted if the American administration exercised some restraints. In the months immediately preceding the "green light" given by ambassador, April Glaspie, a number of Senates including Bob Dole had traveled to Baghdad, met with Saddam, and found him to be a head of state worthy of support. Even Sen. Howard Metzenbaum, a Jewish and supporter of Israel, gave him a seal of approval.

US Army War College reported that 1.4 million Iraqi civilians have died as a result of the economic sanctions, which is 3,000 times more than the number of Kurds who supposedly died of gassing Halabja by Saddam.

Excerpt from Pentagon Report by Stephen C. Pelletiere et al in 1990

Throughout the war the United States practiced a fairly benign policy toward Iraq. Although initially disapproving of the invasion, Washington came slowly over to the side of Baghdad. Both wanted to restore the status quo ante to the Gulf and to reestablish the relative harmony that prevailed there before Khomeini began threatening the regional balance of power. Khomeini's revolutionary appeal was anathema to both Baghdad and Washington; hence they wanted to get rid of him. United by a common interest, Iraq and the United States restored diplomatic relations in 1984, and the United States began to actively assist Iraq in ending the fighting. It mounted Operation Staunch, an attempt to stem the flow of arms to Iran. It also increased its purchases of Iraqi oil while cutting back on Iranian oil purchases, and it urged its allies to do likewise. All this had the effect of repairing relations between the two countries, which had been at very low ebb. Having looked at all of the evidence that was available to us, we find it impossible to confirm the State Department's claim that gas was used in this instance. To begin with there were never any victims produced. International relief organizations who examined the Kurds—in Turkey where they had gone for asylum—failed to discover any. Nor were there ever any found inside Iraq the claim rests solely on testimony of the Kurds who had crossed the border into Turkey, where they were interviewed by staffers of the Senate Foreign Relations Committee We would have expected, in a matter as serious as this, and that the Congress would have exercised some care. However, passage of the sanctions measure through the Congress was unusually swift—at least in the Senate where a unanimous vote was secured within 24 hours. Further, the proposed sanctions were quite draconian. Fortunately for the future of Iraqi-U.S. ties, the sanctions measure failed to pass on a bureaucratic technicality (it was attached as a rider to a bill that died before adjournment it appears that in seeking to punish Iraq, the Congress was influenced by another incident that occurred five months earlier in another Iraqi-Kurdish city, alabjah. In March 1988, the Kurds at Halabjah were bombarded with chemical weapons, producing a great many deaths. Photographs of them Kurdish victims were widely disseminated in the international media. Iraq was blamed for the Halabjah attack, even though it was subsequently brought out that Iran too had used chemicals in this operation, and it seemed likely that it was the Iranian bombardment that had actually killed the Kurds Thus, in our view, the Congress acted more on the basis of emotionalism than factual information, and without sufficient thought for the adverse diplomatic effects of its action. As a result of the outcome of the Iran-Iraq War, Iraq is now the most powerful state in the Persian Gulf, an area in which we have vital interests. To maintain an uninterrupted flow of oil from the Gulf to the West, we need to develop good working relations with all of the Gulf States, and particularly with Iraq, the strongest.

Ref

www.nytimes.com/2003/01/31/opinion/31PELL.html

Stephen C. Pelletiere. "A War Crime or an Act of War" New York Times Friday 31 January 2003

(Stephen Pelletiere is author of "Iraq and the International Oil System: Why America Went to War in the Persian Gulf)

38

Israel plans

Summe2003 Israeli intelligence in Iraq reported that the insurgents had the support of Iranian intelligence operatives and some foreign fighters, who were crossing the unprotected border between Iran and Iraq at will. The Israelis urged the United States to seal the nine-hundred-mile-long border, at whatever cost.

The border stayed open the occupation took no steps to close the borders, the American attitude was that it was more useful for Iraqis to have contacts with Iranians people coming across the border, and thousands were coming across every day. The warnings of increased violence proved accurate, Israelis warned the Americans about the possibility of Iranians attack on the American army.

August 2003, the insurgency against the occupation exploded, with bombings in Baghdad, at the Jordanian Embassy and the United Nations headquarters that killed forty-two people. The Administration then decided, to deploy the Guantánamo jail model in Iraq and to use its rules of interrogation. That decision failed to stop the insurgency and eventually led to the scandal at the Abu Ghraib prison.

Ehu Barak, the former Israeli Prime Minister had privately warned Vice-President Dick Cheney that America had lost in Iraq, Cheney did not respond to Barak's advice. Prime Minister Ariel Sharon's government decided, according to Seymour Hersh, to minimize the damage that the war was causing to Israel's strategic position by expanding its long-standing relationship with Iraqi Kurds and establishing a significant presence in the region of Kurdistan. Sharon's decision involved a heavy financial commitment; this is suspected to have contributed to the chaos in Iraq.

Israeli intelligence and military operatives are now working silently in Kurdistan, providing training for Kurdish commando units and, most important in Israel's view, running covert operations inside Kurdish areas of Iran and Syria. Israel's foreign-intelligence service work undercover in Kurdistan as businessmen and do not carry Israeli passports. A senior C.I.A. official (according to Hersh) acknowledged that the Israelis were indeed operating in Kurdistan despite Israel's denial.

Turkish officials reported that Turks are increasingly concerned by the increasing Israeli influence in Kurdistan and alleged encouragement of Kurdish ambitions to create an independent state. Iran, Syria, and Turkey, all those countries fear that Kurdistan, despite public pledges to the contrary, may declare its independence from the Iraqi government if conditions deteriorate. Israeli involvement in Kurdistan is not new. Throughout the nineteen-sixties and seventies, Israel actively supported a Kurdish rebellion against Iraq, as part of its strategic policy of seeking alliances with non-Arabs in the Middle East. In 1975, the Kurds were betrayed by the United States, when Washington along with the Shah decided to stop Kurdish assistance in their hopes for autonomy in Iraq. A declaration of Kurdish independence would trigger a Turkish response—and possibly a war

"Israel's immediate goal after June 30thof 2004 was to build up the Kurdish commando units to balance the Shiite militias—especially those which would be hostile to the kind of order in southern Iraq that Israel would like to see, if a fanatic Sunni Baathist militia took control—one as hostile to Israel as Saddam was; Israel would unleash the Kurds on it. The Kurdish armed forces (the peshmerga), is estimated to be seventy-five thousand strong, a total number that far exceeds the known Sunni and Shiite militias together. The former Israeli intelligence officer acknowledged (again according to Seymour Hersh)that since late last year Israel has been training Kurdish commando units to operate in the same manner and with the same effectiveness as Israel's most secretive commando units, the Mistaravim. The initial goal of the Israeli assistance to the Kurds to allow them to penetrate, gather intelligence on, and then kill off the leadership of the Shiite and Sunni insurgencies in Iraq. This notion is extremely dangerous, because the definition of insurgency is relative, depends on the motives and interests. Indeed the Pesh Merga was accused of waves of assassinations across the country.

Some Israeli operatives have crossed the border into Iran, accompanied by Kurdish commandos, to install sensors and other sensitive devices that monitors suspected Iranian nuclear facilities. It is likely that the Bush administration is complacent about those activities. German officials that there is evidence that Israel are using its new leverage inside Kurdistan, and within the Kurdish areas of Syria, Turkey and Iran. Syrian officials believe that Israeli intelligence played a role in violent protests in Syria in mid-March 2004. Syrian President and his government had evidence that Israel was "preparing the Kurds to fight all around Iraq, in Syria, Turkey.

Iran seemingly aware of the risks of Israeli influence on the Kurds, started to focus on the south and middle part of Iraq by supporting the militia and by backing some sectarian politicians to demand federal state in that region. With Iranian clandestine weapons program probably running, the imminent danger to Iraq stability is very clear. Iraq is already a battlefield for different parties and the escalation of Iranian-Israeli conflicts about the nuclear issues, the situation is even ore volatile. It is not known but it seems likely that Israel will initiate an attack on the nuclear facilities of Iran. Israel is working hard to help the Kurds as they seem to be the only potential friend to Israel in the Middle East. Turkey has growing relations with the Israelis but the Kurds problem is putting tension on the relations because Turkey's interest is to keep Iraq united and prevent the formation of an independent Kurdish sate in the north, for obvious reasons, but the future of united Iraq is far from being clear

Ref

SEYMOUR M. HERSH, As June 30th approaches, Israel looks to the Kurds. New Yorker 28.06.2004.

39

Daily massacres

Throughout the three-year history of the US-led occupation of Iraq, we have had one instance after another of brutality committed against innocent Iraqi people, by way of direct executions or air strikes.

When some rare reportage of the civilian carnage pops up on the media, albeit briefly, the American public get shocked. Private and public statements of denial and dismissal immediately start to fill the air. We hear, "American soldiers would never do such a thing," or "Who would make such a ridiculous claim?" Many people in the US today somehow seriously believe that American soldiers would never kill civilians. It is ongoing guerrilla war that continues to claim more civilian lives. Robert J. Lifton is a prominent American psychiatrist who lobbied for the inclusion of post-traumatic stress disorder (PTSD) in the Diagnostic and Statistical Manual of Mental Disorders after his work with Vietnam War veterans. He believes that it does not require an unusual level of mental illness or of personal evil to carry out such crimes. Rather, these crimes are nearly guaranteed to occur in "atrocity-producing situations." Iraq today is most certainly an "atrocity-producing situation," as it has been since the early days of the occupation.

Here some examples outlined; US military raid on the al-Mustafa Shiites mosque in Baghdad on March 26th 2006, which killed at least 16 people, was an example of. An AP video of the scene shows male bodies tangled together in a bloody mass on the floor of the Imams' living quarters—all of them with shotgun wounds and other bullet holes. The tape also shows shell casings of the calibre used by the US military scattered about on the floor. An official from the al-Sadr political group reported that American forces had surrounded the hospital where the wounded were taken for treatment after the massacre. The occupying army denied responsibility.

On March 15th 2006, 11 Iraqis, mostly women and children, were massacred by US troops in Balad. Witnesses told reporters that US helicopters landed near a home, which was then stormed by US troops. Everyone visible was rounded up and taken inside the house where they were killed. The victims' ages ranged from six months to 75 years. The US military acknowledged the raid, but claimed to have captured a resistance fighter and insisted that only four people had been killed. Available evidence presents the photographs that the AP reporter took of the scene reveal a collapsed roof, three destroyed cars and two dead cows. The second evidence was from the detailed report of the incident prepared by Iraq Police, which matches witness accounts and accuses the American troops of murdering Iraqi civilians. The police reported: "The American forces gathered the family members in one room and executed 11 persons, including five children, four women and two men. Then they bombed the house, burned three vehicles and killed the animals. The report includes the observation of local medics that all of the bodies had bullet wounds in the head".

Ahmed Khalaf, the nephew of one of the victims said, "The killed family was not part of the resistance, they were women and children. The Americans have promised us a better life, but we get only death."

Another appalling example of the effect of the atrocities was experienced last November 19th 2005 in Haditha (on the Euphrates). American troops, in retaliation against a roadside bomb attack, stormed nearby homes and shot dead 15 members of two families, including a three-year-old girl. US military reported that as "All 15 civilians were killed by the blast of the roadside bomb". This massacre is reported by the Brussels Tribunal as a war crime, for the overwhelming evidence of the atrocity.

During the aftermath of the November 2004 assault on Fallujah, scores of Iraqis were killed by US Army; Khaled Ahmed Rsayef, whose brother and six other relatives were killed by the troops, described to Dhar Jamail the emotional frustration of the American soldiers and their blind revenge at losing one of their own. "American troops immediately cordoned off the area and raided two nearby houses, shooting at everyone inside. It was a massacre in every sense of the word," said Rasayef. Arab media reportage had shown large numbers of atrocities yet we find no mention in the American corporate media.

March 20, 2006, the Daily Dar Al-Salam news paper reported: "US forces destroyed houses in Hasibah and displaced the inhabitants. In December 2003, Dhar Jamail witnessed US soldiers raiding a secondary school in the al-Amiriyah district of Baghdad and detaining 16 children.

March 19, 2006, Al-Arabia reported: "In another development, seven people, including a woman, were killed in a raid carried out by joint American-Iraqi forces in Al-Dulu'iyah at dawn today. The US Army has so far not confirmed this information."

March 9, Al Sharqiyah TV channel reported: "US troops opened fire at a civilian vehicle as it passed by Al-Hadba district in the western part of Mosul, northern Iraq. The three occupants of the vehicle were martyred in the incident."

During an attack on a wedding in May 2004, US troops killed over 40 people, mostly women and children, in a desert village on the Syrian-Iraqi borders.

AP footage showed musical instruments, blood stains, the headless body of a child, and clumps of women's hair in a destroyed house that was bombed by US warplanes in the middle of the night. Other photographs showed dead women and children, and an AP reporter identified at least 10 of the bodies as those of children. Relatives, who gathered at a cemetery outside of Ramadi where all the bodies were buried, told reporters that each of the 28 fresh graves contained between one and three bodies.

Mrs. Shihab, a 30-year-old woman who survived the massacre, told the Guardian, "We went out of the house and the American soldiers started to shoot us. They were shooting low on the ground and targeting us one by one." She added that she ran with her two little boys before they were all shot, including herself in the leg. "I left them because they were dead," she said of her two little boys, one of whom was decapitated by a shell. Thereafter, armoured military vehicles entered the village, shooting at all the other houses and the people who were starting to assemble in the open. Following these, two Chinook helicopters offloaded several dozen troops, some of who set explosives in one of the homes and a building next to it. Both exploded into rubble as the helicopters lifted off.

Hamdi Noor al-Alusi, the manager of al-Qa'im general hospital, the nearest medical facility to the scene of the slaughter, said that of the 42 killed, 14 were children and 11 women. "I want to know why the Americans targeted this small village," he said, "These people are my patients. I know each and every single one of them. What has caused this disaster?"

US military ran a disinformation campaign saying the target was a "suspected safe-house" for foreign fighters and denied that any children were killed.

Topping his ridiculous claim was the statement of Maj. Gen. James Mattis, commander of the 1st Marine Division. "How many people go to the middle of the desert…to hold a wedding 80 miles (130km) from the nearest civilization?"

Perhaps someone should have informed him that these farmers and nomads often "go to the middle of the desert" because they happen to live there.

"These were more than two dozen military-age males. Let's not be naïve," Mattis stated before being asked by a reporter to comment on the footage on Arabic television which showed a child's body being lowered into a grave. His response was: "I have not seen the pictures but bad things happen in wars. I don't have to apologize for the conduct of my men."

Dr. Lifton. In an article he wrote for the New England Journal of Medicine in July 2004, Lifton addressed the issue of US doctors being complicit in torturing Iraqis in Abu Ghraib.

Lifton writes, "American doctors at Abu Ghraib and elsewhere have undoubtedly been aware of their medical responsibility to document injuries and raise questions about their possible source in abuse. But those doctors and other medical personnel were part of a command structure that permitted and sometimes orchestrated torture to a degree that it became the norm—with which they were expected to comply—in the immediate prison environment."

He continues, "The doctors thus brought a medical component to what I call an "atrocity-producing situation"—one so structured, psychologically and militarily, that ordinary people can readily engage in atrocities. Even without directly participating in the abuse, doctors may have become socialized to an environment of torture and by virtue of their medical authority helped sustain it. In studying various forms of medical abuse, I have found that the participation of doctors can confer an aura of legitimacy and can even create an illusion of therapy and healing."

Dhar Jamail wrote "I have personally experienced this. Standing with US soldiers at checkpoints and perimeters of operations in Iraq, I have seen them curse and kick Iraqis, heard them threatening to kill even women and children and then look at me as if they had merely said hello to them. My status of journalist did not deter them because they saw no need for checks".

US troops shot dead and injured scores of Iraqi demonstrators in several incidents. For example, seven people were shot dead and dozens injured in Mosul on 15 April 2003. In a similar fashion 15 people, including children, were shot dead and more than 70 injured in Fallujah on 29 April, 2003.

Two demonstrators were shot dead outside the Republican Palace in Baghdad on 18 June 2005. On 14 May 2005, two US armed vehicles broke through the perimeter wall of the home of Sa'adi Suleiman Ibrahim al-'Ubaydi in Ramadi. Soldiers beat him with rifle butts and then shot him dead as he tried to flee.

On 17 September, a 14-year-old boy was killed and six people were injured when US troops opened fire at a wedding party in Fallujah.

Ramadi in November 23rd, 2003, during Ramadan, US soldiers raided a home where a family was just sitting down together to break their fast. Three men of the family had their hands tied behind them with plastic ties and were laid on the ground face down while the women and children were made to stand inside a nearby storage closet. Khalil Ahmed, 30 years old, the brother of two of the victims and cousin with a third described to Dahr Jamail how after executing the three men the soldiers completely destroyed the home, using Humvees with machine guns, tanks, and gunfire from the many troops on foot and helicopters.

This is only a very small sampling. The only way to prevent any of this from being repeated ad infinitum is to remove US soldiers from their "atrocity-producing situation" in Iraq. For it is clearer than ever that the longer the failed, illegal occupation persists, the larger will be the numbers of Iraqis slaughtered by the occupation forces

I interviewed with Nagem Salam, 55-year-old woman who used to work as an English teacher who was detained for four months, in as many prisons: Samarra, Tikrit, one in Baghdad and of course, Abu Ghraib. She was never allowed to sleep through a night; she was interrogated, not given enough food or water, no access to a lawyer or her family. Verbally and psychologically abused. But that isn't the worst part. Her 70-year-old husband was detained and beaten to death. That took 7 months. "Why are they doing this to us?" She didn't understand what was happening—two of her sons were also detained, her family completely shattered. "We didn't do anything wrong," she said

At the gates of the infamous Abu Ghraib torture prison. Men, women and crying children congregated at that desolate place, expressing bewilderment and outrage at their continuing inability to visit or gain information about loved ones held inside.

"I am sitting here on the ground now, waiting for God's help." On man told Nagem Salam. His son had been in Abu Ghraib for 6 months following a raid on his home that produced no weapons. He had never been charged with anything.

Nagem Salam described the unbreakable pride and dignity of the Iraqi people in his visit to Baghdad. Al-Aadamiyah, a mostly Sunni area of Baghdad. Scores of people were crowded about the Abu Hanifa mosque. Small trucks outside were being loaded with bags of food, boxes of bottled water, and death shrouds for the martyred people of Fallujah during the heavy fighting there. The people of Aadamiyah, in solidarity with the people of Fallujah who were under siege by the US military, were gathering supplies to attempt to get them inside the city which was sealed off at the time. One man told Nagem, "This is Islam! We give all of this aid on our own. We are calling for more trucks, because we already have five Lories full of supplies."

Meanwhile the loudspeaker from the nearby mosque was giving instructions as people frantically loaded bags of potatoes, rice, flour, and other foodstuffs into the trucks. Each time a truck was loaded another empty one pulled up and began to be filled. Salam Khasil, with tears in eyes, told Nagem, "All Muslims have one heart. We help each other no matter what. We want the Americans to leave Iraq. It is the right of a people to be free in their own country. We are all one now—Sunni and Shiites! Kerbala, Najaf, Shu'ala, we will help them all." He pointed to what I estimated to be at least a thousand people crowding towards the mosque and said, "All of these people are coming to give blood to help their brothers! We will send it to Sadr City, and to anyone else who needs it"

He then looked me in the eye and firmly said, "Why are 60 innocent people in Fallujah killed because four Americans were killed there if the American Army wants to stay in Iraq, you must kill all of the Iraqi people!". Later that night, the blood of Al-Aadamiyah was trying to make its way into the veins of bleeding Iraqis in Fallujah, Ramadi, and elsewhere where it flowed throughout Iraq during that time.

Haditha Massacre

Since the Abu Ghraib prisoner abuse scandal became public, Amnesty International and other nongovernmental organizations have been calling for an independent commission to investigate all aspects of U.S. detention policies, including the use of secret detention sites and unlawful civilian killing, the Congress has been lax over those issues.

The incident that happened in Haditha is like so many others that happen on daily basis during the occupation, the kind of tragedy that has become numbing routine amid the daily reports of violence in Iraq. On the morning of Nov. 19, 2005, a roadside bomb struck a Humvee carrying Marines from the 3rd Battalion, 1st Marines, on a road near Haditha, a town in western Iraq. The bomb killed Lance Corporal Miguel (T.J.) Terrazas, 20, from El Paso, Texas.

The next day a Marine communiqué from Camp Blue Diamond in Ramadi reported that Terrazas and 15 Iraqi civilians were killed by the blast and that "gunmen attacked the convoy with small-arms fire," prompting the Marines to return fire, killing eight insurgents and wounding another one. The Marines from held a memorial service for Terrazas at their camp in Haditha. What happened in Haditha is a reminder of the horrors faced by civilians caught in the middle of war.

But the truth and the details of what happened in Haditha are more disturbing, more horrific than the military initially reported. According to eyewitnesses and local officials interviewed by various media, the civilians who died in Haditha on Nov. 19 were killed not by a roadside bomb but by the Marines, who went on a rampage of street type of justice in the village, killing 15 unarmed Iraqis in their homes, including seven women and three children. Human-rights activists say that if the accusations are true, the incident ranks as the worst case of deliberate killing of Iraqi civilians by U.S. occupation army since the beginning of the war. The attack was in revenge of killing Terrazas by a roadside bomb.

TIME obtained videotaped evidence that showed the aftermath of the Marines' assault and provides documentation of lost lives. In January 2006, TIME Magazine Journalists presented military officials in Baghdad with the Iraqis' version of the killing story, U S military officials opened an enquiry and investigated the killing, and 28 people were interviewed, including the Marines, the families of the victims and doctors at Haditha Hospital. According to military officials, the inquiry acknowledged that, contrary to the military's initial report, the 15 civilians killed on Nov. 19 died at the hands of the Marines, not the insurgents. The military announced latter that the evidence of the enquiry was handed over to the Naval Criminal Investigative Service, which will conduct a criminal investigation to determine whether the troops broke the laws of war by deliberately targeting civilians, spokeswoman for the Multi-National Force—Iraq, told TIME the involvement of the NCIS does not mean that a crime occurred. And she says "the fault for the civilian deaths lies squarely with the insurgents, who placed non-combatants in the line of fire as the Marines responded to defend themselves." In a manner similar to Madeline Albright response the debacle of the sanctions that killed hundreds of thousands of people, by Blaming Saddam.

TIME had interviewed six people whose family members were killed that day told reporters the devastatingly violent response by a group of U.S. troops who had lost one of their own to a deadly insurgent attack and believed they were under fire.

At around 7:15 a.m. on Nov. 19, a U.S. Humvee was struck by improvised explosive road side device attached to a large propane canister, triggered by remote control. The bomb instantly killed Terrazas, who was driving, and injured two other Marines.

Eman 9 years was a witness(story taken from Time Magazine)

Eman Waleed, 9, lived in a house very close the site of the blast, which shattered all the windows in her home. "We heard a big noise that woke us all up," she recalls two months later. According to military officials familiar with the investigation, the Marines say they came under fire from the direction of the Waleed house immediately after being hit by the road side bomb. A group of Marines headed toward the house. Eman says she "heard a lot of shooting, so none of us went outside. Besides, it was very early, and we were all wearing our nightclothes." When the Marines entered the house, they were shouting in English. "First, they went into my father's room, where he was reading the Koran," she claims, "and we heard shots." According to Eman, the Marines then went to the living room. "I couldn't see their faces very well—only their guns sticking into the doorway. I watched them shoot my grandfather, first in the chest and then in the head. Then they killed my granny." She said the troops started firing toward the corner of the room where she and her younger brother Abdul Rahman, 8, were hiding; the other adults shielded the children from the bullets but died in the process. Eman says her leg was hit by a piece of metal and Abdul Rahman was shot near his shoulder. "We were lying there, bleeding, and it hurt so much. Afterward, some Iraqi soldiers came. They carried us in their arms. I was crying, shouting 'Why did you do this to our family?' And one Iraqi soldier tells me, 'We didn't do it. The Americans did.'"

Marines said they heard the clack-clack sound of an AK-47 being racked and readied for fire. (According to Eman there were no guns in that house.) Believing they were about to be ambushed, the Marines broke down the two doors simultaneously and fired their weapons. The officials say the military has confirmed that seven people were killed inside the house—including two women and a child.

According to military officials, the Marines say they then started taking fire from the direction of a second house, prompting them to break down the door of that house and throw in a grenade, blowing up a propane tank in the kitchen. The Marines then began firing, killing eight residents—including the owner, his wife, the owner's sister, a 2-year-old son and three young daughters.

The Marines raided another house belongs to a man called Ahmed Ayed. One of a witness told TIME that after hearing the gunfire from his father's house, he rushed over. The Americans didn't let anybody into the house until 6:30 the next morning." the bodies of the dead zipped into body bags and taken by Marines to a local hospital morgue. "But we could tell from the blood tracks across the floor what happened," Ayed claims. "The Americans gathered my four brothers and took them inside my father's bedroom, to a closet. They killed them inside the closet."

The military has a different account of what transpired. According to officials familiar with the investigation, the Marines broke into the third house and found a group of 10 to 15 women and children. The troops say they left one Marine to guard that house and pushed on to the house next door, where they found four men, one of whom was wielding an AK-47. A second seemed to be reaching into a wardrobe for another weapon, the officials say. The Marines shot both men dead; the military's initial report does not specify how the other two men died. The Marines deny that any of the men were killed in the closet, which they say is too small to fit one adult male, much less four.

According to the military officials, the series of raids took five hours and left at least 23 people dead. In all, two AK-47s were discovered. So the killing an act of legitimate self-defence or a homicide It is innocent people who were asleep and killed in cold blood. Dr. Wahid, director of the local hospital in Haditha, who asked that his family name be withheld because, he says, he fears reprisals by U.S. troops, says the Marines brought 24 bodies to his hospital around midnight on Nov. 19. Wahid says the Marines claimed the victims had been killed by shrapnel from the roadside bomb. "But it was obvious to us that there were no organs slashed by shrapnel," Wahid says. "The bullet wounds were very apparent. Most of the victims were shot in the chest and the head from close range."

A day after the incident, a Haditha journalism student videotaped the scene at the local morgue and at the homes where the killings had occurred. The video was obtained by the Hammurabi Human Rights Group, which cooperates with Human Rights Watch. It shows the victims, especially the women and children, were still in their nightclothes when they died. The scenes from inside the houses show that the walls and ceilings are hit with shrapnel and bullet holes as well as spray of blood. Houses, which may cast doubt on the Marines' contention that after the IED exploded, the Marines and the insurgents engaged in a fierce gun-fight.

The military insisted that the Iraqis had been killed by an insurgent bomb—until January when TIME gave a copy of the video and witnesses' testimony to Colonel Barry Johnson, a U.S. military spokesman in Baghdad.

February an infantry colonel went to Haditha and conducted investigations in that matter in which he interviewed Marines, survivors and doctors at the morgue. The investigations concluded that the civilians were in fact killed by Marines and not by an insurgent's bomb. The disturbing events though were the military declaration that those killings happened as a collateral damage.

Anther story from Haditha

Aws Fahmi, a Haditha resident he watched and listened from his home as Marines went from house to house killing three families, his neighbour, Younis Salim Khafif, plead in English for his life and the lives of his family members. Saying: 'I am a friend. I am good,' "Fahmi said. "But they killed him, and his wife and daughters.". Witnesses told a Washington Post special correspondent in

Haditha this week and U.S. investigators said in Washington. The girls killed inside Khafif's house were ages 14, 10, 5, 3 and 1, according to death certificates.

Today the entire world knows that the situation in Iraq is hopeless, but the US officials don't have the will to withdraw. And we certainly will face more Hadithas and more atrocities. Those that committed the atrocities must be investigated and charged with war crimes. Innocent civilians are killed every day unnecessarily; it is a conflict under false pretence, for which the White House Officials are responsible they too must be investigated and held accountable.

Larry Cox, Amnesty International USA's Executive Director, made the following statement in response to the alleged civilian massacre in Haditha, Iraq:

"Amnesty International is deeply disturbed by allegations that U.S. Marines massacred civilians in Haditha, Iraq. These accusations, if proven true, may rise to the level of war crimes. We welcome General Pace's public commitment to both investigate the alleged massacre and the alleged resulting cover-up. However Amnesty International is concerned about the amount of time that passed before these allegations were taken seriously".

Targeting Iraqi academics

Even according to conservative estimates, over 250 professors and academics have been assassinated during the first three years of the occupation, and many hundreds more have disappeared. Thousands fled the country in fear for their lives, Iraq undergoing a major brain drain, with far-reaching consequences for the future of Iraq.

July 14, 2004, Robert Fisk reported from Iraq that: *"University staff suspect that there is a campaign to strip Iraq of its academics, to complete the destruction of Iraq's cultural identity which began when the American army entered Baghdad."*

The wave of assassinations appears to be non-sectarian, targeting women as well as men countrywide. It is indiscriminate of expertise: professors of geography, history and Arabic literature, science as well as prominent doctors are among the dead. Not one individual has been apprehended in connection with these assassinations.

According to the United Nations University, some 84 per cent of Iraq's institutions of higher education have already been burnt, looted or destroyed. Iraq's educational system used to be among the best in the Middle East; one of the country's most important assets was its educated and professional people, which make Iraq stands out among other countries in the region.

It is catastrophe of staggering proportions unfolding in a climate of organised crime. As an occupying power, and under international humanitarian law, final responsibility for protecting Iraqi citizens, including academics, lies with the United States.

Ref

1. Dahr Jamail, Tue 04 Apr 2006

2. Nagem Salam Journalist—Baghdad In the Face of Despair Unbreakable Dignity and Pride, Baghdad 17/06/2004. Nagem Salam is an American journalist of Lebanese descent who has worked in Iraq for a total of four months since the Anglo-American invasion of spring 2003. His articles focus on Iraqis and how the occupation of their country affects their daily life.

3. Rory McCarthy in Ramadi 'US soldiers started to shoot us, one by one'. Survivors describe wedding massacre as generals refuse to apologise. Friday May 21, 200

4. AMNESTY INTERNATIONAL USA. PRESS RELEASE. May 31, 2006

5. Time Mgazine Mar. 27, 2006

6. Amnesty International Deeply Disturbed by Allegations of Civilian Massacre in Haditha.

• Will harsh weed-out allow Iraqi academia to flower?—THES, 25 July 2003

• Another Voice of Academia Is Silenced in Iraq—LA Times, 21 Jan 2004

• Assassinations Tear Into Iraq's Educated Class—New York Times, 7 Feb 2004

• Iraqi intellectuals under siege—Al Jazeera, 29 Feb 2004.

• Iraqi intellectuals flee 'death squads'—Al Jazeera, 30 March 2004.

• Death to those who dare to speak out—CS Monitor, 30 April 2004.

- Iraqi intellectuals appeal for security—Al Jazeera, 19 May 2004.

- "It has begun."—Dahr Jamail, 13 June 2004.

- Where is this going?—Al Ahram, 16 June 2004.

- Academics targeted as murder and mayhem hits Iraqi colleges—Robert Fisk, 14 July 2004.

- Death threats, assassinations teaching Iraqi academics to watch what they say, 16 July 2004.

- —The slaughter of Iraq's intellectuals; The New Statesman, 06 Sept 2004.

- Murder of lecturers threatens Iraqi academia—THES, 10 Sept 2004.

- Iraq's universities face catastrophe, 16 Sept 2004.

- Iraq losing its best and brightest, Christian Science Monitor 21 Sept 2004.

Samaraa

Resistance from Sunni Iraqis over 2005 has been fierce and a bloody guerrilla war had destroyed the city. Samaraa had many military check-points positioned where residents must show identification. Following the destruction of the al-Askari shrine, Shiites militia assisting the US and Iraqi troops with reprisal attacks on the Sunni's. No group claimed responsibility for bombing the Golden Mosque of Al-Askari shrine, but four men, three disguised in black and one in military uniform, entered the building and detonated explosives which destroyed the dome. The Western media immediately implicated extremist groups linked to 'al Qaeda' Iraqis said the work of "a foreign hand aiming to create differences among Iraqis."

It worked, and Iraq is moving closer to civil war, with an escalation in sectarian violence which could lead to the break-up of the country beyond any repair. This coincided with a surprise visit to Baghdad by UK foreign secretary Jack Straw trying to repair the tenuous democratic process is even more fragile after Samaraa events.

American soldiers have patrolled the streets and seized telephones with build-in cameras Samarra. Atwar Bahjat, a journalist of al-Arbiya, were kidnapped and shot by gunmen while she was on her way the city to report on the situation.

This act of desecration of holy places is offensive to any Muslim regardless of their background. It serves the interest of those who wish to ignite the civil war, which will eventually fragment the mostly eroded unity of Iraq. The blame was at neighbouring countries specifically Iran and Syria. The Americans blamed the terrorists and "the enemies of freedom".

Evidently there were "unusual activities" taking place at the mosque the night before the bombing. "Cars the whole night until the next morning". Iraqi National Guard and American troops "patrolled the area until the next morning". At 6:30 AM the American troops left. At 6:40 the first explosion went off

Ref

Samarra is the new Falluja; Hazel McKinlay Prison Planet.com

February 24 2006

Death squads
Corpses in Baghdad's mortuary show signs of torture and execution

Scores of Iraqis are being tortured or summarily executed every month in Baghdad mainly and other cities by death squads working from the Ministry of the Interior, the United Nations' previous human rights chief (John Pace) in Iraq had concluded. Signs of torture such as wounds to the head or injuries caused by drill-bits or burning cigarettes. Much of the killing according to John Pace was carried out by Shiites Muslim groups under the control of the Ministry of the Interior.

The statistical information provided to Mr Pace and his team comes from the Baghdad Medico-Legal Institute. He said figures show that in July 2005 the Baghdad morgue received 1,100 bodies, about 900 of which have evidence of torture or summary execution. These atrocities continued to happen.

These activities of the death squads and the suicide bombings and attacks on Shiites holy places carried out by Sunnis, some of whom are followers of Abu Musab al-Zarqawi, al-Qa'ida's leader in Iraq, are pushing Iraq ever closer to a sectarian civil war.

Mr Pace said the Ministry of the Interior was "acting as a rogue element within the government". It is controlled by the main Shiites party, the Supreme Council for Islamic Revolution in Iraq (Sciri); the Interior Minister, Bayan Jabr, is a former leader of Sciri's Badr Brigade militia, which is groups accused of running the death squads. The Mahdi militia is also blamed.

There are also paramilitary commandos, dressed in black uniforms and driving around Baghdad Sunni neighbourhoods in trucks. People whom they have openly arrested have frequently been found dead several days later, with their bodies bearing obvious marks of torture.

Sunnis are caught between a rock and a hard place (the death squads and the desire the insurgents to start a civil war). The Salafi (Sunni fundamentalists), want to the Americans to withdraw and to build a theocratic Islamic state. They see Shiites, as heretics allied to the US and should be slaughtered.

The current cycle of violence after the bombing of the shrine in Samarra had claimed at least 200 lives so far, including those of 47 factory workers pulled from buses and shot on the outskirts of Baghdad.

The Americans have been trying blame Jabr Sollagh as Interior Minister, accusing him of turning his ministry into a Shiites militia dedicated for assassinations. Shiites blamed US and its allies simply want to prevent the majority community from gaining full power despite winning elections in 2005.

There's an active, undeniable and undeclared civil war and ethnic cleansing. People are being killed according to their ID card. Extremists from both sides (Sunnis and Shiites) are making life unbearable. Some of them work for 'Zarqawi', and the others work for the Ministry of Interior. We hear about Shiites being killed in the 'Sunni triangle' and corpses of Sunnis named 'Omar' (a Sunni name) arriving by hundreds into Baghdad morgue.

Ref:

Andrew Buncombe and Patrick Cockburn Iraq's death squads: On the brink of civil war. 26 February 2006

Iraq: focus on threats against progressive women" *IRIN news*

Iraqi women defy death in fight for political clout" *Reuters*

Rebels kill Iraqi women as 'betrayers' of Islam" *London Times*

Death at 'immoral' picnic in the park" *London Times*

Iraq: Decades of suffering, now women deserve better" *Amnesty International*

Interview with Iraq's Ibrahim Jaafari" *Der Spiegel*

Iraq: The dilemma of government formation" *Morocco Times*

Statement by the Organization of Women's Freedom in Iraq" *OWFI*

Women fear losing rights in new Iraq" *Chicago Tribune*

Democracy may set back Arab women" *Philadelphia Inquirer* Rise of Extremism

Islamic Law Threaten Iraqi Women by Chris Shumway

40

Afterward

Iraqi people have suffered all forms of tragedies in the last 40 years.

President Bush declared the end of Saddam era as not only the end of tyranny, but it is the end of torture chambers and rape, and it is the time for the people of Iraq to choose the government that they want.

Sure enough that the tyranny is gone, but the torture came back under a different name (called liberation). Well, during Saddam time we knew who torturing people was; at least the ruling thug admitted that. Now it is impossible to know who your enemy is. Wars beget atrocities; immoral wars beget immoral inhuman acts. There is no possible positive outcome now for Iraq and the continued presence of US troops will only make the situation worse for the Iraqi people

People getting abducted from their homes disappear and found few days latter dead by a bullet in the back of the head (execution style), whether the internal ministry police or one of the militia organisation or terrorists or other unknown groups it is not really known and remains everyone guess.

In fact the feeling of the American solders who went to Iraq have hatred and disgust for the people of Iraq, they fought a war that they did not believe in, and they fought an enemy that did not threaten them in any way. No one could comprehend the reason of a war that started as an action to remove the non existing weapons of mass destruction and now has changed to be a war on terror. What war is it again? It is certainly confusing to everybody, it is not surprising that the American solders turn on the very people they came to help.

An Iraqi girl stands in front of her house—destroyed March 2003

Those Iraqis who rule the country are no more than US-installed puppets, they have no control on the country or its security or economy. Most of them are opportunists who came on the back of American tanks. Moreover they established themselves firmly in the secured and heavily guarded "Green Zone," with very little contact with ordinary Iraqi people. The dilemma of the Iraqi people continued to be beyond any description. Before the invasion Bush had promised that there will be no more torture chambers, after the invasion he said the torture chambers and the secret police are gone forever.

We saw later that American soldiers and intelligence torturing the Iraqi people in Abu Graib and Camp Boca and elsewhere, the torture was widespread and the possibly approved by the pentagon, army generals knew about such abuses of human rights and reported that the to their higher officials. American media and officials played down the extent of the abuse and rationalized it to certain mitigating circumstances. People who were the victims of abuse had no apologies from the American administration, no compensation, not even counselling for their stress. Reports of human rights abuse continued coming to date confirming that torture is being committed against Iraqis in American detention camps.

The British Army was also involved in torturing Iraqi detainees and abusing them. We know through reports of Human Rights Watch that the Iraqi Army created and trained by the occupying force, was also involved in torturing Iraqis. During the Saddam era the enemy was known and the source of human rights abuse was known as a single entity of the tyrannical regime. After the alleged "liberation of Iraq", Iraqi people are being tortured by so many powers; the occupying army, the militia, death squads, foreign terrorists and other unknown parties. It does seem that the torture chambers and the rapes and the confiscation of the Iraqi freedom have just begun.

In 1991 Iraq refineries were bombed and badly damaged. Iraqi people were able despite the sanctions and without help from Halliburton or Bechtel—to fix the oil refineries in a few months only. We kept them working and going for 13 years and Iraq was exporting oil products. In a similar effort the Iraqi people were able to restore the electricity within few months. The Iraqi people reconstructed every bridge and building damaged by 1991 war in a matter of few months. The occupation had spent billions of dollars from Iraqi oil revenues, yet Iraq had some painted school's walls, no electricity, no running water, no jobs no nothing three years under the occupation.

The general lawlessness that continued up till now three years under the occupation, which is a direct result of the invasion, continued to ruin the daily life of the millions of Iraqi people; kidnaps, organised crimes, gangs roaming the streets, assassinations roadside bombs and political militia had taken over the entire country. And last but not the least is the shooting by a nervous occupation soldiers. More innocent Iraqi civilians are killed by the occupation army than those killed by criminal gangs and assassinations. Trigger-happy soldiers have immunity from prosecution for unlawful killings of large number civilians. The victims of that killing are totally forgotten, no investigations or prosecution, not even apologies.

The US Congress issued a report on Iraq at the end of June 2004. The report states that in May 2003 (just after the invasion) seven out of the 18 governorates of Iraq had more than 16 hours of electricity per day. It also says that this number was reduced to one governorate in May 2004, one year after the invasion. In 2005 people in Baghdad (a city of five million people)are lucky if they get six hours of electricity per day.

The health system has disintegrated throughout the three years of occupation. Hospitals still lack the simplest equipments. Medicines are in severe shortage. Fewer patients seek medical treatment or examination because of the security situation and the cordoned suburbs and streets. Doctors are not safe at hospitals because they have been physically attacked by militia, police, and frustrated relatives who vent their frustration at helpless medical staff, criminal gangs have kidnapped for ransom a few hundred doctors. Some were threatened, hundreds fearing for their lives of highly qualified doctors had left the country. Those doctors were the courageous people who faced the frustration of the long years of sanction and did not leave the country.

Prices of petrol and diesel had skyrocketed, added to it the shortages of petrol, people wait in lines for long hour at petrol stations. Records show that the Iraqi government officials had smuggled up to a hundred thousand barrels of refined diesel fuel each day through under the nose of the occupation. These figures indicate that the Iraqi refineries had an excess refining capacity allowing it to export refined oil products.

Iraq continues to import refined oil products from Turkey, Kuwait, and Saudi Arabia, and even from Israel. No one knows how the oil revenues are being spent.

In 1991 Americans had bombed Iraq back to the "pre-industrial" ages, and they nearly did that by bombing and destroying everything. The Iraqi people reconstructed what had been bombed despite the sanctions and got it to function in reasonable conditions, at least there were no petrol shortages. The government of Iraq used to spend about 150 million dollars a month to import and distribute food rations. According to your CPA Inspector General, 8.8 billion dollars were unaccounted for in one year. These 8.8 billion dollars are enough to feed all the people of Iraq for few years.

Those people are traumatized and broken; nothing will bring their life and hope back together.

While Iraqis largely blame foreign forces for the relative loss of security and free-dom, secular Iraqis fear other products of the 2003 invasion—fundamentalist militants and the prospect of religious rule—as much as protracted occupation and daily

Sanctions against Iraq were lifted by the United Nations May 22, 2003. United States sanctions were not lifted until July 29, 2004, a few days shy of fourteen years of economic warfare.

Although sanctions are no longer in place, their effects continue to be felt. Economic manipulation, theft, and occupation have intensified as multi national corporations divide and contract out the lives and resources of Iraqis, backed by the barrel of the US military and its corporate complex.

Through continued war, bombing, and economic sanctions, the United States has been responsible for infanticide masquerading as foreign policy. As it deci-mated Iraq, the US meanwhile sold weapons of mass destruction, maintained military bases and training of foreign armies, and supplied huge amounts of eco-nomic and military aid, including to Saudi Arabia, Turkey, Kuwait, Israel, Jor-dan, Egypt, and Bahrain.

The Fallujah offensive has virtually disappeared from the news cycle. But his-tory—if written by Iraqis—may well enshrine it as the new Guernica that was brutally bombed by the Nazis in 1937. After Jean-Paul Sartre writing about the Algerian War (1956-62), "after Fallujah no two Americans shall meet without a corpse lying between them". The Iraqi people need modern day Picasso to pic-ture the humanitarian tragedy of Fallujah.

Those of us who managed to escape over the years or forced into exile, we are very lucky, at least we are still alive; the present and future of our families and friends who stayed behind is shattered by a civil conflict and a foreign occupation and remains largely shrouded by a dark veil of poverty, disease, strife and uncer-tainty. Lets make sure we tell the tales of this dark era and ensure that our plight be remembered for generations to come.

Lets not forget we the Nation of Iraq regardless of our creed of ethnicity, we are 9000 years of civilization.

As of now Iraq remains a place where time stood still and the clock switched off on the 2nd of August 1990. It remains a monument of oppression, misery, human endurance, shattered lives and broken spirits.

By the end of 2004 we had up to 500,000 victims of the sanctions in the 1990s, according to United Nations experts. And then according to the British medical paper The Lancet up to 100,000 victims since the beginning of the invasion of Iraq; and at least 6,000 victims in Fallujah, according to the Iraqi Red Crescent. The disaster the US has unleashed on the Iraq is horrifying, and we all must resist it.

The eyes of Iraqis in Diaspora will remain on the home land. During Saddam almost every single Iraqi dream was to see the end of Saddam, hopefully to go back to a friendly homeland; however were very disappointed to see the new Iraq is even worse. My heart goes to my family and my relatives and friends who experienced the grief and the sorrow of the loss of their young men in the wars; and lived under crushing poverty for long years under the sanction, and experienced the miseries of the new Iraq.

Riverbend is Iraqi woman who wrote on the internet

"I'll meet you 'round the bend my friend, where hearts can heal and souls can mend…" In response to that I say, I wonder if we will ever meet again, while the hearts may heal I wonder if the souls will mend.

978-0-595-41602-8
0-595-41602-0

www.ingramcontent.com/pod-product-compliance
Lightning Source LLC
Chambersburg PA
CBHW022243290526
45785CB00015B/73